DBKDA 2018

The Tenth International Conference on Advances in Databases, Knowledge, and Data Applications

May 20 - 24, 2018

Nice, France

DBKDA 2018 Editors

Andreas Schmidt, Karlsruhe Institute of Technology / University of Applied Sciences
Fritz Laux, Reutlingen University, Germany

Printed from e-media with permission by:

Curran Associates, Inc.
57 Morehouse Lane
Red Hook, NY 12571

Some format issues inherent in the e-media version may also appear in this print version.

Printed by Curran Associates, Inc. (2018)

International Academy, Research, and Industry Association (IARIA)
412 Derby Way
Wilmington, DE 19810

Phone: (408) 893-6407
Fax: (408) 527-6351

petre@iaria.org

Additional copies of this publication are available from:

Curran Associates, Inc.
57 Morehouse Lane
Red Hook, NY 12571 USA
Phone: 845-758-0400
Fax: 845-758-2633
Email: curran@proceedings.com
Web: www.proceedings.com

Table of Contents

DBKDA 2018

Foreword

The Tenth International Conference on Advances in Databases, Knowledge, and Data Applications (DBKDA 2018), held between May 20 - 24, 2018 - Nice, France, continued a series of international events covering a large spectrum of topics related to advances in fundamentals on databases, evolution of relation between databases and other domains, data base technologies and content processing, as well as specifics in applications domains databases.

Advances in different technologies and domains related to databases triggered substantial improvements for content processing, information indexing, and data, process and knowledge mining. The push came from Web services, artificial intelligence, and agent technologies, as well as from the generalization of the XML adoption.

High-speed communications and computations, large storage capacities, and load-balancing for distributed databases access allow new approaches for content processing with incomplete patterns, advanced ranking algorithms and advanced indexing methods.

Evolution on e-business, ehealth and telemedicine, bioinformatics, finance and marketing, geographical positioning systems put pressure on database communities to push the 'de facto' methods to support new requirements in terms of scalability, privacy, performance, indexing, and heterogeneity of both content and technology.

We take here the opportunity to warmly thank all the members of the DBKDA 2018 Technical Program Committee, as well as the numerous reviewers. The creation of such a high quality conference program would not have been possible without their involvement. We also kindly thank all the authors who dedicated much of their time and efforts to contribute to DBKDA 2018. We truly believe that, thanks to all these efforts, the final conference program consisted of top quality contributions.

Also, this event could not have been a reality without the support of many individuals, organizations, and sponsors. We are grateful to the members of the DBKDA 2018 organizing committee for their help in handling the logistics and for their work to make this professional meeting a success.

We hope that DBKDA 2018 was a successful international forum for the exchange of ideas and results between academia and industry and for the promotion of progress in the fields of databases, knowledge and data applications.

We are convinced that the participants found the event useful and communications very open. We also hope that Nice provided a pleasant environment during the conference and everyone saved some time for exploring this beautiful city.

DBKDA 2018 Chairs:

DBKDA Steering Committee

Fritz Laux, Reutlingen University, Germany
Andreas Schmidt, Karlsruhe Institute of Technology / University of Applied Sciences
Florin Rusu, University of California Merced, USA
Sergio Ilarri, University of Zaragoza, Spain
Jerzy Grzymala-Busse, University of Kansas, USA
Filip Zavoral, Charles University Prague, Czech Republic
Konstantinos Kalpakis, University of Maryland Baltimore County, USA

DBKDA Industry/Research Advisory Committee

Peter Kieseberg, SBA Research, Austria
Mike Gowanlock, Northern Arizona University, USA
Shin-ichi Ohnishi, Hokkai-Gakuen University, Japan
Thomas Triplet, Ciena inc. / Polytechnique Montreal, Canada
Stephanie Teufel, iimt - international institute of management in technology | University of Fribourg, Switzerland
Rajasekar Karthik, Oak Ridge National Laboratory, USA
Erik Hoel, Esri, USA
Daniel Kimmig, solute GmbH, Germany

GraphSM Special Track Chairs

Dimitar Hristovski, Faculty of Medicine, Ljubljana, Slovenia
Andreas Schmidt, Karlsruhe Institute of Technology / University of Applied Sciences Karlsruhe, Germany

DBKDA 2018

Committee

DBKDA Steering Committee

Fritz Laux, Reutlingen University, Germany
Andreas Schmidt, Karlsruhe Institute of Technology / University of Applied Sciences
Florin Rusu, University of California Merced, USA
Sergio Ilarri, University of Zaragoza, Spain
Jerzy Grzymala-Busse, University of Kansas, USA
Filip Zavoral, Charles University Prague, Czech Republic
Konstantinos Kalpakis, University of Maryland Baltimore County, USA

DBKDA Industry/Research Advisory Committee

Peter Kieseberg, SBA Research, Austria
Mike Gowanlock, Northern Arizona University, USA
Shin-ichi Ohnishi, Hokkai-Gakuen University, Japan
Thomas Triplet, Ciena inc. / Polytechnique Montreal, Canada
Stephanie Teufel, iimt - international institute of management in technology | University of Fribourg, Switzerland
Rajasekar Karthik, Oak Ridge National Laboratory, USA
Erik Hoel, Esri, USA
Daniel Kimmig, solute GmbH, Germany

DBKDA 2018 Technical Program Commiittee

Taher Omran Ahmed, Aljabal Algharby University, Azzentan, Libya / College of Applied Sciences, Ibri, Sultanate of Oman
Baris Aksanli, San Diego State University, USA
Markus Aleksy, ABB AG, Germany
Jose L. Arciniegas H., Universidad del Cauca, Columbia
Zeyar Aung, Masdar Institute of Science and Technology, UAE
Gilbert Babin, HEC Montréal, Canada
Zouhaier Brahmia, University of Sfax, Tunisia
Erik Buchmann, Hochschule für Telekommunikation Leipzig, Germany
Martine Cadot, LORIA-Nancy, France
Ricardo Campos, Polytechnic Institute of Tomar, Portugal
Paola Carrara, CNR IREA, Italy
Chin-Chen Chang, Feng Chia University, Taiwan
Yung Chang Chi, National Cheng Kung University, Taiwan
Byron Choi, Hong Kong Baptist University, Hong Kong
Gabriel David, INESC TEC | University of Porto, Portugal
Maria del Pilar Angeles, UNAM, Mexico
Vincenzo Deufemia, University of Salerno, Italy
Juliette Dibie, AgroParisTech, France
Efrén Díez Jiménez, Universidad de Alcalá, Spain

Lammari Ilham Nadira, Conservatoire National des Arts et Métiers, France
Khaled M. Nagi, Alexandria University, Egypt
Joshua C. Nwokeji, Gannon University - Erie Pennsylvania, USA
Shin-ichi Ohnishi, Hokkai-Gakuen University, Japan
Rasha Osman, University of Khartoum, Sudan
Benoît Otjacques, LIST - Luxembourg Institute of Science and Technology, Luxembourg
Francesco Parisi, University of Calabria, Italy
Bernhard Peischl, Institute for Software Technology | Graz University of Technology, Austria
Hai Phan, New Jersey Institute of Technology, USA
Gianvito Pio, University of Bari Aldo Moro, Italy
Elaheh Pourabbas, National Research Council | Institute of Systems Analysis and Computer Science "Antonio Ruberti", Italy
Praveen R. Rao, University of Missouri-Kansas City, USA
Manjeet Rege, University of St. Thomas, USA
Jan Richling, South Westphalia University of Applied Sciences, Germany
Miguel Romero, Simons Institute | UC Berkeley, USA
Florin Rusu, University of California Merced, USA
M. Saravanan, Ericsson Research, India
Idrissa Sarr, Université Cheikh Anta Diop, Dakar, Sénégal
Andreas Schmidt, Karlsruhe Institute of Technology / University of Applied Sciences Karlsruhe, Germany
Sebastian Schrittwieser, TARGET Research Center, Austria
Erich Schweighofer, University of Vienna, Austria
Nematollaah Shiri, Concordia University, Canada
Patrick Siarry, Université Paris-Est Créteil, France
Sergio Tessaris, Free University of Bozen-Bolzano, Italy
Olivier Teste, University of Toulouse 2 Jean Jaurès - IRIT
Stephanie Teufel, iimt - international institute of management in technology | University of Fribourg, Switzerland
Nicolas Travers, CNAM-Paris, France
Thomas Triplet, Ciena inc. / Polytechnique Montreal, Canada
Robert Ulbricht, Robotron Datenbank-Software GmbH, Dresden, Germany
Lucia Vaira, University of Salento, Italy
Maurice van Keulen, University of Twente, Netherlands
Genoveva Vargas-Solar, French Council of Scientific Research, LIG-LAFMIA, France
Ismini Vasileiou, Plymouth University, UK
Damires Yluska de Souza Fernandes, Federal Institute of Education, Science and Technology of Paraíba, Brazil
Feng George Yu, Youngstown State University, USA
Filip Zavoral, Charles University Prague, Czech Republic
Qiang Zhu, University of Michigan, USA

GraphSM Special Track Chairs

Dimitar Hristovski, Faculty of Medicine, Ljubljana, Slovenia
Andreas Schmidt, Karlsruhe Institute of Technology / University of Applied Sciences Karlsruhe, Germany

GraphSM Special Track Technical Program Committee

Copyright Information

Comparative Analysis of Supervised Machine Learning Techniques on K-12 Educational Data

Ravi Mattani
Intel Corporation
ravi.mattani@intel.com

Manjeet Rege
University of St. Thomas
Graduate Programs in Software
St. Paul, MN 55105
rege@stthomas.edu

Brandan Keaveny
Data Ethics, LLC
brandan@dataethics.net

Abstract— **The Anonymous School District (ASD) presented in this paper is implementing a comprehensive plan to intensify the information intelligence capacity to pinpoint educational needs of every student. Their main goal is to create analytical intelligence processes specific to the research needs of the school district and deploy an infrastructure that includes implementation of state of the art data analytics tools. The initial effort towards that goal is to research several machine learning techniques. The focus of this project is to assist the ASD research team in deployment of appropriate standards and procedures for efficiently forecasting and utilizing the large amount of data collected by the district. The goal of the project is to evaluate the most efficient machine learning techniques to forecast future trends. As a result, we developed a framework to transform raw data into minable data and apply several supervised learning techniques. Experiments were conducted to analyze the best technique.**

Keywords—supervised; machine; learning; k-12; analytics

I. INTRODUCTION

One of the most important challenges educational organizations face is to make effective use of the large volumes of data collected. Educational administrators and other decision makers would want to make decisions based on facts and trends that emerge from these huge data repositories. Data analytics is the practice of applying different algorithms and statistical techniques to extract interesting, unknown trends and predict future outcomes. Specifically, it comprises of applying machine learning algorithms, and other statistical methods for data analysis. This knowledge discovery can enable educational administrators to discover trends in data and assist in decision making [1] [2].

Machine Learning [3] techniques can broadly be classified into two types: Supervised [14] and Unsupervised [15]. The latter comprise of techniques that are used to extract interpretable patterns and correlations that exist in the data. Supervised Machine Learning on the other hand includes methods to perform inference on the available data with the intention to predict future outcomes and values. Classification and regression are two types of prediction problems. Classification problems comprise of predicting categories. For example, by examining samples from past data one can generalize if a student will pass or fail a particular exam. Regression involves predicting a numerical value for a particular attribute based on historical data. Predicting graduation rate for a school based on past data would be a regression problem.

In this paper, we present our work on a project that focuses on applying supervised machine learning techniques to K-12 educational data. The Office of Accountability of the Anonymous School District (ASD) we worked on in this project is implementing a comprehensive plan to intensify the information intelligence capacity to pinpoint educational needs of every student. Their main goal is to create analytical intelligence processes specific to the research needs of the school district and deploy an infrastructure that includes implementation of data mining tools and state of the art data analytics. The initial effort is to research several supervised machine learning techniques and provide a tool which is fine tuned for knowledge discovery on data from multiple sources. The ASD collects and maintains large amounts of student data. This data is collected from different sources like student management systems, excel spreadsheets and other sources. This data varies in both size and scope. These data banks have considerable potential for information discovery and pattern analysis. The main focus of this project is to assist the ASD research team in deployment of appropriate standards and procedures for efficiently forecasting and utilizing the large amount of data collected by the district. The goal of the project is to evaluate the most efficient supervised machine learning techniques to forecast future trends. As a result, we develop a framework to transform raw data into minable data and apply several predictive data mining techniques to the same.

Rest of the paper is organized as follows. Section II is Related Work that provides a discussion of applications of data mining and machine learning techniques to educational data. In Section III we provide an overview of the overall work in terms of the machine learning techniques applied. Section IV explains the structure of the educational datasets that we have analyzed and the preprocessing done before applying the machine learning techniques. The experiments and results appear in Section V with conclusions and a discussion of future work appearing in Section VI.

II. Related Work

Romero et al [4] survey the applications of data mining in the education industry. They analyze how educational data mining is different from traditional systems. The data, mining-objectives and techniques used in traditional e-commerce systems are significantly different. The most important goal in e-commerce mining is monetary and measured in terms of fixed business objectives. Educational data mining is more subjective and its primary goal is to improve the learning experience of students and provide decision makers with trends and analytics. They also highlight how some traditional data mining techniques can be successfully used in education-mining but due to the special characteristics of data in educational systems traditional techniques have to be modified so as to meet the requirements. They appraise the various data-mining techniques like clustering, outlier detection, statistics, visualization and sequential pattern mining that have been applied in education systems. The need for data mining techniques specifically designed to an educational perspective is classified as one of the future research areas of data mining. In [5], Agathe Merceron et al demonstrate how data mining techniques and algorithms can assist in extracting trends and patterns from data obtained from web-based educational systems. Baker et al in [6] review the current advancements in educational data mining. They pinpoint the key areas of research particularly in the field of education mining. They provide a comparative analysis of the emerging research areas. Relationship mining, clustering and prediction have been classified as methods that are gaining popularity in education data mining. Zaiane et al [7] outline how data mining can help in information extraction and analysis of online courses. In [8], Tang et al explain how methods like clustering, association rules and collaborative filtering assist in developing optimized e-learning systems. Beck et al in [9] demonstrate how predictive data mining methods can help in predicting student behavior. Siegel in [10] provides a step by step methodology for effective implementation of predictive data mining methods. This guide provides an excellent introduction to successfully implement a predictive data mining project. It provides a thorough analysis of predictive methods and historical references with regards to advancements in predictive data mining. In [11] Samui et al provide an introduction to predictive data mining process and introduce some of the most widely used predictive techniques like neural networks ,decision trees rule induction and genetic algorithms.

Our current work builds some of the aforementioned research by applying a number of supervised machine learning algorithms to educational data. Before considering advanced models, in the current work we have focused on applying some of the commonly used machine learning models such as Decision Tress, k-Nearest Neighbor, Neural Networks, and Naïve Bayes Classifier.

III. Generalized Framework

In this section, we investigate the various predictive analytics techniques for applying to the educational datasets. The objective is to mine the data collected by the school district and provide a tool which is fine tuned for knowledge discovery of educational data. The tool used for conducting these experiments is Rapid Miner. The tool is very powerful and supports almost all machine learning procedures as well as data preprocessing, modeling, transformation and data visualization. Figure 1 shows the different steps that are performed on the raw data.

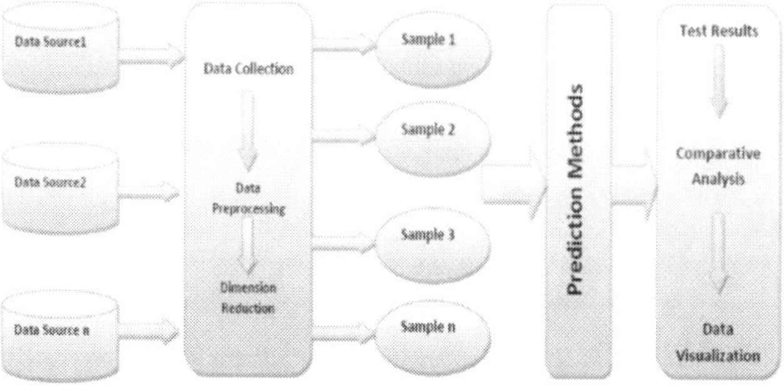

Fig. 1. Predictive data analytics and visualization process

A. *Steps in Data Analytics and Visualization*

Data Preprocessing: Understanding the complexity and inconsistencies that exists in the data will help us decide the most effective methods to make the data minable and achieve our objective. The activities performed in this step are:

Outlier Detection: Outliers are instances in the data that deviate from other instances and appear inconsistent. There are several algorithms and methods that can be used to detect such instances. In our case we used the statistical search based methods based on the distance measure techniques available in Rapid Miner.

Replacing Missing Values: This data cleansing process involves replacing missing instances with appropriate values to make the data complete. Several predictive mining techniques cannot handle missing values so it's important we replace these instances.

Data reduction and transformation: This step involves removing superfluous attributes from the data. If large numbers of instances in an attribute are missing, then we can eliminate that attribute. Certain techniques have limitations on the type of data that can be handled. It is necessary to transform the data into the suitable format to make it minable. For example, wherever necessary tasks such as discretizing the data, converting numerical values to binomial, converting nominal values to binomial, etc. were performed.

Perform Predictive Analytics using different techniques & evaluate performance measures: This step involves performing predictive analysis using the data mining tool and generating performance indicators that will assist in evaluating and analyzing the technique used.

B. *Predictive Analytics Techniques*

Decision Trees: Prediction using decision trees is one of the most popular and widely used logical methods for predictive analytics. The decision tree structure can be easily incorporated with data that is in standard spreadsheet format. There are two fundamental data preparation and learning tasks involved with decision trees. The first task is to establish the nodes in the trees based on the data. The second task is to formulate tests for non-terminal nodes. There are several algorithms to perform these two tasks. The process involves first selecting a feature from the data which is then used to partition the data. This process is performed in recursion and applied to subdivision of data. Finally, terminal nodes are assigned with the appropriate values. One of the advantages of the decision tree approach is that it can handle high dimensional data. One can apply the various dimension reduction techniques to raw data in order to make it suitable for decision modeling. Decision trees that cover all the cases of the training data can get very complex and techniques like pruning have to be applied to reduce the complexity. Overall decision tree induction method is one of the fastest prediction techniques. Another advantage is the explanatory capability and ease of inferring the solution in decision trees. In our work, we have used the Random forest algorithm [12] to generate the decision tree. This approach is characterized by examining the data and classifying the cases on similarity measures. The solution to a new case can be found by looking for a match learnt from training data. Distance measures are used to relate a new case to an already defined case to predict the solution. This method is suitable for both classification and regression problems.

k-nearest neighbor: A distance metric is used to calculate the distance to known cases. In the k-nearest neighbor technique, k represents the number of neighbors to retrieve. Normalization of data is required to make the data suitable for this method. Feature selection plays an important role in the success of this method and it requires extensive experimentation. Overall this method produces satisfactory knowledge discovery which is based on prior experience. The k-NN approach [3] does not support missing values. Therefore, for the model to effectively predict it was important to eliminate instances with missing values.

Neural Networks: Neural Networks is a nonlinear mathematical solution for predictive analytics. This method is characterized by a network of neurons. Each neuron has a threshold value and it accepts a set of input values. A weighted sum of all the inputs to a neuron is calculated and this sum is compared to the threshold. The inputs to a neural network are features. Initially, the computation between nodes is linear. Several data preparation steps are required to make raw data suitable for neural networks. Neural networks are complex when compared to linear prediction techniques and several optimization methods have to be applied to improve the performance. Significant data reduction is required so as to limit the input. One of the drawbacks of neural network approach in predictive analytics is that the time required for training the network is high compared to other methods. For building our neural network model, we used the Nominal to Numerical operator. This operator is used to map all non-numeric attributes to numeric values. Neural network models cannot handle non-numeric instances. This operator does not change any numeric attributes, binary attributes are converted to 0/1 and nominal attributes are converted using effect coding which is implemented in the tool. This model learns and predicts based on feed forward neural network which is trained by back propagation algorithm. We used one hidden layer along with a sigmoid activation function.

Naïve Bayes classifier: This predictive technique is based on the Bayesian Theorem [3]. It is a very popular technique as it can handle data with high dimensionality. This technique is relatively easy to understand and can generate high accuracy rates.

IV. DATA ANALYSIS AND PREPROCESSING

It is important to analyze the raw values and attributes before we undergo data preprocessing. The design approach to perform the experiments has been based on [13].

The data sets used in this comparative analysis were provided by the ASD. All these data sets were drawn from different educational contexts. It included Student transcript GPA data, Course data (ELA) and enrollment data. In order to better understand the data distribution and the nature of the data, first an exploratory data analysis was performed. Table I shows the number of cases/instances in each dataset and the corresponding attributes. These files were extracted from the Student management system for analysis. This data was collected from 2000-2004. Each row within these files represents a student and its respective performance in each marking period. There were four marking periods that were included in our experimental analysis.

The ELA dataset has three class labels high, average and low. The number of features or predictors is 5 in the ELA dataset and the number of instances is 32936. There are two class labels pass and fail and the number of predictors is 8 in the ERSphase4GPA dataset. There are 3103 instances. In the Enrollment dataset there are 20 class labels. The data provided by ASD is the raw data dump obtained from their student management systems. We first performed data preprocessing and eliminated some of the inconsistencies in the data. After unwanted attributes were discarded the next step in the cleansing process is to remove or replace missing values in the example set with relevant instances. Many predictive techniques cannot handle missing data. We decided to replace the missing value of a numerical attribute with the mean of that attribute. If the attribute with missing value was nominal, we have used the mode of attribute for replacement. We also dropped instances that had majority of its values missing.

V. EXPERIMENTS

We now describe the experiments conducted to perform comparative analysis of different predictive analytics techniques on the pre-processed ELA, ERSphase4GPA and Enrollment datasets. We compare the classification accuracy of the four methods on three different datasets and derive the best method across all. Specifically, for comparison we used the following performance measures:

- Accuracy: Percentage of correctly classified instances.
- Kappa: The kappa value presents the measure of agreement. A value of '0' signifies poor agreement, i.e. the prediction was made by chance whereas '1' signifies excellent prediction agreement.

TABLE I. RAW DATA ANALYSIS ON THE ASD DATASETS

Data Set	No. of cases/instances	No. of Attributes	Class/ Label	Comments
ELA 2001.csv	20359	26	**Performance** based on marking periods High, Low, Average	Dataset describes student ELA performance over four marking periods along with their final mark and course information. Raw data had large number of missing values and non significant attributes. Dataset had both numeric and nominal variables.
ELA 2002.csv	18567			
ELA 2003.csv	11585			
ELA 2004.csv	23454			
ERSphase4GPA.csv	25476	23	**Outcome** : pass or fail based on GPA	Dataset describes student GPA info over a period and student related information. Dataset had some missing values and was numeric in nature.
EOYEnrollment0102d.csv	13486	30	**Enrollment Status**: 12 different dimensions/ classes	Dataset describes student enrollment status data over years along with related student information. DOB, Area, School etc. Raw data had large number of missing values and no significant attributes Dataset had both numeric and nominal variables.
EOYEnrollment0203d.csv	10485			
EOYEnrollment0304d.csv	15785			

- Root mean square error: Measurement of error. A low root mean square error signifies that the prediction is more correct than it is wrong.

TABLE II: PERFORMANCE MEASURES FOR ELA DATASET

	Accuracy		Kappa	Root mean square error
K-NN	K=1	K=500		
	46.14 %	83.58 %	0.712	0.157
Naïve Bayes	85.84 %		0.751	0.005
Random Forest	82.80 %		0.634	0.235
Neural Net	90.11 %		0.084	0.203

Table II shows the classification accuracy, classification error, kappa and root mean square error for the ELA dataset. For K-NN, Performance measures were compared at different values of 'k'.' k' determines the flexibility of the classifier. For low 'k', we observed high bias making the classifier very flexible. Through cross validation and experimenting with various values of k we found a value that did not under fit or over fit. The accuracy increased as 'k' was increased. We achieved the highest classification accuracy at k=500. The kappa values suggest that the method has good prediction agreement. The performance of Naïve Bayes was better compared to K-nn and Random Forest method. Random forest model learns and predicts based on a set of random trees. The model created comprises of numerous random tree models. The parameters used to fine tune the model are the number of trees, the criteria used in selecting the attributes and splits. Naïve Bayes method produced the best prediction agreement. Although the best classification accuracy was obtained via the neural net method, the kappa value suggests that it had low agreement.

TABLE III: PERFORMANCE MEASURES FOR ERSPHASE4GPA DATASET

	Accuracy	Kappa	Root mean square error
K-NN	88.04%	0.743	0.275
Naïve Bayes	91.04%	0.815	0.260
Random Forest	89.81%	0.774	0.259
Neural Net	99.58%	0.014	0.074

For 'ERSphase4GPA' dataset, the K-NN performance measures remained constant at different values of 'k'. The kappa values suggest that all methods other than neural net have good prediction agreement. The performance of Naïve Bayes was better compared to K-nn and Random Forest method. This method produced the best prediction agreement. Although the best classification accuracy was obtained via the neural net method, the kappa value suggests that it had low agreement but the root mean square error was also low. Additionally, this dataset was numeric in nature, well suited for neural net method.

TABLE IV: PERFORMANCE MEASURES FOR ENROLLMENT DATASET

	Accuracy	Classification Error	Kappa	Root mean square error
K-NN	73.62%	26.38%	0.304	0.275
Naïve Bayes	72.08%	27.92%	0.459	0.260
Random Forest	68.71%	31.29%	0.053	0.514
Neural Net	76.65%	23.35%	0.481	0.468

For the 'Enrollment' dataset the K-NN performance measures remained constant at different values of 'k'. The performance of K-NN was better compared to Naïve Bayes and Random Forest methods. The kappa values suggest that all methods produced poor prediction agreement when compared to other datasets. The root mean square error was comparatively high for this dataset signifying that the prediction is more wrong than it is correct. The best classification accuracy was obtained via the neural net method; additionally, the kappa value suggests that it had higher agreement compared to other methods.

VI. Conclusions and Future Work

We evaluated the performance of four supervised machine learning algorithms on three different data sets drawn from distinct educational contexts. The ERSphase4GPA dataset produced the best classification accuracy. Neural net emerged as a method producing the highest accuracy rates but this method had low agreement, i.e. prediction was made by chance for some datasets. Naive Bayes emerged as a consistent method producing reliable performance across all datasets.

There are a number of research avenues that can be followed thereby increasing the scope of this work. More experimentation with parameters within each method could effectively improve the performance. Using Deep Learning models is another interesting direction to pursue as well.

References

[1] E. A. Amrieh, T. Hamtini, and I. Aljarah, "Mining Educational Data to Predict Student's academic Performance using Ensemble Methods", International Journal of Database Theory and Application, 9(8), 119-136, 2016

[2] E. A. Amrieh, T. Hamtini, and I. Aljarah, "Preprocessing and analyzing educational data set using X-API for improving student's performance", In proc. of IEEE Jordan Conference on Applied Electrical Engineering and Computing Technologies (AEECT), 2015

[3] Hands-On Machine Learning with Scikit-Learn and TensorFlow, O'Reilly Media, ISBN: 1491962291

[4] C. Romero, and S. Venture, Educational Data Mining: A Survey from 1995 to 2005.Expert Systems with Applications 33, 125-146, 2007

[5] A. Merceron and K. Yacef, Educational Data Mining: a Case Study. In Proceedings of the conference on Artificial Intelligence in Education: Supporting Learning through Intelligent and Socially Informed Technology, Chee-Kit Looi, Gord McCalla, Bert Bredeweg, and Joost Breuker (Eds.). IOS Press, Amsterdam, The Netherlands, The Netherlands,467-474, 2005

[6] R. Baker and K. Yacef, the State of Educational Data Mining in 2009: A Review and Future Visions JEDM - *Journal of Educational Data Mining, Volume 1, Issue 1, October 2009 Pages 3-17, 2009*

[7] O. Zaiane, Web usage mining for a better web-based learning environment. In Proceedings of conference on advanced technology for education, 2001

[8] T. Tang and G. Mccalla, Smart recommendation for an evolving e-learning system: architecture and experiment. International Journal on E-Learning 4, 105-129, 2005

[9] J. Beck, and B. Woolf, High-level student modeling with machinelearning. Proceedings of the 5th International Conference on IntelligentTutoring Systems, 584–593, 2000

[10] E. Siegel, Predictive Analytics: The Power to Predict Who Will Click, Buy, Lie, or Die, Wiley, ISBN: 1119145678, 2016.

[11] P. Samui, S Roy, and V. Balas, Handbook of Neural Computation, ISBN 0128113189, Academic Press, 2017.

[12] C. Smith, Decision Trees and Random Forests: A Visual Introduction For Beginners, ISBN 1549893750, 2017.

[13] L. Talavera, E. Gaudioso, Mining student data to characterize similar behavior groups in unstructured collaboration spaces, In Workshop on AI in CSCL (2004), pp. 17-23.

[14] N. Moseley, C. O. Alm and M. Rege, "Toward inferring the age of Twitter users with their use of nonstandard abbreviations and lexicon," *2014 IEEE International Conference on Information Reuse and Integration (IRI)*, 2014, pp. 219-226

[15] A. Oest and M. Rege, "Feedback-driven clustering for automated linking of web pages," *8th International Conference for Internet Technology and Secured Transactions (ICITST-2013)*, London, 2013, pp. 344-3

An Analysis of Correlation Between Seat Positions and Achievements of Students

Toshiro Minami and Yoko Ohura
Kyushu Institute of Information Sciences
Saifu, Dazaifu, Fukuoka 818-0117 Japan
Email: minamitoshiro@gmail.com ohura@kiis.ac.jp

Abstract—**It has been a big issue for universities to setup an appropriate environment for their students to learn effectively. Traditionally, professors have been supposed to understand their students, their attitudes to learning, knowledge levels and other factors by themselves. Thanks to the recent development of Information and Communications Technology (ICT), it is possible to collect various kinds of educational data, analyze them, and extract useful knowledge for enhancing education. Such approach is called Educational Data Mining (EDM). This paper, as a part of EDM, deals with the seat occupation data of students in a class. It is often pointed out that students who take seats close to the lecturer tend to have good evaluation scores, or achievements. Our major aim of this paper is to analyze objective data and to investigate how students take their seats, to find if seat locations relate to the students' achievements, and to investigate if distances of seats between students relate to their differences of achievements.**

Keywords-Educational Data Mining; Learning Analytics; Seat Location; Friendship Analysis.

I. INTRODUCTION

In order to let their students learn effectively, universities have been making great efforts. Professors have to educate themselves through faculty development (FD) activities. They are expected to capture what their students are like, including their attitudes to learning, knowledge levels, and other pedagogical features. Recent development of ICT makes it easy to collect various kinds of educational data. In the field of Educational Data Mining (EDM) [11][12], a lot of studies have been carried out for investigating about students.

We have been investigating retrospective evaluation texts of students written in a term-end lectures in some studies on EDM [3] – [10]. Through these studies, we found that students who can study with wider viewpoints have better achievements than those who have narrower viewpoints. In other words, the students who can position new knowledge in their knowledge network what they have already learned are able to get better achievements, such as the term-end examination for evaluating what they have learned in the course.

As was pointed out in [1][2], psychological issues are quite important for students in learning, such as to be well-motivated, to percept meanings of study, and to have appropriate self-images for learning. It is also an important issue for the lectures how and how much they involve the class and help their students have the best achievements out of the lectures. Our studies in educational data analysis intend to contribute to improvements for these issues.

We often observe that the students who take seats close to the lecturer in the classroom are eager to learn more than those who choose far away seats from the lecturer, who seem to have less eagerness for learning. We have been wondering if this observation is true or not.

In this paper, as a part of study about students' attitudes to learning, eagerness to study, etc., we add-up the data of seat positions occupied by students, and investigate further on these issues. We take the term-end examination scores as the index for measuring achievements of students. We investigate how the seat positions of students and their achievements are corelated.

We also observe that students often form groups of friends. They are close to each other, and thus, they like to do things together, including taking nearby seats in the classrooms, chat a lot, and study together. We hypothesize that seat positions and achievements of students in the same group somehow relate to each other. Investigation of this issue is another important aim of this paper.

In the long run, our goal of analysis of educational data is to better understand our students, such as their attitudes towards learning, what they think about their learning style, how we could advise them for better performance, etc. The study conducted in this paper is a part of our approach toward this goal.

The rest of this paper is organized as follows: In Section II, we describe the data we deal with for analysis in this paper. Then, in Section III, we investigate how students take seats in the class and if seat positions relate to the students' achievements. In Section IV, we define the concept of the distance between two students, and then, we investigate if distances of two students relate to the difference of their achievements. Finally, in Section V, we summarize this paper and prospect our future plans.

II. THE TARGET DATA FOR ANALYSIS

The data we deal with in this paper are obtained in a course called "Information Science" in a university in Japan during the semester from September 2013 to February 2014. The course aimed to make the students learn sufficient elementary knowledge about the computer's hardware and software, network, information security, information ethics, etc., and was consisted of 15 lectures.

The number of students who registered for the course was 68. The number of students who actually attended the classes was 67 because one student did not attend the classes at all. The students of the course consisted from the first-year to the fourth-year. The attending students were asked to write a mini-report at the end of every class. There was the term-end examination for assessing the student's achievement, which consisted of 3 questions: The first question asked the students to choose appropriate terms for the 20 fill-in-the-blank-places contained in 6 descriptive sentences. The second and the third questions asked them to answer in free-text style. These questions aimed to assess if the students had sufficient knowledge about the technical terms and concepts which they had learned in the classes. We consider the score of this examination as the measuring index of achievement of the student.

Considering the privacy issue of students, we refer each student by his or her sequential number. The seat position records used in this paper are the ones students recorded themselves at each class.

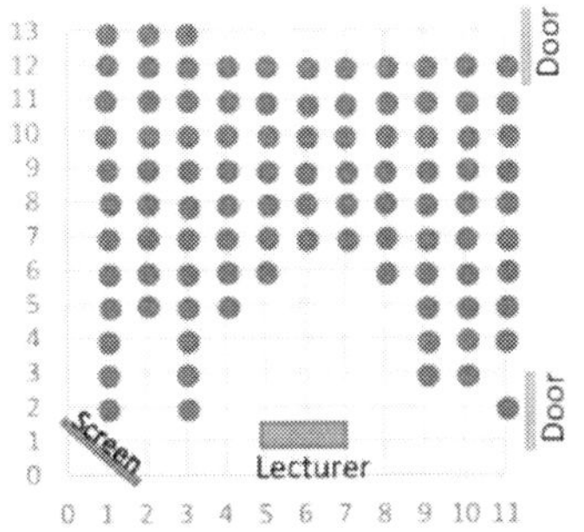

Figure 1. Seats occupied by students at least once

Figure 1 shows the seats occupied by at least once by some students. The lecturer's table was located at the center area of the lower-end of the figure, and a screen was located at the lower-left corner, and two entrance doors were located at the right; one at the lower-right corner and the other, at the top-right corner.

The seats were spanned from 1 to 11 horizontally (or x-direction) and from 2 to 13 vertically (or y-direction). In this paper, we specify a set position by its x- and y-coordinates. For example, the seat (1, 2) is the left-bottom-end seat, which is the closest seat to the screen. The seats at the topmost line with 13 y-coordinate existed only from 1 to 3 in their x- coordinates. There were no seats from 4 to 11. Thus, the seat at (1, 13) is the left-top-most seat and the seat (11, 12) is the top-right-most seat of the classroom.

As we can see easily, quite a few students avoided the seats that are close to the lecturer and thus some seats had been occupied by no students. For example, the seats from (2, 2) to (10, 2) except (3, 2) are never occupied by any students. Among 124 seats, 26 seats are never used, and the rest 98 seats are used at least once.

Table I shows how many times each seat was occupied during the course. The frequencies range from 1 to 16. The seat (10, 11) is the only one which has the maximum frequency of 16. There are 4 seats which have the minimum frequency of 1, namely, (11, 4), (9, 6), (5, 6), (4, 5), and (2, 5).

The right-most column marked as μ, meaning the mean, shows the mean of the respective line, and the bottom line marked as μ shows the mean value of the respective column.

TABLE I. FREQUENCY OF OCCUPATION OF SEATS

	1	2	3	4	5	6	7	8	9	10	11	μ
13	12	11	12									12
12	15	15	7	8	8	12	13	8	12	12	5	10
11	13	8	11	5	13	15	13	4	14	16	13	11
10	12	11	11	6	7	14	11	4	9	12	14	10
9	12	10	12	5	2	12	15	12	6	15	13	10
8	11	12	8	5	10	10	9	8	5	12	13	9
7	9	7	8	4	4	5	4	6	4	6	11	6
6	11	10	11	2	1			3	1	8	12	7
5	12	1	2	1					4	4	8	5
4	3		9						12	14	1	8
3	11		2						14	15		11
2	11		13								3	9
μ	11	9	9	5	6	11	11	6	8	11	9	

According to Table I, we can say that the seats in the areas which are far-end from the lecturer are very popular. For example, the seats surrounded by the areas from 1 to 3 in horizontal, or x-coordinate and from 8 to 13 in vertical, or y-coordinate (i.e., far-left corner) have high values, where the mean value of frequency in this area is 11.

Also, the seats in the area surrounded by from 9 to 11 horizontally and from 8 to 12 vertically (i.e., far-right corner) is also the one that is highly used by students, where the mean frequency is also 11. Furthermore, the seats in the area from 5 to 7 horizontally and from 9 to 12 vertically (i.e., far-middle) also has mean frequency 11. On the contrary, the seats with 4, 5, 8, and 9 in x-coordinate have very low frequency in average, as we can see in the last line of Table I, specifically, 5, 6, 6, and 8, respectively.

As we compare the mean frequencies between the horizontal lines of seats which are shown at the right-most column marked as μ in Table I, the upper area, or the far-from-the-lecturer area, from 7 to 13 in y-coordinate have high values from 9 to 12, whereas the middle area, or the not-far-away-and-not-too-close-to-the-lecturer area, from 5 to 7 in y-coordinate have small values from 5 to 7 in their mean frequencies. The lower area, or the closest-to-the-lecturer area, from 2 to 4 in y-coordinate has the mean frequency values from 8 to 11.

From these observations, we may roughly conclude that both horizontally and vertically, far-end areas are popularly used by students. As we compare the columns horizontally, left-most, middle, and right-most areas are popular, whereas the area between these areas are not so much popularly used. As we compare the lines vertically, the upper half area is most popularly used, and the lower part of the rest areas are the next, whereas the upper area in the lower part is the least popularly used area.

III. SEAT POSITION ANALYSIS

Each student has his or her own seat choosing preference. Some students prefer to occupy the same seat throughout the classes, whereas some other students transit a lot from a lecture to the next one. We assume that a group of students who are friends each other might transit together by keeping their seat distances as close as possible throughout the course.

A. Correlation between Seat Positions and Achievements of Students

It is often pointed out that students who take seat near the lecturer are more eager to learn, and thus have better achievements than those who take far-away seats from the lecturer. First of all in this section, we would like to make sure if this observation is true or not in our data.

In order to prepare for further analysis, we give a formalized descriptions of the data and important concepts.

We define $S = \{s_1, s_2, \ldots, s_n\}$, the set of all students. Note $n = 68$ in our case. We also define the set of lectures by $L = \{1, 2, \ldots, m\}$. Note $m = 15$ in our case.

Let $s \in S$ and $l \in L$. Then, the seat data is in the form $seat(s, l) = (x, y)$, where $x \in \{1, 2, \ldots, 11\}$ for x-coordinate and $y \in \{2, 3, \ldots, 13\}$ for y-coordinate. Note that $seat(s,l)$ is undefined if the student s is absent at the lecture l. We also define $Achv(s)$ for student s as the achievement, or examination score, of s. Note $0 \leq Achv(s) \leq 100$ for all s.

We define the concept of achievement value for a seat for preparing later discussions. Let p be a seat position, i.e., $p = (x, y)$ for some x and y so that $1 \leq x \leq 11$ and $2 \leq y \leq 13$. The achievement value $\alpha(p)$ is defined by:

$$\alpha(p) = \frac{\sum_{(s,l) \in so(p)} Achv(s)}{|so(p)|} \tag{1}$$

where $so(p) = \{(s, l) \in S \times L \mid seat(s,l) = p\}$, and $|so(p)|$ is the number of elements of the set $so(p)$.

According to the definition, $\alpha(p)$ is the mean of the achievements of the students who occupied the seat p on the basis of occurrences of occupation. For example, if exactly one student takes the seat p, and no other students take it, then the achievement value of the seat is the same value as the achievement of the occupying student; i.e., $\alpha(p) = Achv(s)$. Note that the student may not attended all the lectures.

Table II and Figure 2 show the achievement values of seats. The size of a circle in Figure 2 is proportional to the achievement value of the seat located as the center of the circle. We can see easily that the size of the circles close to the lecturer, i.e., in the lower area, are bigger than those in the upper area. The rightmost column of Table II shows the mean of the achievement values of the line. They also show that the achievement values are larger in the lines with smaller number, i.e., closer to the lecturer, than those with bigger numbers. Thus, we can conclude that our observation that the students closer to the lecturer have better achievements than those who take far-away, or rear seats.

We are also interested in to know if there is a difference in achievements between the students who sit near the enter/exit doors and those who sit far-away seats from the doors. We could not find clear differences of the size of the circles between left and right areas of the classroom, more specifically, the values range from 52 to 68, with small difference. Thus, we may roughly conclude that there are no significant differences in the achievement of seats between left and right positions.

TABLE II. SEAT POSITION ACHIEVEMENT

	1	2	3	4	5	6	7	8	9	10	11	μ
13	52	56	66									58
12	56	60	47	57	64	60	52	79	89	64	67	63
11	64	50	30	62	62	65	61	46	53	48	69	55
10	61	57	63	57	61	69	60	55	14	61	56	56
9	59	50	55	63	73	61	61	60	37	65	58	58
8	60	56	66	51	66	66	68	67	24	70	62	60
7	70	80	61	55	62	68	61	69	46	67	54	63
6	75	79	60	48	59			69	70	65	56	64
5	43	55	82	25					62	75	63	58
4	78		82						57	86	70	75
3	83		97						79	80		85
2	68		95									81
μ	64	60	67	52	64	65	60	64	53	68	62	

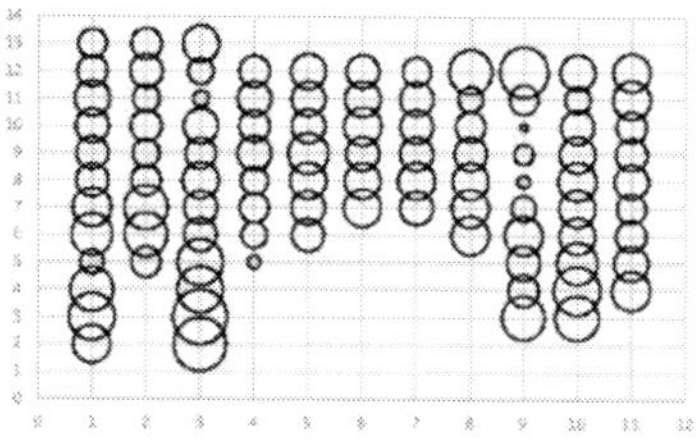

Figure 2. Seat Achevement

TABLE III. COMPARISON OF DOMAIN-ACHIEVEMENTS

	1-3	4-8	9-11
7-13	57.7	62.2	57.9
2-6	73.6	55.3	70.7

We would like to analyze the differences between areas in the classroom. We divide the classroom area into 6 smaller areas; left area by column numbers from 1 to 3, middle area from 4 to 8, and right area from 9 to 11, and front area by line numbers from 2 to 6, and back area from 8 to 13. Table III shows the mean values of achievement of these 6 areas; front-left, front-middle, front-right, back-left, back-middle, and back-right. As we can see easily, front-left and front-right areas have the highest achievement values, followed by the back-middle area, and back-left and back-right areas. The front-middle area has the least, or worst, achievement value.

We investigate a significant difference of the mean of the seat achievement α(p) for the six areas in TABLE III using the analysis of variance (ANOVA) test without assuming equal variance. We obtain the results that F = 3.734, num df = 5.000, denom df = 20.061, p-value = 0.01496. The result of the mean difference of seat achievement degree α(p) with a significance level 5%, the p-value is 0.01496. Thus, we can conclude that significant difference holds in at least one pair of 6 areas.

It is interesting to see that the students who sit in front area are diligent and having good achievements in general. It is also interesting that in the back area, students in front of the lecturer may be more diligent than those who sit far-left and far-right seats. We need to investigate further on these results with other lecture data in order to generalize this observation.

B. Seat Transition Length Analysis

In this section, we pay attention to the transitions of seats of students. According to our observation, some students take same seats at every lecture, whereas some students take different seats frequently. It may happen that the seat transitions reflect the student's attitude to learning or some other attitudes which relate to their achievements. We would like to investigate if such kinds of relations exist or not in this section.

Figure 3 shows sample seat transition trajectories of two students 12 and 27. Student 12 is a typical example who keeps their positions, and student 27 is one who transits a lot. Note that the numbers next to the points indicate the lecture number.

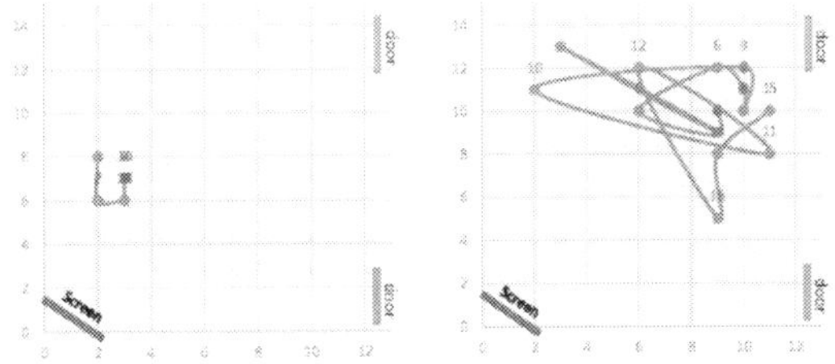

(a) Student 12 (b) Student 27

Figure 3. Sample Seat Transition Trajectories: (a) with Small Transition Length, and (b) with Large Seat Transition Length

For a student s ($\in S$), we define the set of attending lectures L_S by $L_S = \{l \in L \mid seat(s, l) \text{ is defined }\}$. Let $|\cdot|$ be the number of elements of the set. Then, $|L_S|$ is the number of the lectures which the student s has attended. Thus, $0 \leq |L_S| \leq 15$ holds. Where, $|L_S| = 15$ means that the student s attended all the classes, whereas $|L_S| = 0$ means that the student s did not attend the class at all.

Now we define the mean transition length $\tau(s)$ of the student s with $|L_S| > 0$ by:

$$\tau(s) = \frac{\sum_{i=1}^{k-1} d(seat(s.l_i), seatl(s.l_{i+1}))}{k-1} \tag{2}$$

where, there exists a sequence $l_1, l_2, \ldots, l_k (\in L)$ for some k (≥ 2) such that $l_1 < l_2 < \cdots < l_k$ and $L_S = \{l_1, l_2, \ldots, l_k\}$. Here, $d(p_1, p_2)$ is the distance function defined for every seat positions p_1 and p_2. Note that $k = |L_S|$. We define $\tau(s) = 0$ if $k = 1$; i.e., $L_S = \{l\}$ for some $l \in L$.

According to our definition, $\tau(s)$ is undefined if the student s did not attend at all. Note that $\tau(s) = 0$ if the student takes the same seat every time he or she attended. Note that the Σ-part of the definition is the accumulated transition distances. Thus, τ is the mean of transitions by only considering the seats when the student attended.

In this paper, we define the distance function d as follows: For any seats $p_1 = (x_1, y_1)$ and $p_2 = (x_2, y_2)$, $d(p_1, p_2) = |x_1 - x_2| + |y_1 - y_2|$. Note $|\cdot|$ in this definition is the absolute value of the number. In our method of analysis conducted in this paper, we may take other distance functions such as Euclidean distance:

$$d(p_1, p_2) = \sqrt{(x_1 - x_2)^2 + (y_1 - y_2)^2}$$

TABLE IV. SEAT TRANSITION LENGTH DATA FOR THE STUDENTS FROM 1 TO 10, 12 AND 27.

St.	Total.	#Transitions	τ	Achievement
1	61	12	5.1	46
2	69	12	5.8	55
3	13	14	0.9	63
4	7	12	0.6	56
5	9	11	0.8	49
6	23	14	1.6	53
7	2	14	0.1	80
8	44	14	3.1	82
9	35	14	2.5	59
10	37	12	3.1	74
12	7	14	0.5	57
27	82	14	5.9	75

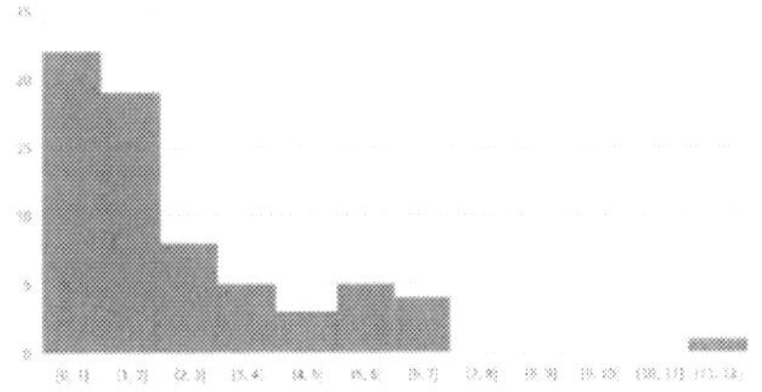

Figure 4. Histogram of Mean Transition Distance

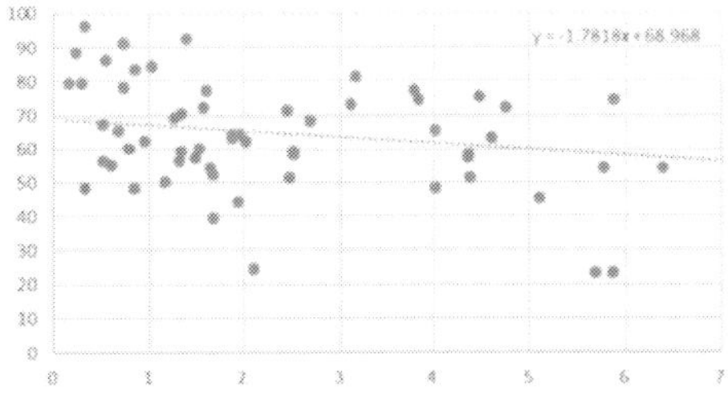

Figure 5. Correlation between mean Seat Transition Length and Achievement

Table IV shows the total transition length, the number of transitions, the value of $\tau(s)$, and the achievement of students from 1 to 10, 12, and 27, as example. As we have pointed out in Figure 3, we can numerically confirm our observation by objective data that $\tau(s_{12}) = 0.5 \ll \tau(s_{27}) = 5.9$.

Figure 4 shows a histogram for τ. We can see that the number of students decreases as τ value increases. Thus, many students do not transit a lot. From this result, we can say that the student 12 is a typical example of those who do not transit a lot, whereas the student 27 represents a rare case who transits a lot.

Figure 5 shows how τ values and achievements of students are correlated. The correlation coefficient is -0.253*, which is weak in negative and not uncorrelated. The p-value is 0.04726 in the Pearson product-moment correlation coefficient test. For the students with long transition length τ, i.e., frequently moving students for each lecture, achievements are not very good.

The results of our regression analysis test show that the explanatory variable coefficient = -1.78* and the intercept = 68.96***, adjusted R-squared = 0.04841, p-value = 0.04726.

The seat transition lengths of the top 10 students in achievement, i.e., those who's achievement values are greater than or equals to 80, are less than 2 except student 8, who has 3.14 in seat transition length. The mean seat transition length of these 10 students is 0.77.

It is interesting to see that the worst 10 students in achievement also have smaller transition length. Their achievement value is $\leq$ 51 and their mean transition length is 2.07. If we avoid the two students who have more than 5 transition length, the remaining 8 students have 1.22 in their transition length.

The students who have roughly from 50 to 80 have a wide range of values in their transition length, where their mean length is 2.39.

IV. Seat Distances between Students

In this section, we investigate the correlation between seat distances and achievement differences of two students. We have a hypothesis that students who are friends tend to take seats close to each other. They communicate a lot, do things together including studying together. As a result, they might have similar achievements in the term-end evaluation examination. We would like to verify if this assumption is true or not in our data.

To begin with, we define the seat distance (or just distance for brevity) between two students. Let s_1 and s_2 be students ($\in S$). We define the seat distance $\delta(s_1, s_2)$ of s_1 and s_2 by:

$$\delta(s_1, s_2) = \frac{\sum_{l \in L_{s_1} \cap L_{s_2}} d(seat(s_1.l), seat(s_2.l))}{|L_{s_1} \cap L_{s_1}|} \quad (4)$$

when $L_{s_1} \cap L_{s_2} \neq \phi$.

The seat distance is the mean distance of two students when both of them are attending. Thus, $\delta(s_1, s_2)$ is undefined when $L_{s_1} \cap L_{s_2} = \phi$; which includes the case when one student is absent at all the lectures, and when one student attends the class, the other one is absent all the time.

Figure 6 shows the histogram of seat distances. The mean distance is 7.4, and maximum and minimum distances are 18.7 and 1, respectively. Figure 7 shows the histogram of differences of achievement of all the combinations of a pair of students. The number decreases as the difference increases. However, as we compare the mean values of achievement differences of all pairs and only the pairs which have less than or equals to 2, the former value is 24 and the latter is 21 as the difference of achievement score increases. The minimum, maximum, and mean values of the differences are 1, 18.7, and 7.4, respectively.

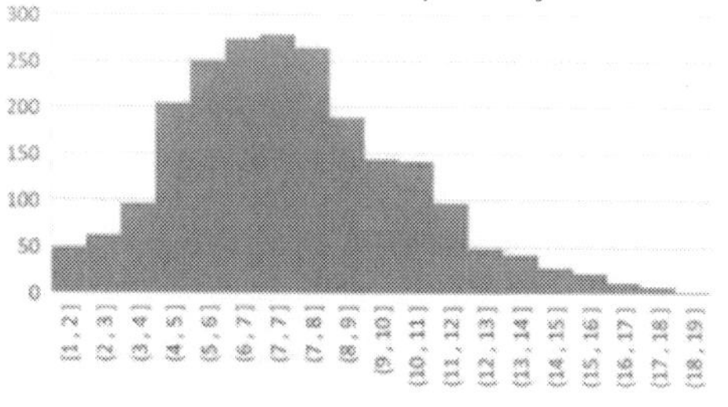

Figure 6. Histogram of Seat Distances between Pairs of Students

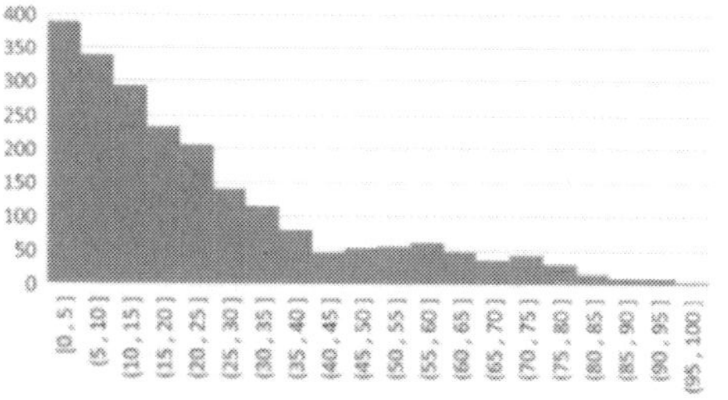

Figure 7. Histogram of Achievement Differences between two Students

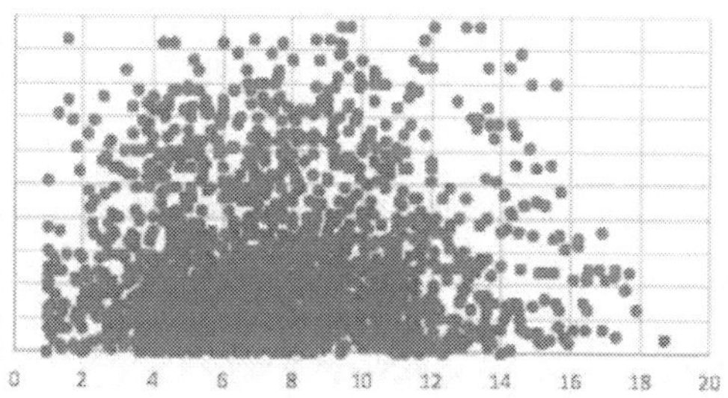

Figure 8. Correlation Between Seat Distance and Achievement Difference Between Two Students

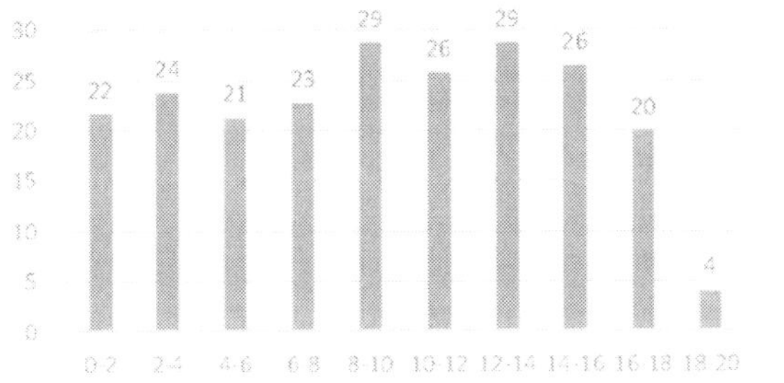

Figure 9. Mean Achievement Differences over the Range of Distance of Students

Figure 8 shows the correlation between the seat distances and achievement difference of every pair of students. From the figure, there seems to have little correlation between them. Actually, their correlation coefficient is a very small positive number of 0.08.

Next, we restrict the range of seat distance to 2 or less than 2, there are 59 cases of pairs of students, which correlation coefficient is 0.08, nearly the same value as that for all data. However, as we compare the mean values of achievement differences of all pairs and only the pairs which have less than or equals to 2, the former value is 24 and the latter is 21, which is somewhat smaller for the intimate student pairs than those in general.

Figure 9 shows the comparison of the mean differences from 0 to 20 by dividing them with the range width of 2. We can see that the values for the intervals 4-6 and 16-18 have smaller difference values than the closest value interval of 0-2. Thus, we cannot say that achievement difference is small when the seat distance is very small. We need to investigate in more detail in order to clarify what conditions are needed in our assumption that friendship of students might induce similarity of their achievements holds.

V. CONCLUDING REMARKS

The major goal of our series of study is to understand about the students, such as their attitudes to the lectures, and to learning in general, their motivation and seriousness to learning, and their styles in learning, and providing them with the best learning environment to them so that they can achieve the most out of the lectures.

Our approach is to extract useful tips for this goal by analyzing objective data obtained in the lectures together with other data collected by the university they are affiliating. By combining these tips and our know-hows obtained from practicing lectures, we should be able to provide them with good and valuable lectures.

In this paper, we take seat position data for analysis. First, we define an index for seat positions which shows how much achievement scores are taken by the students who use the seat. The result showed that the students who take seats close to the lecturer tend to have good achievements, whereas those who take far-away seats achieve rather poorly in general, which supports our observation. However, the result also inspired that some students with high performance may take seats near some far-end corner of the classroom. We need to investigate further with different lecture data on this.

Then, we investigate correlation between the transition lengths and achievements. We found that students who have either high achievements and low achievements rather transit a little length, and achievements of the students in the middle area vary widely from small transition to big transition lengths.

Even though we have some amount of confidence that students who take seat close to each other and transit together in order to keep their close distance might have similar achievement difference. Experimental result inspired that this is not true. One possible interpretation of this result is that there are many students who happen to take seats close to each other without intending to take close seats. We need to investigate further on such possibilities.

Our future study topics include: (1) to investigate the seat data further so that we can extract more valuable tips, (2) to analyze text data of the mini-reports which students had written at the end of each lecture, (3) to apply the similar method presented in this paper to other lecture data and compare them, etc.

ACKNOWLEDGMENT

This work was supported in part by JSPS KAKENHI Grant Number JP17K00502.

REFERENCES

[1] C. Ames and J. Archer, "Achievement Goals in the Classroom: Students' Learning Strategies and Motivation Processes," Journal of Educational Psychology, Vol.80, No.3, 1988, pp. 260–267. Available from: http://citeseerx.ist.psu.edu/viewdoc/ download?doi=10.1.1.536.309&rep=rep1&type=pdf 2018.01.30

[2] C. Ames, "Classrooms: Goals, Structures, and Student Motivation," Journal of Educational Psychology, Vol.84, No.3, 1992, pp. 261–271. Available from: http://llgarcia.educ.msu. edu/910reading/ames199 2 .pdf 2018.01.30

[3] T. Minami and Y. Ohura, "An Attempt on Effort-Achievement Analysis of Lecture Data for Effective Teaching," Database Theory and Application (DTA 2012), in T.-h. Kim et al. (Eds.): EL/DTA/UNESST 2012, CCIS 352, Springer-Verlag, Dec. 2012, pp. 50–57.

[4] T. Minami and Y. Ohura, "Towards Development of Lecture Data Analysis Method and its Application to Improvement of Teaching," 2nd International Conference on Applied and Theoretical Information Systems Research (2ndATISR 2012), Dec. 2012, 14pp..

[5] T. Minami and Y. Ohura, "Lecture Data Analysis towards to Know How the Students' Attitudes Affect to their Evaluations," 8th International Conference on Information Technology and Applications (ICITA 2013), July 2013, pp. 164–169.

[6] T. Minami and Y. Ohura, "Investigation of Students' Attitudes to Lectures with Text-Analysis of Questionnaires," 4th International Conference on E-Service and Knowledge Management (ESKM 2013), Sep. 2013, 7pp..

[7] T. Minami and Y. Ohura, "A Correlation Analysis of Student's Attitude and Outcome of Lectures –Investigation of Keywords in Class-Evaluation Questionnaire–," Advanced

Science and Technology Letters (ASTL), Vol.73 (FGCN 2014), Dec. 2014, pp. 11–16.

[8] T. Minami and Y. Ohura, "Towards Improving Students' Attitudes to Lectures and Getting Higher Grades –With Analyzing the Usage of Keywords in Class-Evaluation Questionnaire–," in Proc. The Seventh International Conference on Information, Process, and Knowledge Management (eKNOW 2015), 2015, pp. 78–83.

[9] T. Minami and Y. Ohura, "How Student's Attitude Influences on Learning Achievement? –An Analysis of Attitude-Representing Words Appearing in Looking-Back Evaluation Texts–," International Journal of Database Theory and Application (IJDTA), Science & Engineering Research Support Society (SERSC), Vol.8, No.2, 2015, pp. 129–144.

[10] T. Minami, Y. Ohura, and K. Baba, "A Characterization of Student's Viewpoint to Learning and its Application to Learning Assistance Framework," Proc. 9th International Conference on Computer Supported Education (CSEDU 2017) Volume 1: A2E, SciTePress, 2017, pp.619–630.

[11] C. Romero and S. Ventura, "Educational data mining: A survey from 1995 to 2005," Expert Systems with Applications, Vol. 33, Issue 1, July 2007, pp. 135–146. Available from: http://citeseerx.ist.psu.edu/viewdoc/download?doi=10.1.1.103.702&rep=rep1&type=pdf, 2018.01.30

[12] C. Romero, S. Ventura, P. Espejo, and C. Hervas, "Data mining algorithms to classify students," 1st International Conference on Educational Data Mining (EDM 2008), June 2008, pp.8–17. Available from: http://www.educationaldatamining.org/EDM2008/uploads/proc/fullproceedings.pdf#page=8 2018.01.30

Partial Order Multi Version Concurrency Control

Yuya Isoda, Atsushi Tomoda, Tsuyoshi Tanaka, Kazuhiko Mogi
Hitachi, Ltd. Research & Development Group
1-280, Higashi-koigakubo, Kokubunji-shi, Tokyo, Japan
email: { yuuya.isoda.sj, atsushi.tomoda.nx, tsuyoshi.tanaka.vz, kazuhiko.mogi.uv } @ hitachi.com

Abstract — **This paper presents the Partial Order Multi Version Concurrency Control (POMVCC), which is a concurrency control technique based on partial ordering of transactions. We claim that timestamp generation can be a bottleneck in multicore, high-throughput systems and POMVCC can execute multiple transactions using same timestamp without losing the consistency level. In this paper, we change the ordering of transaction processing from total order to partial order and propose partial order transaction processing on Multi Version Concurrency Control (MVCC), which numbers a timestamp in partial order per N transactions. This helps the system to reduce the overall number of increments to the timestamp and therefore improves the overall performance of the system. We claim that POMVCC achieves as high as 1.74 times the throughput of the conventional MVCC based system. We implemented a lock-free version of POMVCC in MPDB, which is their under development database system.**

Keywords - Partial Order Transaction Proccessing; In-memory DB; timestamp; Concurrency Control.

I. Introduction

In recent years, the number of CPU cores and the size of memory have increased owing to the progress of hardware technology. In the case of DataBase Management Systems (DBMSs), scalability technology for multicore CPUs [7][12][15] and large-scale and non-volatile in-memory technology [14][16] are advancing rapidly, and the performance of DBMS is close to reaching one million Transactions Per Second (tps) [3][12].

DBMS must guarantee ACID properties to maintain data consistency [22]. However, strictly doing so prevents a DBMS from improving performance because it needs to process Transactions (Tx) as serial processing in strict total order [13]. To increase performance, a DBMS generally uses the isolation level, which mitigates ACID properties step by step, performance in parallel processing is improved.

Recently, Multi Version Concurrency Control (MVCC) has been used for controlling the isolation level. It manages timestamps of both before and after updating a record and enables records to be referenced and updated simultaneously. As a result, it increases the performance of OnLine Transaction Processing (OLTP) and OnLine Analytical Processing (OLAP). Also, recent research has clarified how SERIALIZABLE can be implemented. Therefore, DBMSs with MVCC are thought to prevail in the near future [23][24].

There are two types of Timestamps (Ts) for MVCC, that is, a physical clock and a logical clock. The physical clock is the time used in the real world, such as Coordinated Universal Time (UTC). The Network Time Protocol (NTP) is prevailingly used as a protocol for synchronizing UTC among servers. However, the logical clock is not related to time in the real world, such as UTC and is a counter that determines the order, in which events occur. The Lamport method is known as a mechanism for sharing this counter among servers [28].

The logical clock implementation in DBMSs is common [5]. Spanner implemented a physical clock for DBMSs, but such an example is rare [29]. In recent years, the performance of DBMSs is close to reaching one million tps owing to in-memory technology, multicore technology, and improved transaction management methods [3][12]. In addition, the size of memory and the number of CPU cores, e.g., Hewlett Packard's Memory-Driven Computing, will be increasing more and more [32]. The bigger the system is, the more difficult the conventional timestamp management becomes. For example, in recent computers, it is mandatory for timestamps to be numbered every 1 us. In such an environment, large-scale mutual exclusion with a high CPU clock frequency may be problematic.

Silo is proposed for this problem [3]. Silo is the timestamp based on Epoch. It periodically updates the high-order bits of the timestamp. Transaction threads update low-order bits under the condition that they satisfy the order of dependence. As a result, Silo can reduce the number of updates for the timestamp. However, it cannot be easily adapted for the conventional MVCC-based DBMS because it needs lock processing and management of the Read-Set and Write-Set for concurrency control.

In this paper, we propose Partial Order Multi Version Concurrency Control (POMVCC). POMVCC is technology based on the reduction of the conflict rate, which is caused by a large-scale DB. It mitigates the problems with simultaneous executable transactions. Specifically, it updates the timestamp at an abort. Thus, multiple transactions can be processed at the same timestamp, and the number of timestamp updates can be reduced.

In summary, our contributions are the following.

1. We propose partial order transaction control based on reconsidering the isolation level of MVCC. To update a timestamp at an abort, POMVCC can process multiple transactions at the same timestamp and reduce the number of timestamp updates. In addition, POMVCC is easily implementable for DBMS based on MVCC.

2. We show the cause and the solution of a new anomaly named "HISTORICAL READ" caused by POMVCC.
3. We also show a lock-free implementation of POMVCC.
4. Finally, we implement POMVCC on an in-memory DBMS and evaluate the performance.

The rest of this paper is organized as follows. In Section 2, we introduce research on concurrency control for DBMS. In Section 3, we reconsider the requirement of concurrency control for DBMS and show a problem with performance and scalability. In Section 4, we propose POMVCC. We also show the cause and the solution of a new anomaly named "HISTORICAL READ" with POMVCC. In Section 5, we describe a method for implementing POMVCC that is lock-free. In Section 6, we evaluate the performance and consider the results. Finally, in Section 7, we give concluding remarks and our future work.

II. RELATED WORK

In this section, we show work related to concurrency control for DBMSs. The most notable viewpoint of concurrency control is the persistence of an execution result and the concurrency control of transactions.

Algorithms for Recovery and Isolation Exploiting Semantics (ARIES) is a general persistence processing [17]. ARIES is composed of analysis, REDO, and UNDO. Analysis pinpoints the starting point of a recovery. REDO re-executes a transaction on the basis of a REDO log. UNDO deletes an uncommitted transaction on the basis of an UNDO log. During logging, Write-Ahead Logging (WAL), which can restore logs safely in the case of failure, is used. WAL has a problem in that the speed of writing a log to a storage device is slow. However, in recent years, speedup technology that uses distributed logging with non-volatile memory has been proposed for WAL [14].

Research on the concurrency control of transactions has been made since the 1980s. There are two types of concurrency control, that is, Pessimistic Concurrency Control (PCC) and Optimistic Concurrency Control (OCC) [4][6][1]. For PCC, concurrency control with a 2 Phase Lock (2PL) is mainly used. DORA, PLP, and Shore-MT are proposed as lock-based DBMSs [8][9][11][19]. However, in recent years, DBMSs with MVCC, which enables OCC, have been proposed because the processing cost of locks and latches is high [13][25][26][27].

In past research, it was stated that an isolation level for SERIALIZABLE cannot be realized [2]. However, the proposal of SERIALIZABLE SNAPSHOT ISOLATION enabled this [23] [24]. Using this technology, H-Store/VoltDB [10][18], Hekaton [7][15], and SAP HANA [16] were proposed as MVCC-based DBMS. H-Store creates transaction sites whose number is the same as the number of CPUs, and transaction threads that stick to the logical sites execute SQL. Such a mechanism enables in-memory and lock-free fast processing. To reduce the number of responses between interfaces, Hekaton compiles stored procedures into native codes. SAP HANA manages both the row store whose update efficiency is high and column store whose reference efficiency is high. A lot of MVCC-based DBMSs whose characteristics are diverse are proposed like these examples.

In addition, a Silo in-memory DBMS that manages Epoch-based timestamps as a concurrency control was proposed [3]. In Silo, updates of timestamps are removed from the concurrency control of a transaction. Silo uses a special-purpose thread for managing timestamps. As a result, it achieves high performance. In addition, it creates temporary areas per transaction for references (Read-Set) and updates (Write-Set). Concurrency control with the Read-Set and Write-Set can use cache and memory efficiently. Using these technologies, Silo achieves 700,000 tps for the industry standard benchmark TPC Benchmark™ C (TPC-C) [20]. Moreover, Silo-based transaction control is adopted by Intel's Rack-Scale Architecture, which has become popular these days, and in-memory DBMS Foedus [12], which supposes Hewlett Packard's Memory-Driven Computing [32]. Silo-based concurrency control has become popular.

Research on MVCC-based DBMSs is now advancing. Silo-like concurrency control enables further speedup. However, it is difficult to adopt it for MVCC-based DBMSs because many components, such as thread management, transaction control, and data management must be modified. There, we propose an easier method that is equivalent to Silo's concurrency control for MVCC-based DBMSs.

III. RECONSIDERING ANOMALIES AND CONCURRENCY CONTROL ON MVCC

In this section, we outline concurrency control on MVCC, and we reconsider the update conflict of timestamps, which are a problem in Silo, and clarify the problem.

A DBMS must keep ACID properties, but to do so strictly, transactions must be serialized, and this degrades performance. To avoid this phenomenon, an isolation level, in which ACID properties are mitigated gradually is used. The isolation level is defined as the allowable range for an anomaly, which occurs when transactions are executed in parallel. This mitigation achieves high scalability enabled by the highly parallel and high performance transactions of DBMSs.

The isolation level is different between lock-based control and MVCC-based control [2]. In this paper, we outline the relationship of the isolation level for MVCC and anomalies, and we clarify the order of transactions and the problem with scalability.

In the following, we define Begin (B) as the start of a transaction, Commit (C) as the commit of the transaction, Abort (A) as the abort of the transaction, Read (R) as the reference in the transaction, and Write (W) as the update in the transaction. We also define TX1, TX2, etc., as identifiers of the transaction, X, Y, etc., as a set of records, and i, j, etc., as integers. The time at which commit is completed is the Committed Time (CT). The attribute of transaction type is defined as Type. For Type, Read represents read only, and Write includes write.

A. *Relationship between Isolation Level and Anomalies*

WRITE SKEW (WS), FUZZY READ (FR), READ SKEW (RS), and LOST UPDATE (LU) are general anomalies [2]. Examples of anomalies are shown in Table 1.

For example, LOST UPDATE happens when Tx1 and Tx2 update record X simultaneously and both are successful. This is a problem because the value of the record is either X' or X'', and the update history of the record is not uniquely determined. In the case of one-side failure (W1 W2 C2 A1), LOST UPDATE may occur when Tx2 updates record X to X' and then Tx1 aborts and the record X' is roll-backed to X.

The isolation level is defined as the allowable range for anomalies. SERIALIZABLE SNAPSHOT ISOLATION has the strictest requirement of consistency. The second strictest is READ COMMITTED. READ UNCOMMITED is the least strict. Table 2 shows the relationship between the isolation level and anomalies. For example, in the case of READ COMMITED, WRITE SKEW or FUZZY READ may occur. READ UNCOMMITTED is hardly used because user-unallowable anomalies occur.

TABLE I. ANOMALIES ON MVCC

Anomaly	Formula
LOST UPDATE	W2[X→X'] W1[X→X'']
READ SKEW	W2[X→X', Y→Y'] R1[X, Y']
FUZZY READ	R1[X] W2[X→X'] R1[X']
WRITE SKEW	R1[X] R2[Y] W1[Y→Y'] W2[X→X']

TABLE II. ISOLATION LEVEL ON MVCC

Isolation Level	Anomaly
SERIALIZABLE	-
SNAPSHOT ISOLATION	WS
READ COMMITTED	WS, FR
READ UNCOMMITTED	WS, FR, RS, LU

B. *Concurrency Control*

MVCC controls records and transactions by using timestamps. MVCC manages the update history of records by giving Timestamps at Commit (CTs) to the records. Transactions refer to Timestamps at Begin (BTs) or when SQL executes. They update timestamps at Commit. They refer to the latest record whose timestamp is smaller than BTs. The references of transactions maintain consistency with this method. How BTs are treated is different among the isolation level. SERIALIZABLE and SNAPSHOT ISOLATION use a timestamp that is referred to at Begin. READ COMMITTED uses a timestamp that is referred to at SQL execution. Figure 1 shows the difference between SNAPSHOT ISOLATION and READ COMMITTED. Tx2 and Tx3 are assumed to be SNAPSHOT ISOLATION and READ COMMITTED, respectively. They execute the SQL at the same time. However, Tx2.SQL2 sees record X, but Tx3.SQL2 sees record X'. Such concurrency control protects SNAPSHOT ISOLATION from FUZZY READ. Similarly, READ SKEW is prevented.

Update conflicts at the Commit of transactions generally use First Committer Win, which is optimistic concurrency control. It executes transactions in the order, in which Commits are executed. It keeps consistency by aborting subsequent conflicting transactions.

The concurrency control explained above cannot prevent WRITE SKEW from occurring. It happens when references and updates of multiple transactions mutually conflict (RW-Conflict). Serializable Snapshot Isolation (SSI) was proposed to find such a condition and avoid WRITE SKEW [23][24]. SSI adds a read flag and write flag to the conventional MVCC algorithm and detects RW-Conflict. SSI aborts at least one of the RW-Conflict transactions and avoids WRITE SKEW. Therefore, SERIALIZABLE is enabled. SSI can realize SERIALIZABLE with the same performance of SNAPSHOT ISOLATION [23][24].

We can prevent anomalies from occurring by using these concurrency controls on MVCC.

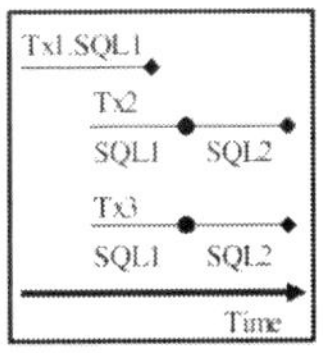

	Formula
Tx1.SQL1	B1 [BTs=10] W1 [X→X'] C1 [CTs=10, Ts=11]
Tx2.SQL1	B2 [BTs=10] R2 [X]
Tx2.SQL2	R2 [X] C2
Tx3.SQL1	B3 [BTs=10] R3 [X]
Tx3.SQL2	B3 [BTs=11] R3 [X'] C3

Figure 1. Difference between SNAPSHOT ISOLATION (Tx2) and READ COMMITTED (Tx3)

C. *Problem of Scalability*

To keep ACID properties strictly, it is necessary for transactions to be processed in strict total order. In this case, scalability is low. To the contrary, MVCC enables high scalability by parallel execution in total order. Table 3 defines D1 as strict total order, D2 as the total order, and D3 as the order of transactions for MVCC.

The CTs of MVCC must be different between the two transactions shown in D3.I, or one of the transactions must be the reference transaction shown in D3.II. That is, multiple update transactions cannot be committed at the same time due to D3.II. Thus, the transactions of MVCC are in strict total order in the case of update transactions only, or it is in total order when transactions include reference transactions.

As described above, MVCC allows D3.II, instead of D1 only, and scalability increases. However, D3.II is applicable only for transactions including reference transactions. In the case of update transactions only, scalability is low, because the conditions of the order are the same as D1. Therefore, mitigating the order of update transactions under D3.II is a problem.

TABLE III. DEFINITION OF MVCC

D1. Definition of Strict Total Order	
i < j <==> i ≦ j AND i ≠ j	
D2. Definition of Total Order	
i ≦ j <==> i < j OR i = j	
D3. Definition of Committed Tx. Order for MVCC	
CTs (Tx i) ⊴ CTs (Tx j) <==> I OR II	
I	CT (Tx i) < CT (Tx j)
II	CT (Tx i) = CT (Tx j) AND Type (Tx i) = Read

IV. PROPOSAL OF POMVCC

In this section, we propose POMVCC, which mitigates the order of update transactions and realizes high scalability. In addition, a new anomaly caused by POMVCC is considered.

In the following, DB is defined as the content of a database, and the execution order of transactions is shown as →.

A. Basic Idea

On the basis of the consistency of a database, transactions can be controlled in partial order. For example, if the concurrency control of DBMS exchanges the execution order of one transaction with other transaction and the result is not changed, these transactions can be executed in non-order, and consistency is kept. Thus, we do not need to update timestamps per update transaction, and we can share one timestamp among multiple update transactions. Therefore, we propose POMVCC as new concurrency control focused on the partial order of transactions. POMVCC gives a same timestamp to two update transactions if they have no dependency. This method mitigates condition D3.II, so scalability can increase.

The concept and definition of POMVCC are shown in Figure 2 and Table 4. By controlling the partial order of transaction processing, POMVCC eliminates the need to update the timestamp every time Tx. process is ended. POMVCC updates the timestamp when it detects Anomaly. For example, in Figure 2, since LOST UPDATE occurred between Tx1 and Tx3, POMVCC will update timestamp. Even if the execution order of all Tx. processes within the same timestamp is changed, POMVCC permits simultaneous execution if the contents of the database same. Then we also show the allowable conditions of transaction processing on the same timestamp for MVCC (D3.II) and POMVCC (D4.II) in Table 5, which shows POMVCC has more conditions that can be executed simultaneously than MVCC. Therefore, POMVCC can reduce the update frequency of timestamps. This means that the scalability of POMVCC is better than that of MVCC.

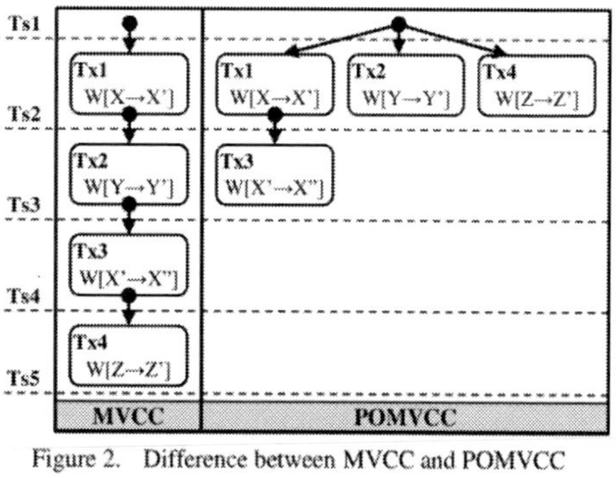

Figure 2. Difference between MVCC and POMVCC

TABLE IV. DEFINITION OF POMVCC

D4. Definition of Committed Tx. Order for POMVCC	
CTs (Tx i) ≤ CTs (Tx j) < = = > I OR II	
I	CT (Tx i) < CT (Tx j)
II	CT (Tx i) = CT (Tx j) AND DB(Tx i → Tx j) = DB(Tx j → Tx i)

TABLE V. ALLOWABLE RANGE OF TRANSACTIONS FOR D3.II AND D4.II ON THE SAME TIMESTAMP

#	Formula	D3. II	D4. II
1	R1[X] R2[X]	**Success**	**Success**
2	R1[X] W2[X→X']	**Success**	**Success**
3	W1[X→X'] R2[X]	**Success**	**Success**
4	W1[X→X'] W2[Y→Y']	Failure	**Success**
5	W1[X→X'] W2[X→X'']	Failure	Failure

B. How to Control POMVCC

The trigger to update a timestamp of POMVCC is different from that of MVCC. MVCC updates a timestamp at the Commit of a transaction, but POMVCC updates it at the Abort of a transaction. Thus, multiple update transactions can be executed at one timestamp.

A schematic diagram of POMVCC is shown in Figure 3. Tx1 and Tx3 have the update conflict of record X. In the case of MVCC, a timestamp is updated at the Commit of Tx1, but in the case of POMVCC, a timestamp is not updated. Therefore, Tx3 refers to old record X, and an update conflict happens. POMVCC updates a timestamp at the Abort of Tx3. Record X can be updated when Tx3 is re-executed. Because a timestamp is updated at the Abort of a transaction caused by an anomaly, partial order transaction control can be realized.

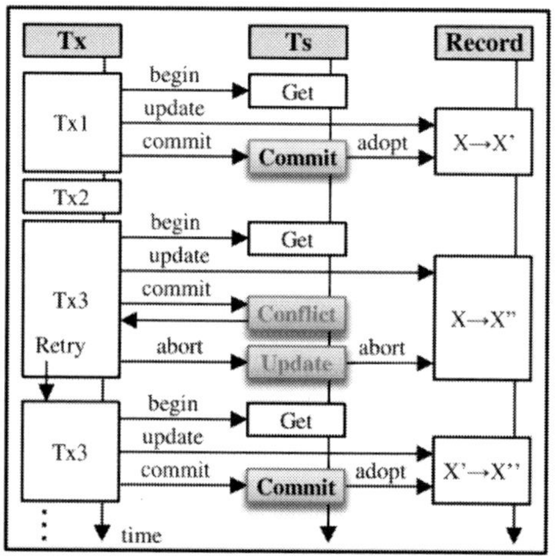

Figure 3. Concurrency Control of POMVCC

C. New Anomaly: HISTORICAL READ

The partial order transactions of POMVCC enable highly scalable concurrency control. However, the execution order of transactions is limited by the APplication (AP) or user. For example, consider that the succeeding transaction refers to the result of the preceding transaction. In this case, a HISTORICAL READ (HR), in which the succeeding transaction cannot refer to the result of the preceding transaction, occurs. It is necessary for POMVCC to provide the result of the preceding transaction to the succeeding transaction when AP requires the result of the preceding transaction.

Table 6 shows the definition of HISTORICAL READ. Tx2 cannot refer to record X', which Tx1 updates after the Commit of Tx1. This is the anomaly. If Tx1 and Tx2 are independent transactions, this does not happen. However, when AP assumes that the execution order is Tx1→Tx2, such an unexpected response occurs.

TABLE VI. DEFINITION OF HISTORICAL READ

Anomaly	Formula
Historical Read	W1[X→X'] C1 B2 R2[X]

D. *How to Avoid HISTORICAL READ*

HISTORICAL READ is avoidable if the BTs of a succeeding transaction is bigger than the CTs of the preceding transaction. That is, when the same user (DB connection) or the same AP executes transactions, the value that is bigger than the CTs of the preceding transaction is given to the BTs of the succeeding transaction. Therefore, HISTORICAL READ can be avoided.

The avoidance method for the same user (User Approach) may include false positives. In the worst case, timestamps are updated at every Commit. For example, the independent transactions that the same user issues do not need timestamp updates. However, in the User Approach, timestamps are always updated at the Begin of the transactions. As a result, performance degradation is a concern due to there being a lot of false positive cases.

In the avoidance method for the same AP (AP Base Method), minimum timestamps which would preferably be referred to, are set when the AP issues transactions. This method can avoid HISTORICAL READ efficiently because false positives are excluded. However, the DB interface, such as Commit and Begin, must be modified, and this is a downside of this method.

Figure 4 shows the solution of the AP Base Method. POMVCC returns CTs at the Commit of Tx1, and BTs (=CTs) is set at the Begin of Tx2. As a result, Tx1.CTs < Tx2.BTs is established, and Tx2 can refer to the execution result of Tx1.

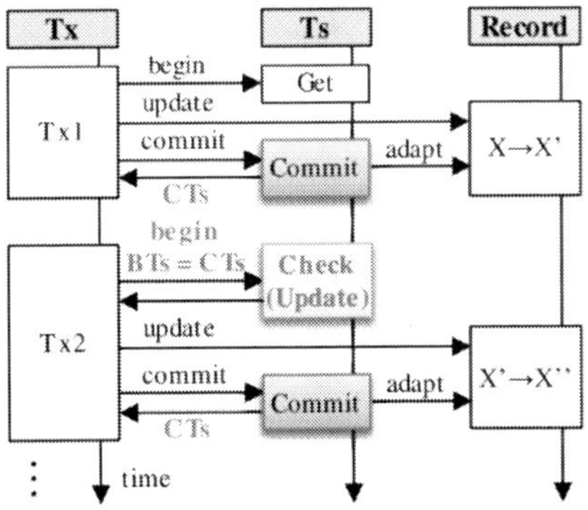

Figure 4. Solution for HISTORICAL READ

V. IMPLEMENTATION OF POMVCC

The lock used in parallel processing may degrade scalability [15]. In this section, to avoid this degradation, we introduce a lock-free implementation for scalable POMVCC.

However, in POMVCC, the implementation related to general DMBS is not different from the MVCC implementation of other pieces of literature [3][7][10][12][15][18][24]. Therefore, in the following, we focus on the extension of MVCC, that is, the concurrency control of transactions and timestamps.

In POMVCC, timestamps are divided into reference timestamps (RTs) and commit timestamps (WTs). Figure 5 shows the data structure of POMVCC. It has RTs, WTs, monotonically increasing timestamps, and the number of transactions at commit per timestamp. RTs are the timestamps that are used for referring to a record. WTs are the timestamps for a Commit. In addition, the state of Commit processing is divided into PreCommit and Commit. The PreCommit state includes the success of solving a conflict and the transfer to the Commit state. The Commit state includes giving CTs to all updated records and the completion of issuing a log. That is, if the timestamp of a PreCommit Counter and the Commit Counter is the same, the record can be referred to by using this timestamp while keeping consistency.

Figure 6 describes the control of POMVCC. In POMVCC, after the state is transferred to the PreCommit, CTs (= WTs) is obtained, and the PreCommit Counter of the CTs is incremented. After the state is transferred to the Commit, the Commit Counter of the CTs is incremented, and the transaction is completed. In case of Abort, WTs is incremented. If the timestamp (ATs) that causes the abort is known, RTs is incremented to ATs+1. At the re-execution of the transaction, this prevents the next abort, which has the same abort reason as the previous abort. RTs can be incremented if the PreCommit Counter and Commit Counter are the same and RTs < WTs. Finally, at Begin, RTs tries to be updated. If BTs is specified as the Begin interface, RTs is incremented till BTs < RTs is satisfied.

These controls enable POMVCC. They can be implemented without a lock by using atomic instructions, such as Compare-And-Swap (CAS).

RTs	WTs
10	12

Ts	PreCommit Counter	Commit Counter
9	14	14
10	3	3
11	6	2
12	1	0
13	0	0

Figure 5. Data Structure of POMVCC

```
Tx.Begin ( TmpTs = CTs or ATs) {
  WTs = Get.WTs ( ) ;
  while ( WTs ≦ TmpTs ) {
    WTs = Increment.WTs ( ) ;
  }
  do {
    BTs = Check.RTs ( ) ;
  } while ( BTs ≦ TmpTs ) ;
  return ( ) ;
}

Tx.Commit ( ) {
  // PreCommit Process
  if ( Tx.Judgement = Success ) {
    CTs = GetWTs ( ) ;
    Increment.PreCommitCnt ( CTs ) ;
    ･･･Commit Completion･･･
    Increment.CommitCnt ( CTs ) ;
  } else if ( Tx.Judgement = Failure) {
    Tx.Abort ( ) ;
  }
  return ( CTs or ATs) ;
}

Tx.Abort ( ) {
  // Abort Process
  IncrementWTs ( ) ;
  return ( ) ;
}

Check.RTs ( ) {
  RTs = Get.RTs ( ) ;
  WTs = Get.WTs ( ) ;
  if ( Diff.Commit.Counter ( RTs ) = 0 and RTs < WTs )
    RTs = Increment.RTs ( ) ;
  return ( RTs ) ;
}
```

Figure 6. Schematic Timestamp Control

VI. EVALUATION OF PROTOTYPE IMPLEMENTATION

In this section, we compare the performance of MVCC and POMVCC. We implemented MVCC and POMVCC on an in-memory DBMS named "MPDB", which we are developing, and evaluated their performance. MPDB is an MVCC-based, lock-free, in-memory DBMS that is characterized by parallel logs and PCC/OCC mixed control [30] [31].

In this experiment, we use the industry standard benchmark TPC-C and repeatedly execute stored procedure calls that model NewOrder [20].

A. *Experimental Environment*

Figure 7 depicts the system configuration. Four blade servers were used. They were Symmetric MultiProcessors (SMP) and had 8 CPUs (80 cores), 1 TB of memory, and 8 ports of an 8-Gb Fiber Channel (FC). Servers and storage were connected via an FC switch and communicate with FC communication.

In the OS (CentOS 6.5) settings, FC ports were assigned to each CPU to distribute the interrupt overhead of FC communication. Hyper-threading was disabled.

In the MPDB settings, one thread was assigned to one core. This means that MPDB uses a maximum of 80 threads. One log file is assigned to one CPU to load balance logs. The isolation level was SNAPSHOT ISOLATION.

The DB was created on the basis of TPC-C. The number of warehouses was 16 and the size of database was 0.72 GB. The item table, stock table, and order_line table were used in TPC-C. In addition, indexes were created for the i_id of the item table, s_w_id and s_i_id of the stock table, and ol_o_id and ol_w_id of the order_line table.

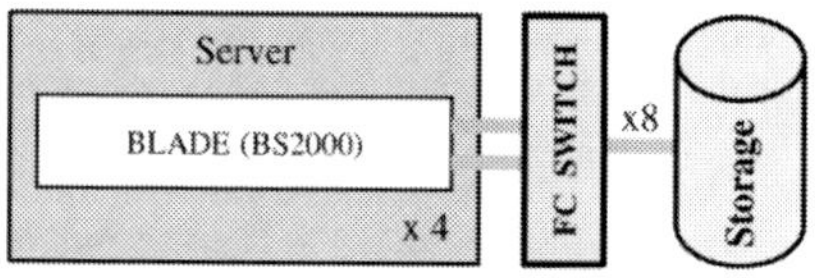

System Configuration

Blade	BS2000
CPU	Xeon(R) E7 8870 x 2
Memory	256GB (16GB x 16)
PCIe	2 Port HBA (8Gb)

Storage	Hitachi Unified Storage VM (HUS-VM)
Cache	54GB
Disk	6.4TB (1.6TB x 4) Hitachi Accelerated Flash
RAID	RAID5(3D + 1P)

Figure 7. System Configuration

B. *Workload*

The workload shown in Figure 8 was created on the basis of TPC-C's New Order. The workload simulates the repeatedly executing part of the New Order. The processing in Figure 8 was repeated 10 times per transaction on average.

1	SELECT	i_price, i_name, i_data
	INTO	:i_price, :i_name, :i_data
	FROM	item
	WHERE	i_id = :ol_i_id
2	SELECT	s_quantity, s_data, s_dist_...
	INTO	:s_quantity, :s_data, :s_dist_...
	FROM	stock
	WHERE	s_i_id = :ol_i_id AND s_w_id = :ol_supply_w_id
3	UPDATE	stock
	SET	s_quantity = :s_quantity
	WHERE	s_i_id = :ol_i_id AND s_w_id = :ol_supply_w_id
4	INSERT	
	INTO	order_line (,,,,,)
	VALUES	(,,,,,,)

While (Repeats 5 ~ 15 times, Ave. 10)

Figure 8. Experiment Workload

C. *Experimental Results and Consideration*

The experiments were done to compare the performance of MVCC and POMVCC corresponding to the number of threads. In Figure 9, the x-axis means the number of threads, and the y-axis means the transactional performance (tps). The performance of both MVCC and POMVCC increased as the number of threads increased. POMVCC ran 1.36-1.60 times faster than MVCC.

To investigate scalability more precisely, we made an experiment, in which the number of warehouses changed corresponding to the number of threads. That is, the number of warehouses was 10 (DB size was 0.45 GB) when the number of threads is 10. The number of warehouses was 80 (DB size was 3.61 GB) when the number of threads was 80. Figures 10 and 11 are the experimental results. From Figure 10, the performance of POMVCC was 1.63 - 1.74 times better than that of MVCC. From Figure 11, the scalability coefficient of MVCC was 87.98 - 97.96 [%], and that of POMVCC was 94.02 –98.32 [%]. This experiment says that the scalability coefficient of POMVCC is greater than that of MVCC.

From these experiments, the scalability coefficients of POMVCC and MVCC depended on the size of the DB and the number of threads. If the size of the DB was large and the conflict rate of the transaction was low, the scalability coefficient of POMVCC was high, and in all experiments, POMVCC ran faster than MVCC.

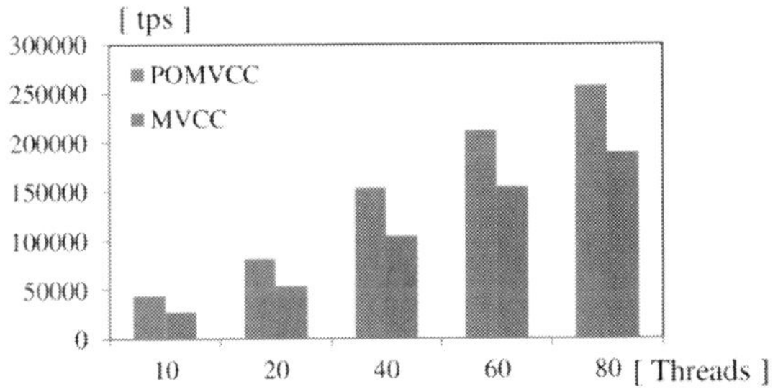

Figure 9. Performance Evaluation

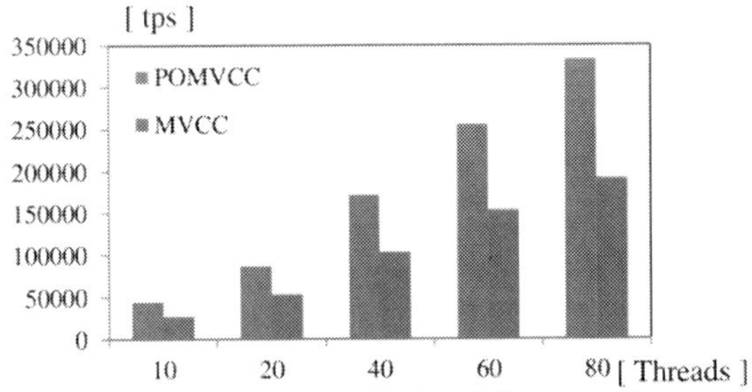

Figure 10. Performance when Number of Warehouses Changes

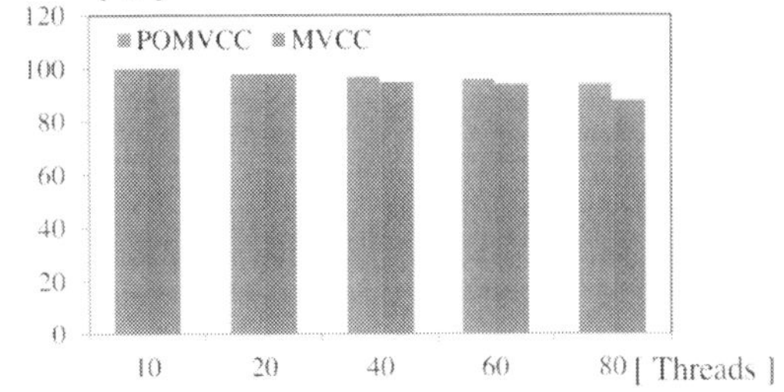

Figure 11. Scalability Coefficient when Number of Warehouses Changes

VII. CONCLUSION

In this paper, we proposed and evaluated POMVCC, which keeps the consistency of MVCC and improves performance and scalability. POMVCC is technology that focuses on the partial order of transactions. The conventional method gives a timestamp to a transaction, but POMVCC gives a timestamp to multiple transactions. POMVCC reduces the number of timestamps that are updated and improves performance and scalability. We show the difference of Isolation Level between MVCC and POMVCC in Figure 12.

We implemented and evaluated POMVCC on an in-memory DBMS named "MPDB" that we are developing. From experiments, the performance of POMVCC was 1.30 - 1.74 times better than that of MVCC. The scalability of the POMVCC was higher than that of the MVCC. Every experiment showed that the performance of POMVCC was 1.30 - 1.74 times higher than that of the MVCC.

We implemented the POMVCC on the MPDB and evaluated it by using SNAPSHOT ISOLATION, for which POMVCC had higher performance than MVCC. However, with SERIALIZABLE, the performance trend was unclear because the probability of WRITE SKEW increased. This occurs when reference and update transactions are executed at the same timestamp. POMVCC increases the number of transactions at the same timestamp. As a result, the number of WRITE SKEWs increases. In addition, it is possible that RW-CONFLICT GRAPH will grow and a large cyclic graph will be created. Therefore, our future work is to implement and evaluate POMVCC by using SERIALIZABLE.

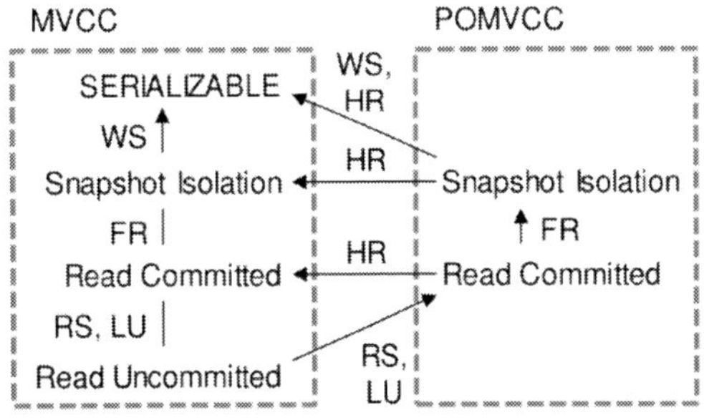

Figure 12. A Diagram of the Isolation Levels and Relationships

REFERENCES

[1] D. A. Menascé, and T. Nakanishi, "Optimistic versus pessimistic concurrency control mechanisms in database management systems," Information Systems Volume 7, Issue 1, pp. 13-27, 1982.

[2] H. Berenson, P. Bernstein, J. Gray, J. Melton, E. O'Neil and, P. O'Neil, "A Critique of ANSI SQL Isolation Levels," ACM SIGMOD '95 Proceedings, pp. 1-10, San Jose, CA, 1995.

[3] S. Tu, W. Zheng, E. Kohler, B. Liskov, and S. Madden, "Speedy Transactions in Multicore In-Memory Databases," SOSP '13 Proceedings, pp. 18-32, Farmington, Pennsylvania, USA, 2013.

[4] H. T. Kung, and J. T. Robinson, "On optimistic methods for concurrency control," ACM Transactions on Database Systems, Volume 6 Issue 2, pp. 213-226, 1981.

[5] P. Larson, S. Blanas, C. Diaconu, C. Freedman, J. M. Patel, and M. Zwilling, "High-performance concurrency control mechanisms for main-memory databases," Proceedings of the VLDB Endowment Volume 5 Issue 4, pp. 298-309, 2011.

[6] K. P. Eswaran, J. N. Gray, R. A. Lorie, and I. L. Traiger, "The notions of consistency and predicate locks in a database system," Communications of the ACM, Volume 19 Issue 11, pp. 624-633, 1976.

[7] C. Diaconu, C. Freedman, E. Ismert, P. Larson, P. Mittal, R. Stonecipher, N. Verma, and M. Zwilling, "Hekaton: SQL server's memory-optimized OLTP engine," SIGMOD '13 Proceedings, pp. 1243-1254, 2013.

[8] I. Pandis, R. Johnson, N. Hardavellas, and A. Ailamak, "Data-oriented transaction execution," Proceedings of the VLDB Endowment, Volume 3 Issue 1-2, pp. 928-939, 2010.

[9] I. Pandis, P. Tozun, R. Johnson, and A. Ailamaki, "PLP: page latch-free shared-everything OLTP," Proceedings of the VLDB Endowment, Volume 4 Issue 10, pp. 610-621, 2011.

[10] M. Stonebraker, S. Madden, D. J. Abadi, S. Harizopoulos, N. Hachem, and P. Helland, "The end of an architectural era: (it's time for a complete rewrite)," VLDB '07 Proceedings, pp. 1150-1160, 2007.

[11] R. Johnson, I. Pandis, N. Hardavellas, A. Ailamaki, and B. Falsafi, "Shore-MT: a scalable storage manager for the multicore era," EDBT '09 Proceedings, pp. 24-35, 2009.

[12] H. Kimura, "FOEDUS: OLTP Engine for a Thousand Cores and NVRAM," SIGMOD '15 Proceedings, pp. 691-706, 2015.

[13] S. Harizopoulos, D. J. Abadi, S. Madden, and M. Stonebraker, "OLTP through the looking glass, and what we found there," SIGMOD '08 Proceedings, pp. 981-992, 2008.

[14] T. Wang, and R. Johnson, "Scalable logging through emerging non-volatile memory," Proceedings of the VLDB Endowment, Volume 7 Issue 10, pp. 865-876, 2014.

[15] P. Larson, S. Blanas, C. Diaconu, C. Freedman, J. M. Patel, and M. Zwilling, "High-performance concurrency control mechanisms for main-memory databases," Proceedings of the VLDB Endowment, Volume 5 Issue 4, pp. 298-309, 2011.

[16] V. Sikka, F. Färber, W. Lehner, S. K. Cha, T. Peh, and C. Bornhövd, "Efficient transaction processing in SAP HANA database: the end of a column store myth," SIGMOD '12 Proceedings, pp. 731-742, 2012.

[17] C. Mohan, D. Haderle, B. Lindsay, H. Pirahesh, and P. Schwarz, "ARIES: a transaction recovery method supporting fine-granularity locking and partial rollbacks using write-ahead logging," ACM Transactions on Database Systems, Volume 17 Issue 1, pp. 94-162, 1992.

[18] R. Kallman, H. Kimura, J. Natkins, A. Pavlo, A. Rasin, S. Zdonik, and et al., "H-store: a high-performance, distributed main memory transaction processing system," Proceedings of the VLDB Endowment, Volume 1 Issue 2, pp. 1496-1499, 2008.

[19] P. A. Bernstein, V. Hadzilacos, and N. Goodman, "Concurrency Control and Recovery in Database System," 1987.

[20] The Transaction Processing Council, "TPC-C Benchmark (Version 5.11.0)," http://www.tpc.org/tpcc/, March 2018.

[21] G. Weikum, and G. Vossen, "Transactional Information Systems: Theory, Algorithms, and the Practice of Concurrency Control and Recovery," Elsevier, 2001.

[22] J. Gray, and A. Reuter, "Transaction Processing: Concepts and Techniques," Elsevier, 1992.

[23] M. J. Cahill, U. Röhm, and A. D. Fekete, "Serializable isolation for snapshot databases," ACM Transactions on Database Systems, Volume 34 Issue 4, Article No.20, 2009.

[24] A. Fekete, D. Liarokapis, P. O'Neil, and D. Shasha, "Making snapshot isolation serializable," ACM Transactions on Database Systems, Volume 30 Issue 2, pp. 492-528, 2005.

[25] ORACLE, "Oracle Database 12c Release 2," https://docs.oracle.com/en/database/oracle/oracle-database/12.2/index.html, March 2018.

[26] MySQL, "MySQL 5.7 Reference Manual," https://dev.mysql.com/doc/refman/5.7/en/, March 2018.

[27] PostgreSQL, "PostgreSQL 9.6.8 Documentation," https://www.postgresql.org/docs/9.6/static/index.html, March 2018.

[28] L. Lamport, D. Malkhi, and L. Zhou, "Reconfiguring a state machine," ACM SIGACT News, Volume 41 Issue 1, pp. 63-73, 2010.

[29] J. C. Corbett, J. Dean, M. Epstein, A. Fikes, C. Frost, J. Furman, and et al., "Spanner: Google's Globally Distributed Database," ACM Transactions on Computer Systems, Volume 31 Issue 3, Article No.8, 2013.

[30] Y. Isoda, A. Tomoda, K. Ushijima, T. Tanaka, T. Uemura, T. Hanai, and et al., "In-Memory Database Engine for Scale-up System," Forum on Information Technology '15, D-035, 2015 (in Japanese).

[31] Y. Isoda, K. Ushijima, T. Tanaka, T. Hanai, and K. Mogi, "Proposal of Multi Version Concurrency Control for Partial Order Transaction," Forum on Information Technology '16, D-015, 2016 (in Japanese).

[32] Hewlett Packard, "Memory-Driven Computing," https://news.hpe.com/content-hub/memory-driven-computing/, March 2018.

QualIe: A Data Quality Assessment Tool for Integrated Information Systems

Lisa Ehrlinger*†
†Software Competence Center Hagenberg
Softwarepark 21, 4232 Hagenberg, Austria
email: lisa.ehrlinger@scch.at

Bernhard Werth*, Wolfram Wöß*
*Johannes Kepler University Linz
Altenberger Straße 69, 4040 Linz, Austria
email: {lisa.ehrlinger, wolfram.woess}@jku.at

***Abstract*—Data is central to decision-making in enterprises and organizations (e.g., smart factories and predictive maintenance), as well as in private life (e.g., booking platforms). Especially in artificial intelligence applications, like self-driving cars, trust in data-driven decisions depends directly on the quality of the underlying data. Therefore, it is essential to know the quality of the data in order to assess the trustworthiness and to reduce the uncertainty of the derived decisions. In this paper, we present QualIe (Quality Assessment for Integrated Information Environments, pronounced [ˈkvɑlə]), a Java-based tool for the domain-independent ad-hoc measurement of an information system's quality. QualIe is based on a holistic approach to measure both schema and data quality and covers the dimensions accuracy, correctness, completeness, pertinence, minimality, and normalization. The quality measurements are presented as machine- and human-readable reports, which can be generated periodically in order to observe how data quality evolves. In contrast to most existing data quality tools, QualIe does not necessarily require domain knowledge and thus offers an initial ad-hoc estimation of an information system's quality.**

***Index Terms*—Data Quality; Information Integration; Estimation; Measurement; Trust.**

I. Introduction

Decision-making is usually based on data. Applications are process data in industry, sales, weather forecast, search engines, self-driving cars, or booking platforms. In order to trust such data-driven decisions, it is necessary to know the quality of the underlying data. Despite the clear correlation between data and decision quality, 84 % of the CEOs in the US are concerned about their data quality [1]. In addition to incorrect decision making, poor Data Quality (DQ) may cause effects like cost increase, customer dissatisfaction, and organizational mistrust [2]. According to an estimation by IBM, the total financial impact of poor quality data on business in the US was $3.1 trillion [3] in 2016. Thus, DQ is no longer a question of "hygiene", but has become critical for operational excellence and is perceived as the greatest challenge in corporate data management [4].

In practice, data of enterprises and organizations are often stored in Integrated Information Systems (IISs), which gather data from different and often heterogeneous information sources [5]. If such a system is queried, it is desirable to select the most appropriate and most trustworthy source with respect to query. Thus, an automated on-the-fly estimation of the eligible Information Sources (ISs) is necessary to judge weather an IS is complete or accurate enough to answer the query sufficiently. For this purpose, we developed QualIe (Quality Assessment for Integrated Information Environments), a modular Java-based tool that automatically performs quality measurement at the data-level and the schema-level. QualIe offers metrics for the quality dimensions accuracy, correctness, completeness, pertinence, minimality, and normalization.

Although the most frequently used definition of data quality is "fitness for use" [6], which expresses the high subjectivity and context-dependency of this concept, we aim at a domain-independent measurement of the quality of ISs. QualIe performs an automated ad-hoc estimation of the qualitative condition of multiple information sources within an IIS and generates a machine- and human-readable XML (extensible markup language) quality report. Such a report can be generated periodically in order to observe how DQ evolves. Our focus is the quality measurement of an IIS in productive use, and automatic data cleansing activities are therefore outside the scope of this research work. In a first step, it is essential to know the quality of the data in order to define goals and to verify the effectiveness of data cleansing activities.

The main contribution of this paper is the presentation of a novel tool that implements automated DQ measurement and estimation, covering the most important dimensions for both, data- and schema-level. To the best of our knowledge, there exists no tool that offers DQ metrics for such a large number of different DQ dimensions in a single application and comprises both data and schema quality. Therefore, we developed QualIe to fill this gap. The advantage of the presented approach is a long term observation of the DQ development, which provides indicators for further DQ improvements and thus, increases trustworthiness for data-driven decisions.

This paper is organized as follows: in Section 2 we discuss existing DQ tools and highlight their differences to QualIe. Section 3 covers the data and schema quality measurement, which was applied in this research. The implementation of QualIe is described, demonstrated and discussed in Section 4.

II. Related Work

Although the interest into DQ, from both research and industry, has increased over the last decade, it is still an underestimated topic in operational information systems. This fact is also reflected by the current market of DQ tools, which is considered a niche market despite its continuous growth [7]. In the following paragraphs, we give a short overview on existing DQ tools and discuss their differences to QualIe.

Gartner lists 39 commercial DQ tools by 16 vendors in their "Magic Quadrant of Data Quality Tools 2017" [7]. Most of the tools offer functionalities to investigate the qualitative condition of different data sources, manage DQ rules, resolve DQ issues, enrich data quality by integrate external data, validate addresses, standardize and cleanse data, and link related data entries using a variety of techniques. The aim of these commercial tools is usually the support of a comprehensive DQ program that involves management, IT, and business users. Thus, the application of such a tool usually requires a domain expert and preparatory work to be effective.

In addition to commercial DQ tools, a number of scientific tools has been proposed over the years, where the most important ones are compared and discussed in [8][9]. Both surveys make clear that the focus of those tools is on the detection and cleansing of specific DQ problems (e.g., name conflicts, missing data). QualIe, in contrast, focuses on the pure measurement (detection) of DQ problems and does not cleanse data, but with the advantage to be unsupervised, domain-independent and applicable for ad-hoc analysis. Additionally, and in contrast to most existing DQ tools, QualIe addresses the DQ topic from the dimension-oriented view. While a lot of research on DQ dimensions and their definition has been proposed in literature [2][6][10], there is no tool that implements metrics for such a broad number of dimensions. QualIe fills this gap and can thus be considered a vital complement in the section of research-oriented DQ tools. The main contributions in QualIe are (1) the combination of data and schema quality measurement and (2) the implementation of such a wide spectrum of different quality dimensions. Of course, more specialized tools might outperform QualIe in specific implementations, like distance calculation or string matching.

III. Data and Schema Quality Measurement

Data quality is usually described as multidimensional concept, which is characterized by different aspects, so called *dimensions* [6]. Those dimensions can either refer to the data values (i.e., *extension* of the data), or to their schema (i.e., the *intension* or data structure) [11]. While the majority of research into DQ focuses on the data values, QualIe covers dimensions for both schema and data quality. In fact, schema quality has a strong impact on the quality of the data values [11]. An example are redundant schema elements, which can lead to data inconsistencies. Thus, it is essential to consider both topics in order to provide holistic DQ measurement.

Since a wide variety of quality dimensions has been proposed over the years, we focus in the following paragraphs on accuracy, correctness, completeness, pertinence, minimality, and normalization. Each dimension can be quantified using one or several metrics, which capture the fulfillment of a dimension in a numerical value [12]. Some metrics require a reference or benchmark (*gold standard*) for their calculation. According to the Oxford Dictionary, a Gold Standard (GS) is "the best, most reliable, or most prestigious thing of its type" [13]. In the vast majority of cases a gold standard does not exist, but if there is one, it would be used in place of the IS under investigation. Thus, in practice, an existing benchmark is employed as gold standard, e.g., a single IS can be compared to the integrated data from the complete IIS. Although in practice, there is usually no complete gold standard for large data sets available, there are often reference data sets of good quality for a subset of the data. Examples are purchased reference data sets for customer addresses or a manually cleaned part of the original data. The quality estimation in QualIe (cf. Section III-F) allows to extrapolate the exact measurement for a part of the data to other parts that are required for a query but have not been yet measured. For more details to the schema quality dimensions applied in this paper, we refer to [14] and more information on the DQ dimensions can be found in [15].

A. Accuracy and Correctness

The terms *accuracy* and *correctness* are often used synonymously in literature and a number of different definitions exist for both terms [6][11][16]. In the DQ literature, accuracy can be described as the closeness between an information system and the part of the real-world it is supposed to model [11]. From the natural sciences perspective, accuracy is usually defined as the magnitude of an error [16]. In this research work, we refer to correctness for a calculation, which has been presented by Logan et al. [17], who distinguish between correct (C), incorrect (I), extra (E) and missing (M) elements after comparing a data set to its reference:

$$Cor(c, c') = \frac{C}{C + I + E}. \qquad (1)$$

Here, the data correctness of, for instance, a relational table or class in an ontology, denoted as concept c, is measured by comparing it to its "correct" version c'. In this notion, C is the number of elements that correspond exactly to an element from the reference c'. The incorrect elements I have a similar element in the gold standard, but are not identical. While M describes the number of missing elements in the IS under investigation that exist in the gold standard, its complement E is the number of extra elements that exist in the investigated IS, but have no corresponding element in the gold standard. We refer to the values as CIEM counts.

In QualIe, however, an accuracy metric is implemented, which has its origins in the field of machine learning and is usually used to measure the accuracy of classification algorithms [18]. This accuracy metric can also be mapped to the notion by Logan et al. [17]:

$$Acc(c, c') = \frac{|c|}{|c \cup c'|} = \frac{C}{C + I + E + M} \qquad (2)$$

where $|c|$ gives the number of records in a data set or concept c. In the rest of this paper, we refer to accuracy when discussing quality metrics for data values (since QualIe implements the metric for accuracy on data-level), and to correctness when discussing the corresponding schema dimension.

On the schema-level, Vossen [19] describes a database (DB) schema as correct, if the concepts of the related data model are applied in a syntactically and semantically appropriate way. Thus, he considers the model (e.g., Entity-Relationship model) as reference, which is assumed to be correctly available. In [11], the authors distinguish between correctness with respect to the model and with respect to the requirements. The correct representation of the schema requirements are considered a manual task, because requirements are rarely available in machine-readable form. Despite unknown quality, the content of an IS can be added as third possibility to validate a schema, in order to measure whether a schema fits its values. This includes for instance the correct usage of attributes (e.g., an attribute `first_name` actually contains a person's first name and no numeric value).

In QuaIIe, the formula by Logan et al. [17] for data correctness is also employed as a metric for schema correctness with C_s, I_s, E_s, and M_s denoting the correct, incorrect, extra, and missing elements of a schema s:

$$Cor(s, s') = \frac{C_s}{C_s + I_s + E_s}. \tag{3}$$

B. Completeness

Completeness is broadly defined as the breadth, depth, and scope of information contained in the data [10]. A number of authors [6][11] calculate data completeness according to:

$$Com(c, c') = \frac{|c|}{|c'|}. \tag{4}$$

Despite differences in expressions, most existing completeness metrics are correspondent to (4) and compare the number of elements in a data set $|c|$ to the number of elements in the gold standard $|c'|$. In this metric, scope for interpretation lies in selecting the gold standard or reference c' and in the similarity calculation (i.e., determining whether an element has a reference element in c'). In QuaIIe however, extra records, which exist in the gold standard, but have no counterpart in the data set under investigation are excluded and therefore have no influence on the completeness calculation. We use the formula presented by Logan et al. [17]:

$$Com(c, c') = \frac{C + I}{C + I + M}. \tag{5}$$

Schema completeness describes the extent to which real-world concepts of the application domain and their attributes and relationships are represented in the schema [11]. The metric for schema completeness in QuaIIe corresponds to the metric for data completeness in (5):

$$Com(s, s') = \frac{C_s + I_s}{C_s + I_s + M_s}. \tag{6}$$

Batista and Salgado [20] applied a schema completeness metric, which is equivalent to the data completeness in (4). In the calculation, the number of elements in the reference schema $|s'|$ is determined by counting the number of distinct elements in all schemas of an IIS. While the authors in [20] assume pre-defined schema mappings to be provided, QuaIIe implements the distance or similarity calculation between the schema elements on-the-fly.

In addition, Nauman et al. [21] proposed a comprehensive IIS completeness metric, which incorporates the *coverage* (i.e., data completeness of the extension of an IS), and *density* (i.e., schema completeness of the intension of an IS). The authors use the entire IIS as gold standard. The density of a schema is calculated according to the population of attributes with non-null values [21]. In contrast, the schema completeness metric in QuaIIe implements a data-value-independent calculation, which considers the existence of specific schema elements (e.g., relations in a relational DB).

C. Pertinence

Pertinence on the data-level equates to the notion of precision (in contrast to recall [18]) from the information retrieval field and complements data completeness. Data pertinence describes the prevalence of unnecessary records in the data. The classic precision metric is defined as the probability to select a correct element from a list [18] and in terms of correct, incorrect, extra, and missing records, is defined as:

$$Per(c, c') = \frac{C + I}{C + I + E}. \tag{7}$$

Schema pertinence describes a schema's relevance, which means that a schema with low pertinence has a high number of unnecessary elements [11]. A schema that is perfectly complete and pertinent represents exactly the reference schema (i.e., its real world representation), which means that the two dimensions complement each other. In accordance to (7), schema pertinence is calculated in QuaIIe as

$$Per(s, s') = \frac{C_s + I_s}{C_s + I_s + E_s}, \tag{8}$$

where the number of schema elements with a (correct or incorrect) correspondence in the gold standard is divided by the total number of elements in the schema under investigation.

D. Minimality

Information sources are considered minimal if no parts of them can be omitted without losing information, that is, the IS is without redundancies and no duplicate records exist [11]. The detection of duplicate records is a widely researched field that is also referred to as record linkage, data deduplication, data merging, or redundancy detection [22]. In order to determine which records of a data set are duplicates, different approaches exist. The most prominent approaches can be assigned to one of the following types [22]: (1) *probabilistic assignment* using the Fellegi-Sunter model [23], (2) *machine learning techniques* like support vector machines, clustering algorithms, or decision trees, (3) *distance-based methods*, which are based on a function that calculates the distance between two objects, and (4) *rule-based methods*, which are usually based on the work of domain experts.

In QualIe, duplicate detection is done by hierarchical clustering, which requires a distance function between the records. A distance function $\delta : o \times o \rightarrow [0, 1]$ is a function from a pair of elements to a normalized real number expressing the distance or dissimilarity between the two elements [24]. Analogous, some techniques calculate the similarity $\sigma : o \times o \rightarrow [0, 1]$ between two elements, which can be transformed to a distance value using the formula $\delta = 1 - \sigma$.

Since each data record consists of multiple attribute values, the distance function is a weighted-average of individual attribute distance functions. QualIe offers the following distance functions for data values: `AffineGapDistance`, `CosineDistance`, `LevenshteinDistance`, and `SubstringDistance` for strings, `AbsoluteValueDistance` for double values, `EqualRecordDistance` for entire records, as well as `EnsembleDistance` for any data type. The latter one combines an arbitrary number of other distances and a weight for each one. Thus, it allows the creation of distances that are adjusted to a specific IS schema, for example, to calculate the distance between persons by applying a string distance to the first and last name and a distance for numeric attributes to the age, and giving higher weights to the name than the age.

The main advantage of clustering in our approach is the automatic resolution of multiple correspondences. It thus, however, requires a threshold to be defined. QualIe sets a predefined clustering threshold which has been evaluated in experiments presented in [14]. In an automated test run, similarity matrices with different parameter combinations have been compared to a similarity matrix created by a domain expert using the mean squared error (MSE). The parameter combination yielding the closest similarity results (having a MSE of 0.0102) were used as standard parameters. However, QualIe also allows to overwrite those values by the user to adjust for specific domains. Hierarchical clustering initially creates one cluster for each observed record and continuously combines different clusters until all records are subsumed into one large cluster. QualIe offers seven different linkage strategies (single linkage, complete linkage, median linkage, mean linkage, pair group method with arithmetic mean, centroid linkage, and Ward's method). We refer to [25] for in-depth information on hierarchical clustering.

Following, the minimality metric in QualIe is based on a three-step approach, which is used for the data values and the schema elements likewise. Consequently, we refer to the observed objects as "elements", using the more generic term for both, records, as well as schema elements.

1) *Element-wise distance calculation.* All elements are compared to each other, which yields a distance matrix.
2) *Clustering.* All elements are hierarchically clustered according to their distance values. In a perfectly minimal IS, the number of elements $|c|$ should be equal to the number of clusters $|clusters|$. If two or more elements are grouped together into one cluster, the minimality score drops to a value below 1.0.
3) *Minimality calculation.* Finally, the minimality can be calculated according to

$$Min(c) = \begin{cases} 1.0, & \text{if } |c| = 1 \\ \frac{|clusters|-1}{|c|-1}, & \text{else} \end{cases} . \quad (9)$$

Schema minimality is of particular interest in the context of IIS, where redundant representations are common. The minimality of a schema is an important indicator to avoid redundancies, anomalies and inconsistencies. QualIe calculates schema minimality according to the three-step approach described above. For the schema similarity, the following distance functions are available: `DSDAttributeDistance` on attribute-level, `DSDConceptAssocDistance` on concept- or association-level, and `SimilarityFloodingDistance` on schema-level. DSD (data source description) is a vocabulary to semantically describe IS schemas [26] and is explained in more detail in Section IV-B. The first two distances are ensemble distances, which are adjusted to the DSD representation of attributes or concepts and associations respectively. In addition, we implemented the Similarity Flooding (SF) algorithm proposed in [27], which calculates the similarity between nodes in a graph-based schema representation, and can thus only be applied to a complete DSD schema (in contrast to single concepts). Subsequently, (9) can be reformulated for schema minimality according to

$$Min(s) = \begin{cases} 1.0, & \text{if } |s| = 1 \\ \frac{|clusters|-1}{|s|-1}, & \text{else} \end{cases} , \quad (10)$$

where $|s|$ is the number of elements (concepts and associations) in a schema s.

E. Normalization

Normal Forms (NFs) can be used to measure the quality of relational DBs, with the aim of obtaining a schema that avoids redundancies and resulting inconsistencies as well as insert, update, and delete anomalies [19]. In contrast to all other schema quality dimensions listed in this paper, normalization requires access to the extension of the information source, i.e., the data values themselves. Although this quality dimension refers to relational data only, it is included in QualIe, because of the wide spread use of relational DBs in enterprises. Several modern DBs use denormalization deliberately to increase read and write performance. Hence, depending on the type of IS, a NF evaluation is not always helpful in deducing the quality of its schema. It can however, serve as checking mechanism to ensure that only controlled denormalization exists.

Identifying *functional dependencies* (FDs) forms the basis for determining the NF of a relation. A FD $\alpha \rightarrow \beta$, where α

and β are two attribute sets of a relation $\mathcal{R}$, describes that two tuples that have the same attribute values in α must also have the same attribute values in β. Thus, the α-values functionally determine the β-values [28].

In QualIe, the second, third, and Boyce Codd normal form (2NF, 3NF, and BCNF, respectively) can be determined. The applied algorithm can be classified as a bottom-up method [29], in which the FDs of a relation are analyzed by comparing all attributes' tuple values with all other attributes' tuple values. Then, the minimal cover is determined by performing left- and right-reduction so that all FDs are in canonical form and without redundancies [19]. Following, all attributes are classified as key or non-key attributes and based on all information gathered, the correct NF is determined. Each schema element is annotated with quality information about its NF, key attributes, and minimal cover.

F. Estimation of Integrated Quality Values

In Big Data applications there is usually no gold standard for the entire data set, which makes it impossible to calculate DQ metrics that require a GS in the formula. However, there exist often reference data sets of good quality, for example, purchased customer addresses or a manually cleaned subset of the data. In such cases, DQ can be estimated by extrapolating exact measurements for parts of the data to the entire data set. An estimated quality rating allows to draw conclusions whether to include a data source in a query result or not.

QualIe provides a heuristic estimation of DQ values for a number of query results, views, and integrated record sets. Assuming a composite record set can be defined by applying only relational algebra operators (projection π, selection σ, rename ρ, union $\cup$, set difference $-$, and cross product $\times$ [28]) to existing data, queries can be treated as relational syntax trees. From these trees, estimations about the DQ metrics of the composite set can be made without actually evaluating DQ again. Hence, a gold standard is only required for the exact measurement of the leaf components and the DQ estimation for larger (integrated) data is possible without further need of a gold standard [15]. Currently, estimates for the DQ dimensions accuracy, completeness, and pertinence have been implemented in QualIe. The DQ metrics of the composite set are estimated by traversing the relational algebra syntax tree in a bottom up fashion utilizing the formulas we present in Tables I and II. Here, $D(c)$ is the proportion of records in a data set c, for which at least one duplicate entry exists in c, and p is a selection-specific factor denoting $\frac{|\text{selected records}|}{|\text{original records}|}$.

IV. Implementation Architecture and Demonstration

Fig. 1 shows the architecture of our modular Java-based tool QualIe (pronounced [ˈkvalə]) for measuring IIS data and schema quality. The tool consists of three main components: (a) data source connectors to establish an IS connection and load schema information, (b) quality calculators that store information about the schema and data quality in the DQ Store, and (c) reporters to generate a human- and machine-readable quality report. The tool has been implemented with a focus on maximum flexibility and extensibility, which makes it easy to add new connectors, calculators, or reporters, due to a standardized interface for each component. In addition to a pre-configured automatic execution, it also allows user input in form of rules and parameters for specific quality calculations.

In the following paragraphs, each component as well as the DSD Environment and the Data Quality Store are described in more detail and are underpinned with code examples. Fundamentals on the DSD vocabulary are provided in Section IV-B. Recently, a call for more empiricism in DQ research has been proposed in [30], promoting both, (1) the evaluation on synthetic data sets to show the reproducibility of the measurements, and (2) evaluations on large real-world data sets. In this paper, we target the first part since the main contribution is an introduction of QualIe and how it can actually be used. We plan to extend the evaluation on real-world data in future work.

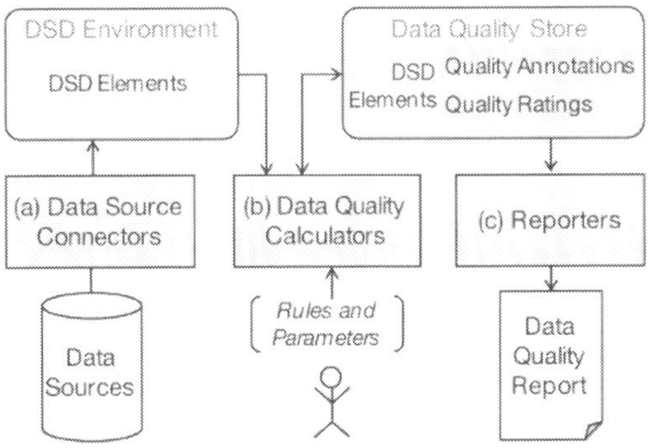

Fig. 1. Implementation Architecture of QualIe

A. Demonstration Data Sources

Three different data sources have been employed for this demonstration: employees DB, Sakila DB, and a Comma-Separated Values (CSV) file "Department". We selected those data sources because of their manageable size and well-known qualitative condition, which allows manual tracking and verification of the calculated quality ratings, cf. [30] (in contrast to large real-world data sets with unknown quality).

a) Employees: The employees DB contains six tables with about three million records in total and models the administrations of employees in a company [31]. We employ the `Datasource` object *dsEmpGS* as gold standard for our demonstration, which represents the original employees DB. In addition, we created two variants that have been automatically populated with randomly inserted errors in the original data: *dsEmp1* (501 records in the main table "employees") and *dsEmp2* (4,389 records in the "employees" table). Table III shows the error types that were used in the script. The added noise n is an absolute error that is normally distributed.

TABLE I. DATA QUALITY ESTIMATION - COMPLETENESS AND PERTINENCE

Operator	Composite	Completeness of Composite	Pertinence of Composite
Projection	$\pi(c)$	$Com(c)$	$Per(c)$
Selection	$\sigma(c)$	$p * Com(c)$	$Per(c)$
Union	$c_1 \cup c_2$	$Com(c_1) + Com(c_2) - D(c_1 \cup c_2) * \frac{Com(c_1) + Com(c_2)}{2}$	$\frac{Per(c_1) * \lvert c_1 \rvert + Per(c_2) * \lvert c_2 \rvert}{\lvert c_1 \rvert + \lvert c_2 \rvert}$
Set Difference	$c_1 - c_2$	$Com(c_1) - D(c_1 \cup c_2) * \frac{Com(c_1) + Com(c_2)}{2}$	$\frac{2 * Per(c_1) * \lvert c_1 \rvert - D(c_1 \cup c_2) * (Per(c_1) * \lvert c_1 \rvert + Per(c_2) * \lvert c_2 \rvert)}{2 * \lvert c_1 \rvert - D(c_1 \cup c_2) * (\lvert c_1 \rvert + \lvert c_2 \rvert)}$
Cross Product	$c1 \times c_2$	$Com(c_1) * Com(c_2)$	$Per(c_1) * Per(c_2)$

TABLE II. DATA QUALITY ESTIMATION - ACCURACY

Operator	Composite	Accuracy of Composite
Projection	$\pi(c)$	$Acc(c)$
Selection	$\sigma(c)$	$\frac{Com(c) * p * Acc(c)}{Com(c) * p + (1 - p) * Acc(c)}$
Union	$c_1 \cup c_2$	$\frac{\left(1 - \frac{D(c_1 \cup c_2)}{2}\right) * (Com(c_1) + Com(c_2))}{1 + \left(1 - \frac{D(c_1 \cup c_2)}{2}\right) * \left(Com(c_1) * \left(\frac{1}{Acc(c_2)} - 1\right) + Com(c_2) * \left(\frac{1}{Acc(c_2)} - 1\right) - 1\right)}$
Set Difference	$c_1 - c_2$	$\frac{2 * Com(C_1) - D(c_1 \cup c_2) * (Com(c_1) + Com(c_2))}{2 * \frac{Com(c_1)}{Acc(c_1)} - D(c_1 \cup c_2) * \left(\frac{Com(c_1)}{Acc(c_1)} - \frac{Com(c_2)}{Acc(c_2)}\right)}$
Cross Product	$c1 \times c_2$	$\frac{Com(c_1) * Com(c_2)}{1 + Com(c_1) * \left(\frac{Com(c_2)}{Acc(c_2)} - 1\right) + Com(c_2) * \left(\frac{Com(c_1)}{Acc(c_1)} - 1\right) + \left(\frac{Com(c_1)}{Acc(c_1)} - 1\right) * \left(\frac{Com(c_2)}{Acc(c_2)} - 1\right)}$

TABLE III. ERROR TYPES

Error type	Domain	Example
`LetterSwap`	String	"Bernhard" $\rightarrow$ "Bernhrad"
`LetterInsertion`	String	"Bernhard" $\rightarrow$ "Bernnhard"
`LetterDeletion`	String	"Bernhard" $\rightarrow$ "Bernhrd"
`LetterReplacement`	String	"Bernhard" $\rightarrow$ "Burnhard"
`AddedNoise`	Numeric	$a \rightarrow a + n$, where $n \sim N(0, 1)$
`NullFault`	Any	"Bernhard" $\rightarrow$ NULL
`RecordDuplication`	Record	{("Werth", 9)} $\rightarrow$ {("Werth", 9), ("Werth", 9)}
`RecordDeletion`	Record	{("Werth", 9)} $\rightarrow \emptyset$
`RecordInsertion`	Record	{("Werth", 9)} $\rightarrow$ {("Werth", 9), ("Ehrlinger", 5)}
`RecordCrossOver`	Record	{("Werth", 9), ("Wöß", 2)} $\rightarrow$ {("Werth", 2), ("Wöß", 9)}

b) Sakila: The Sakila DB has 16 tables and models the administration of a film distribution [32]. While the employees DB contains a large number of records for quality measurement on the data-level, Sakila consists of a more advanced schema for schema quality measurement. We employed the `Datasource` object *dsSakilaGS*, which represents the original Sakila DB, as gold standard. In addition, we created *dsSakila1*, *dsSakila2*, and *dsSakila3*, which are excerpts of Sakila including schema modifications to downgrade correctness, completeness, and pertinence respectively.

c) Department CSV: Additionally, a CSV file that contains a list of people affiliated to the department of "Application-oriented Knowledge Processing" at Johannes Kepler University was used.

As supplement to the demonstration in this paper, we published an executable (`QuaIIe.jar`) on our project website [33], which allows to reconstruct the schema quality measurement described in this section. The program takes one mandatory and one optional command line parameter: (1) the path to the DSD schema to be observed and (2) the path to the gold standard schema, and generates a quality report in XML format. Schema descriptions for all four versions of the Sakila DB, as well as a description for the employees DB are provided in form of DSD files.

B. Data Source Connectors and DSD Environment

A connector's task is to guarantee data model independence by accessing a data source and transforming its schema into a harmonized schema description, which is based on the the DSD vocabulary. The transformation process from various data models and details of the DSD vocabulary are described in [26]. The transformation from schema elements to DSD elements is a prerequisite for performing cross-schema calculations and obtaining information about a schema's similarity to other schemas in the IIS. In QuaIIe, DSD elements are represented as dynamically created objects in the Java environment. Below we list the most important terms of the DSD vocabulary that are used in this paper.

- A `Datasource` s represents one schema in an IIS and has a type (e.g., relational DB, spreadsheet) and an arbitrary number of concepts and associations, which are also referred to as schema elements.

- A `Concept` *c* is a real-world object and is usually equivalent to a table in a relational DB or a class in an object-oriented DB.
- An `Association` is a relationship between two or more concepts. There are three types of association: (i) a reference association describes a general relationship between two concepts (e.g., employment of a person with a company); (ii) an inheritance association represents an inheritance hierarchy (e.g., specific types of employees are inherited from a general employee concept); and (iii) an aggregation association describes the composition of several concepts (components) to an aggregate.
- An `Attribute` is a property of a concept or an association; for example, the column "first_name" provides information about the concept "employees".

Fig. 2 shows an example transformation of two relations from the employees DB: `employees {emp_no: int, birth_date: date, first_name: string, last_name: string}` and `dept_emp {emp_no: int, dept_no: int, from_date: date, to_date: date}` into a DSD file in Turtle syntax (cf. [34]). The attribute descriptions are omitted for brevity. The example shows that a relational table can be transformed into a concept or an association, for example, `dept_emp` is a reference association since it models the assignment of an employee to a department.

```
ex:employees a dsd:Concept ;
  rdfs:label "employees" ;
  dsd:hasAttribute ex:employees.emp_no, ex:employees
      .birth_date, ex:employees.first_name, ex:
      employees.last_name;
  dsd:hasPrimaryKey ex:employees.pk .

ex:dept_emp a dsd:ReferenceAssociation ;
  rdfs:label "dept_emp" ;
  dsd:hasAttribute ex:dept_emp.emp_no, ex:dept_emp.
      dept_no, ex:dept_emp.from_date, ex:dept_emp.
      to_date;
  dsd:hasPrimaryKey ex:dept_emp.pk ;
  dsd:referencesTo ex:employees, ex:departments .
```

Fig. 2. Example Schema Description

While this harmonization step enables comparability and quality measurement of schemas from different data models, it does not guarantee access to the original information sources' content after transformation. Consequently, the schema quality metrics in QualIe primarily use the schema's metadata instead of the IS content. An exception is the determination of the normal form, which is impossible without considering the semantics of the attributes that can be derived from the content.

There are two different types of connectors in QualIe: (1) data source connectors (`DSConnector`), which load the meta data of an IS to describe its schema, and instance connectors (`DSInstanceConnector`), which additionally provide access to the data values of an IS. The interface-oriented design of QualIe allows new connectors to be added by implementing one of the two abstract classes `DSConnector` or `DSInstanceConnector`. Currently, three different connectors are supported:

- `ConnectorMySQL` creates a connection to a MySQL DB as representative for relational DBs by using the functionality of the MySQL Java Connector (cf. [35]). This connector allows access to the DB data values. Information on the selected DB schema is retrieved from the data dictionary, including all tables, columns, foreign keys and column properties.
- `ConnectorCSV` allows to access CSV files and is also is a subclass of `DSInstanceConnector`. Due to little meta data available in plain CSV files, schema information is solely extracted from the given file (i.e., column headers as attribute names).
- `ConnectorOntology` uses the Apache Jena framework (cf. [36]) to access a DSD file. Since DSD files hold only schema information and not a connection to the original database, this connector does not provide any possibilities for accessing the DB content and can be used for schema quality measurement only.

Fig. 3 shows an example instantiation for each of the connector types. In addition to opening a connection, it is necessary to load the schema and thus trigger the conversion of schema elements to DSD elements in the Java DSD environment. For our demonstration, we created a connection to all data sources described in Section IV-A, adhering to the same naming standard. For example, for the employees DB we created the connectors *connEmp1* and *connEmp2* to access the MySQL databases with the inserted errors, and load their schema in form of two `Datasource` objects *dsEmp1* and *dsEmp2* into the DSD environment.

```
// Opening and loading a MySQL data source
DSInstanceConnector connEmpGS = ConnectorMySQL.
    getInstance("jdbc:mysql://localhost:3306/", "
    employees", "user", "pw");
Datasource dsEmpGS = connEmpGS.loadSchema();

// Opening and loading a DSD schema description
DSConnector connSakilaGS = new ConnectorOntology("
    filepath/sakila_gs.ttl", "Sakila_Goldstandard");
Datasource dsSakilaGS = connSakilaGS.loadSchema();

// Opening and loading a CSV file
DSInstanceConnector connDept = new ConnectorCSV("
    filepath/department.csv", ",", "\n", "
    FAW_Department");
Datasource dsDept = connDept.loadSchema();
```

Fig. 3. Data Source Connectors

In QualIe, each data source connectors also offers at least one gold standard implementation, in order to allow the calculation of reference-based DQ dimensions (e.g., completeness). Fig. 4 shows the creation of two different gold standards: (1) `empGS`, which can be used for quality measurement at the data-level, and (2) `hsGS1`, a `HierarchicalSchemaGS` that is solely used for schema quality measurement. Since specific gold standard implementation might have different tasks, each implementation requires a different set of parameters. However, all gold standards in QualIe inherit from the abstract class `GolStandard`, which offers methods to retrieve referenced records or schema elements. The object *empGS* in Fig. 4 shows the instantiation of a gold standard object for a single concept (table), for DQ calculations on different aggregation levels (i.e., when only parts of the content of a data source should be analyzed).

The `HierarchicalSchemaGS` for schema quality calculations extends the idea of simply representing a perfect reference to an information source; rather it is a "container" that holds the reference to another information source and calculates the similarity or dissimilarity between schema elements on-the-fly. Thus, it is, for example, possible to compare one MySQL DB schema to a DSD description as shown in Fig. 4, to overcome data model heterogeneity.

```
// Creation of a gold standard from a single concept
GoldStandard empGS = new StrictConceptMySQLGS(
    dsEmpGS.getConcept("employees"), connEmpGS);

// Creation of a schema gold standard
GoldStandard hsGS1 = new HierarchicalSchemaGS(
    dsSakila1, dsSakilaGS);
```

Fig. 4. Gold Standards

C. *Data Quality Calculators and DQ Store*

Each DQ calculator is dedicated to one of the quality dimensions described in Section III and links the measurements to the corresponding DSD elements in the DQ store. Quality measurements in the DQ store can be used for reporting or reused by other calculators, and can be divided into two different types: *quality ratings* or *quality annotations*. A rating is a double value between 0.0 and 1.0, which is calculated by a specific metric that is assigned to a quality dimension. An example would be a value of 0.85 for the dimension "completeness" on data-level using the metric "ratio". A quality annotation can be an arbitrary object that is linked to a DSD element in the DQ store in order to provide additional information about the quality. An example would be the annotation of functional dependencies to a concept.

Fig. 5 shows the application of all non-time-related DQ calculators that are implemented in the current version of QuaIIe. Initially, the concept "employees" from the erroneous `Datasource` *dsEmp1* is selected for closer investigation. As an example for a distance function, which is required for the minimality calculation, line 5-7 cover the creation of an `EnsembleDistance`, which is a weighted combination of an arbitrary number of specific distance functions. In the demo, we use a combination of two string distances for the attributes `first_name` and `last_name` in the "employees" table. However, QuaIIe allows the creation of arbitrary complex distance functions for each record. Finally, ratings for the DQ dimensions accuracy, completeness, pertinence, and minimality are calculated. Line 16 shows how to programmatically retrieve those stored DQ values from the DQ store. One data quality rating or annotation is uniquely identifiable in the DQ store by a reference to the DSD element (e.g., a reference to the concept "employees" in *dsEmp1*), the `DIMENSION_LABEL` of the measured quality dimension (e.g., "completeness") as well as a `METRIC_LABEL` (e.g., "ratio"), which describes the metric used for calculating the dimension.

```
1  // Select concept "employees" from employees DB
2  Concept c = dsEmp1.getConcept("employees");
3
4  // Create a custom distance measure
5  EnsembleDistance<Record> dist = new EnsembleDistance
       <Record>();
6  dist.addDistance(new StringRecordDistance(c.
       getAttribute("first_name"), new
       LevenshteinDistance()), 0.5);
7  dist.addDistance(new StringRecordDistance(c.
       getAttribute("last_name"), new
       LevenshteinDistance()), 0.5);
8
9  // Perform quality calculations
10 RatioAccuracyCalculator.calculate(c,empGS,connEmp1);
11 RatioCompletenessCalculator.calculate(c,empGS,
       connEmp1);
12 RatioPertinenceCalculator.calculate(c, empGS,
       connEmp1);
13 RecordMinimalityCalculator.calculate(c, dist, 0.1,
       connEmp1);
14
15 // Retrieve DQ measurements from the DQ store
16 DataQualityStore.getDQValue(c,
       RatioPertinenceCalculator.DIMENSION_LABEL,
       RatioPertinenceCalculator.METRIC_LABEL)
```

Fig. 5. Data Quality Calculations

In addition to the measurement of *dsEmp1* (501 records), we applied the same calculations on the "employees" table of *dsEmp2* (4,389 records). The results can be compared in Table IV. The low quality values for accuracy and completeness are due to the small subsets of the erroneous tables in contrast to the original employees table with 30,0024 records.

TABLE IV. DQ MEASUREMENT OF ERRONEOUS DATA SOURCES

Dimension	*dsEmp1*	*dsEmp1*
Accuracy	0.0013	0.0116
Completeness	0.0013	0.0116
Pertinence	0.7725	0.7938
Minimality	0.7180	0.7532

For the schema quality calculations, we employed a DSD description of the original Sakila DB as gold standard and accessed the three additional data sources (*dsSakila1*, *dsSakila2*, *dsSakila3*) through the MySQL connector. Each data source contains schema modifications that tackle one of the schema quality dimensions correctness, completeness, and pertinence, and are justified in the following paragraphs. For the demonstration using `QuaIIe.jar` on our project website [33], we provided all four schemas as DSD files in order to facilitate data exchange and reproduction.

The 16 tables from Sakila were transformed into 14 DSD concepts and two DSD reference associations (`film_category` and `film_actor`). For the *hierarchical schema similarity*, standard parameters have been used with a less restrictive attribute similarity threshold of 0.8. The determination and evaluation of the schema similarity standard parameters is justified in [14]. Fig. 6 shows the application of the schema quality calculators.

```
HierarchicalSchemaCorrectness.calculate(dsSakila1,
    hsGS1);
HierarchicalSchemaCompleteness.calculate(dsSakila2,
    hsGS2);
HierarchicalSchemaPertinence.calculate(dsSakila3,
    hsGS3);
RatioMinimalityCalculator.calculate(dsEmpGS);
NormalFormCalculator.calculate(dsEmpGS, connEmpGS);
```

Fig. 6. Schema Quality Calculations

The schema quality measurements that have been generated in Fig. 6, are 0.8125 for correctness, 0.8125 for completeness, 0.8824 for pertinence, and 0.8 for minimality. The results are discussed in more detail in the following subsections.

a) Schema Correctness: In order to demonstrate the correctness dimension, we performed changes in the observed schema but did not remove or add new schema elements. The corresponding DQ report can be generated by executing `java -jar QuaIIe.jar sakila_correctness.ttl sakila_gs.ttl`. First, the concept `film` was renamed to "movie", which did not change the ratings for pertinence and completeness, but decreased correctness slightly to 0.9375 due to the additional incorrect element. Second, all occurrences of film (e.g., `film_id`) in the DB were replaced with "movie". While completeness and pertinence retained a rating of 1.0, because all concepts and associations were assigned (even if incorrectly) to their original correspondences in the GS, correctness achieved only a rating of $\frac{13}{13+3+0} = 0.8125$.

b) Schema Completeness: The completeness calculation was demonstrated by removing schema elements. The DQ report for this demo can be generated by assessing `sakila_completeness.ttl`. Initially, the two tables `category` and `film_category` were removed, which resulted in a completeness rating of $\frac{14+0}{14+0+2} = 0.875$ because two elements were classified as missing. Then, the attribute `picture` was deleted from the table `staff`. Removals at the attribute level did not directly affect the result of the completeness calculation, since `staff` is still correctly assigned to its gold standard representation due to the tolerance of the distance calculation. Concluding, three additional attributes were removed from `staff`, which resulted in a similarity rating of 0.6923 between `staff` and its correspondence in the GS. Consequently, both tables were not mapped because they were too different and completeness dropped to $\frac{13+0}{13+0+3} = 0.8125$.

c) Schema Pertinence: For the demonstration of pertinence, we added additional elements to the schema and the quality report can be generated by assessing the file `sakila_pertinence.ttl`. In a first step, the "employees" table from the employees DB was added to *dsSakila3*, dropping pertinence to 0.9412. This demo correctly classifies the concept `employees` as an extra element, although the new concept has a relatively low distance to the concept `actor`. Second, we modified the concept `actor` in *dsSakila3*, such that no assignment to its corresponding concept in the GS was created and the pertinence rating dropped to $\frac{15+0}{15+0+2} = 0.8824$. Following, the newly added `employees` table was aligned with the `actor` concept in the GS by removing and altering attributes. This resulted in a similarity value of 0.8333 between `employees` and the concept `actor` from the GS and increased completeness to 1.0 (all elements could be assigned to the GS). However, the pertinence dimension (0.9412) indicated the extra `actor` concept in the observed schema, which did not match any of the GS elements.

We conclude that an examination of all three dimensions (correctness, completeness, and pertinence) is advisable when measuring the quality of a schema. Note that the correctness metric is particularly strict, because it is decreased by every incorrect element in the schema, whereas completeness and pertinence do not distinguish between correct and incorrect.

d) Schema Minimality: Analogous to the data minimality, schema minimality requires a distance function. Currently, two schema distance functions are offered: the similarity flooding algorithm introduced in [27] and hierarchical schema similarity, which we use in the following calculations with standard parameters that have been evaluated in [14]. First, we observed the Sakila DB schema (`sakila_gs.ttl`), which achieves an ideal minimality rating of $\frac{16-1}{16-1} = 1.0$, because all schema elements are sufficiently different to each other.

Second, we evaluated the employees schema, which yields the similarity matrix in Table V. Interestingly, the two associations `dept_emp` and `dept_manager` achieve a very high similarity of 0.875, which reduces the minimality rating to $\frac{5-1}{6-1} = 0.8$. In practice, this rating indicates an IS architect that the two associations should be further analyzed. However, in our case, no further action is required since the employees schema contains a special modeling concept of parallel associations (i.e., two different roles) which does not represent semantic redundancy, but leads to very similar relations in the schema model (cf. [31]). Since it is known that this modeling construct yields high similarity values (e.g., also for schema matching applications), it was specially suited to demonstrate our minimality metric. The full quality report for this demo can be generated by executing "`java -jar QuaIIe.jar employees.ttl`".

TABLE V. SIMILARITY MATRIX FOR EMPLOYEES SCHEMA

	depts*	dept_emp	dept_mgr*	employees	salaries	titles
depts*	1.0	0.125	0.125	0.1	0.125	0.125
dept_emp	0.125	1.0	0.875	0.1818	0.2222	0.1
dept_mgr*	0.125	0.875	1.0	0.1818	0.2222	0.1
employees	0.1	0.1818	0.1818	1.0	0.1818	0.1818
salaries	0.125	0.2222	0.2222	0.1818	1.0	0.375
titles	0.125	0.1	0.1	0.1818	0.375	1.0

*Departments is abbreviated with "depts" and dept_manager with "dept_mgr".

e) Normal Form Calculation: The NF calculator was applied to the employees DB and yields BCNF for each concept. The minimal cover of the FDs is shown in Table VI.

Due to the large number of records in the employees database, calculating these results took about 22 minutes and 45 seconds on a Macbook Pro with an Intel Core i7 processor with 2,2 GHz and 16 GB main memory. In addition to FDs, candidate keys are also annotated to the observed schema elements, and attributes are annotated with a Boolean value that indicates whether they are classified as key or non-key. Note that, particularly in terms of performance, more sophisticated methods of discovering FDs exist [29]. However, since the main aim of our work was to provide a comprehensive approach to data and schema quality measurement, the normalization dimension was included for completeness to support full FD discovery (i.e., without approximation).

TABLE VI. NF CALCULATION - EMPLOYEES SCHEMA

Concept	Functional Dependencies
departments	{dept_no}→{dept_name}, {dept_name}→{dept_no}
dept_emp	{emp_no, dept_no}→{from_date, to_date}
dept_manager	{emp_no}→{dept_no, from_date, to_date}
employees	{emp_no}→{first_name, last_name, gender, birth_date, hire_date}
salaries	{emp_no, from_date}→{to_date, salary}
titles	{emp_no, title, from_date}→{to_date}

D. Data Source Integration

In IIS, it is often necessary to estimate the quality of data stemming from different IS. QualIe supports the virtual integration of different concepts, which is realized with the Java classes `IntegratedDatasource` and `IntegratedConcept`. Fig. 7 shows an example integration, where all records from the table "employees", which is present in both erroneous data sources *dsEmp1* and *dsEmp2*, are unified. The data is stored in form of a virtual integrated data source (`ids`), which exists only during runtime.

```
IntegratedDatasource ids = DSDFactory.
    makeIntegratedDatasource("integratedEmp");

ISQLIntegrator integrator = new ISQLIntegrator(ids);
integrator.add(dsEmp1, connEmp1);
integrator.add(dsEmp2, connEmp2);

IntegratedConcept ic = integrator.
    makeIntegratedConceptFromString("SELECT * FROM
    dsEmp1.employees UNION SELECT * FROM dsEmp2.
    employees", "integratedEmployees");
```

Fig. 7. Data Integration

An integrated concept contains an *operator tree*, which specifies the data sources, concepts, connectors, and integration transformations that are required for its creation. After generating such an integrated concept, it can be assessed likewise to an ordinary concept from a single data source in QualIe (cf. lines 3-6 in Fig. 8). Additionally, it is possible to estimate the quality (cf. Section III-F), which is not a complete measurement of the new integrated concept, but is based on the prior quality ratings of each IS. Thus, an estimation requires the prior measurement of each IS that takes part in the integration.

```
1  DSInstanceConnector integrConn = new
       IntegratedInstanceConnector(ic);
2
3  RatioCompletenessCalculator.calculate(ic, gsEmp,
       integrConn);
4  RatioAccuracyCalculator.calculate(ic, gsEmp,
       integrConn);
5  RatioPertinenceCalculator.calculate(ic, gsEmp,
       integrConn);
6  RecordMinimalityCalculator.calculate(ic, dist, 0.1,
       integrConn);
7
8  RatioCompletenessCalculator.estimate(ic);
9  RatioAccuracyCalculator.estimate(ic);
10 RatioPertinenceCalculator.estimate(ic);
```

Fig. 8. DQ Estimation of an integrated Concept

The ratings for the DQ calculations and estimations from Fig. 8 are compared in Table VII and show high conformance. In the current version of QualIe, quality estimation is only available for the dimensions accuracy, completeness, and pertinence. However, an extension of the DQ estimators to other dimensions, like minimality, is planned as future work.

TABLE VII. DQ CALCULATION OF AN INTEGRATED CONCEPT

Dimension	Measurement	Estimation
Accuracy	0.0129	0.0130
Completeness	0.0129	0.0128
Pertinence	0.7916	0.7916
Minimality	0.7494	-

E. Data Quality Report

In order to present the quality ratings and annotations contained in the DQ store in a human- and machine-readable way, QualIe offers several reporter classes that generate a quality report. The most comprehensible end-user report is `XMLTreeStructureDQReporter`, which is created in Fig. 9 and exports a description of all connected data sources with their DSD elements, quality ratings and annotations. Since such a report tends to be large and verbose for large IIS, the hierarchical structure of the XML document allows to drill-down and roll-up on different aggregation levels by using a suitable viewer. In addition, languages like XSLT, XQuery, or XPath allow a user to search within such a report. The advantage of an XML report in our use case is however the fact that it can be reused automatically for further analysis and benchmarking (e.g., for data quality monitoring). When measuring the quality of the published DSD schemas with `QuaIIe.jar` (cf. [33]), the output is such a report.

```
XMLTreeStructureDQReporter reporter = new
    XMLTreeStructureDQReporter();
reporter.buildReport();
reporter.writeReport("path/DQReport.xml");
```

Fig. 9. Data Quality Report Generation

V. CONCLUSION AND FUTURE WORK

In this paper, we have described QualIe, a tool to estimate and measure the data and schema quality of an IIS.

QualIe generates a machine- and human-readable quality report, which allows for repetitive quality measurement and comparison of different reports from the same IIS. The DQ measurement covers the dimensions accuracy, correctness, completeness, pertinence, minimality, and normalization for both, the schema and the data of an IS. To the best of our knowledge, there exists no tool that measures such a large number of different DQ dimensions in a single application. However, our major contribution is the unsupervised and automated ad-hoc analysis of both data and schema quality.

Our ongoing and future work focuses on a practical evaluation of QualIe on real-world data with respect to the benefits of the measured DQ metrics. Coupled to the evaluation, we plan to extend the theoretical foundations by more deeply considering research from related fields, like data cleansing and integration. In addition, several implementation extensions like a calculator for the readability dimension as well as a connector for Oracle DBs and a connector for Apache Cassandra are currently under development. An implementation of a graphical user interface to visualize the DQ measurements is also planned.

Acknowledgment

The research reported in this paper has been partly supported by the Austrian Ministry for Transport, Innovation and Technology, the Federal Ministry of Science, Research and Economy, and the Province of Upper Austria in the frame of the COMET center SCCH.

References

[1] KPMG International, "Now or Never: 2016 Global CEO Outlook," 2016.

[2] T. C. Redman, "The Impact of Poor Data Quality on the Typical Enterprise," *Communications of the ACM*, vol. 41, no. 2, pp. 79–82, Feb. 1998.

[3] ——, "Bad Data Costs the U.S. $3 Trillion Per Year," Harvard Business Review, 2016, https://hbr.org/2016/09/bad-data-costs-the-u-s-3-trillion-per-year [retrieved: March, 2018].

[4] B. Otto and H. Österle, *Corporate Data Quality: Prerequisite for Successful Business Models*. Berlin, Germany: Berlin: Springer Gabler, 2016.

[5] F. Naumann, U. Leser, and J. C. Freytag, "Quality-driven Integration of Heterogenous Information Systems," in *Proceedings of the 25th International Conference on Very Large Data Bases*, ser. VLDB '99. San Francisco, CA, USA: Morgan Kaufmann Publishers Inc., 1999, pp. 447–458.

[6] Y. Wand and R. Y. Wang, "Anchoring Data Quality Dimensions in Ontological Foundations," *Communications of the ACM*, vol. 39, no. 11, pp. 86–95, Nov. 1996.

[7] M. Y. Selvege, S. Judah, and A. Jain, "Magic Quadrant for Data Quality Tools," Gartner, Tech. Rep., October 2017.

[8] J. Barateiro and H. Galhardas, "A Survey of Data Quality Tools," *Datenbank-Spektrum*, vol. 14, no. 15-21, p. 48, 2005.

[9] V. Pushkarev, H. Neumann, C. Varol, and J. R. Talburt, "An Overview of Open Source Data Quality Tools," in *Proceedings of the 2010 International Conference on Information & Knowledge Engineering, IKE 2010, July 12-15, 2010, Las Vegas Nevada, USA*, 2010, pp. 370–376.

[10] R. Y. Wang and D. M. Strong, "Beyond Accuracy: What Data Quality Means to Data Consumers," *Journal of Management Information Systems*, vol. 12, no. 4, pp. 5–33, Mar. 1996.

[11] C. Batini and M. Scannapieco, *Data and Information Quality: Concepts, Methodologies and Techniques*. Springer International Publishing, 2016.

[12] "Standard for a Software Quality Metrics Methodology," Institute of Electrical and Electronics Engineers, IEEE 1061-1998, 1998.

[13] Oxford University Press, "Definition of Gold Standard in English," Online, 2017, http://www.oxforddictionaries.com/definition/american-_english/gold-standard [retrieved: March, 2018].

[14] L. Ehrlinger, "Data Quality Assessment on Schema-Level for Integrated Information Systems," Master's thesis, Johannes Kepler University Linz, 2016.

[15] B. Werth, "Identifikation von Datenqualitätsproblemen in integrierten Informationssystemen [Identification of Data Quality Issues in Integrated Information Systems]," Master's thesis, Johannes Kepler University Linz, 2016.

[16] T. Haegemans, M. Snoeck, and W. Lemahieu, "Towards a Precise Definition of Data Accuracy and a Justification for its Measure," in *Proceedings of the International Conference on Information Quality (ICIQ)*, 2016, pp. 16:1–16:13.

[17] J. R. Logan, P. N. Gorman, and B. Middleton, "Measuring the Quality of Medical Records: A Method for Comparing Completeness and Correctness of Clinical Encounter Data," in *AMIA 2001, American Medical Informatics Association Annual Symposium, Washington, DC, USA, November 3-7, 2001*, 2001, pp. 408–4012.

[18] G. Salton and M. J. McGill, "Introduction to Modern Information Retrieval," 1986.

[19] G. Vossen, *Datenmodelle, Datenbanksprachen und Datenbankmanagementsysteme [Data Models, Database Languages, and Database Management Systems]*. Oldenbourg Verlag, 2008.

[20] M. C. M. Batista and A. C. Salgado, "Information Quality Measurement in Data Integration Schemas," in *Proceedings of the Fifth International Workshop on Quality in Databases, QDB 2007, at the VLDB 2007 Conference, Vienna, Austria*. ACM, September 2007, pp. 61–72.

[21] F. Naumann, J.-C. Freytag, and U. Leser, "Completeness of Integrated Information Sources," *Information Systems*, vol. 29, no. 7, pp. 583–615, Sep. 2004.

[22] A. K. Elmagarmid, P. G. Ipeirotis, and V. S. Verykios, "Duplicate Record Detection: A Survey," *IEEE Transactions on knowledge and data engineering*, vol. 19, no. 1, pp. 1–16, 2007.

[23] I. P. Fellegi and A. B. Sunter, "A Theory for Record Linkage," *Journal of the American Statistical Association*, vol. 64, no. 328, pp. 1183–1210, 1969.

[24] J. Euzenat and P. Shvaiko, *Ontology Matching*. Secaucus, NJ, USA: Springer-Verlag New York, Inc., 2007.

[25] A. K. Jain, M. N. Murty, and P. J. Flynn, "Data Clustering: A Review," *ACM Computing Surveys (CSUR)*, vol. 31, no. 3, pp. 264–323, 2000.

[26] L. Ehrlinger and W. Wöß, "Semi-Automatically Generated Hybrid Ontologies for Information Integration," in *Joint Proceedings of the Posters and Demos Track of 11th International Conference on Semantic Systems – SEMANTiCS2015 and 1st Workshop on Data Science: Methods, Technology and Applications (DSci15)*. CEUR Workshop Proceedings, 2015, pp. 100–104.

[27] S. Melnik, H. Garcia-Molina, and E. Rahm, "Similarity Flooding: A Versatile Graph Matching Algorithm and its Application to Schema Matching," in *Proceedings of the 18th International Conference on Data Engineering*, ser. ICDE '02. Washington, DC, USA: IEEE Computer Society, 2002, pp. 117–128.

[28] E. F. Codd, "A Relational Model of Data for Large Shared Data Banks," *Communications of the ACM*, vol. 13, no. 6, pp. 377–387, 1970.

[29] J. Liu, J. Li, C. Liu, and Y. Chen, "Discover Dependencies from Data – A Review," *IEEE Transactions on Knowledge and Data Engineering*, vol. 24, no. 2, pp. 251–264, 2012.

[30] S. Sadiq, T. Dasu, X. L. Dong, J. Freire, I. F. Ilyas, S. Link, M. J. Miller, F. Naumann, X. Zhou, and D. Srivastava, "Data Quality: The Role of Empiricism," *ACM SIGMOD Record*, vol. 46, no. 4, pp. 35–43, 2018.

[31] Oracle Corporation, "Employees Sample Database," Online, https://dev.mysql.com/doc/employee/en [retrieved: March, 2018].

[32] ——, "Sakila Sample Database," Online, https://dev.mysql.com/doc/sakila/en [retrieved: March, 2018].

[33] L. Ehrlinger, "Data Quality Assessment for Heterogenous Information Systems," Online, http://dqm.faw.jku.at [retrieved: March, 2018].

[34] W3C Working Group, "RDF 1.1 Turtle," Online, 2014, https://www.w3.org/TR/turtle [retrieved: March, 2018].

[35] Oracle Corporation, "MySQL Connectors," Online, https://www.mysql.com/products/connector [retrieved: March, 2018].

[36] The Apache Software Foundation, "Apache Jena," Online, https://jena.apache.org [retrieved: March, 2018].

Real-Time Scheduler For Consistent Query Execution of Big Data Analytics

Shenoda Guirguis[1]
Graph DB
LinkedIn
Sunnyvale , USA
sguirguis@linkedin.com

Sabina Petride[1]
Oracle SQL Execution
Oracle
Redwood City, USA
sabina.petride@oracle.com

Abstract—**Analytical queries on big data consume a lot of resources and typically run for long time. Both resource utilization and execution time can be reduced by order of magnitude by transitioning to main memory systems, as well as by offloading part of the analytic computation to in-memory clusters of special purpose analytic engines. These systems are highly optimized for certain patterns of query execution on main memory data, and can support high level of concurrency. Trading off optimization and specialization for operational completeness, such secondary systems are not always fully fledged transactional: they hold copies of the data and rely on refreshes being coordinated from the primary. In such heterogeneous systems, it is particularly challenging to support applications with *strict consistency guarantees* requiring transaction consistent query execution. The eventually-consistency model does not fit in this setup, yet eager propagation of changes imposes a huge unnecessary overhead. In this paper, we formalize the challenge of strictly consistent query execution in hybrid (primary plus in-memory secondary) systems as a *real-time scheduling problem*, and propose a scheduler that ensures consistent query execution and minimal overhead at both primary and secondary systems. We detail the system design with a focus on the query and change propagation scheduler and its interaction with other processes, explaining the advantages of our solution over alternatives. We argue that the proposed framework is easily extendable to incorporate different customized optimization goals. We conclude with preliminary promising performance evaluation of the implemented infrastructure part of the Data Processing Unit (DPU)-based hybrid database system.**

Keywords - Big Data Analytics; Replication; Consistency; Change Propagation; Real-time Scheduling.

I. INTRODUCTION

Analytical queries on Big Data consume a lot of resources and typically run for long time [8][17]. In-memory databases speed up query performance by orders of magnitude - factor of 100x for some applications [7][9][16][21][22]. One opportunity is to use a cluster of in-memory databases, as a secondary database to speed up the performance of analytical queries [12][13][19][20]. One can consider such secondary database as a huge cache. In this setup, and in presence of data updates or changes, there is a need to ensure consistent query execution. That is, whenever a query runs against data in the secondary in-memory database, it should return the same results as when it runs against the data in the primary database. Eventually-consistent model [10] does not fit in this setup, since analytical queries are typically used to support decision making and policy changes. Therefore, analytical queries need to return accurate up-to-date results. Yet, eager propagation of changes imposes a huge unnecessary overhead. In this paper, we propose a framework that ensures consistent query execution and minimal overhead at both primary and secondary databases. This framework includes all components of a consistent query execution starting with the capture of data changes, and the propagation and deployment of changes at the secondary system. In our solution, the secondary database does not need to run the same query execution engine as the primary, which makes the framework applicable to any hybrid database, as long as there is an agreed upon data exchange format that can be understood by both systems. Further, out design allows optimizing performance for user-defined performance goals.

Our contributions can be summarized in the following points:

1) We formalize change propagation from the primary to the secondary systems and query submission on the secondary system as a *real-time scheduling* problem. While real-time scheduling is a well-known subject [2]-[6][11], its applicability to change and query propagation in heterogeneous systems is new, to the best of our knowledge. In particular, while the mechanism of capturing Data Manipulation Language (DML) activity may be common with the hybrid periodic change propagation method (of [1]), the formalization of DML activity as jobs and the definition of job granularity and job metadata are novel.

2) We explain the design of a query and DML activity scheduler that runs on the primary, its system placement in database and interaction with database processes. The scheduler is a new component of the database, and subsequently its interaction with other activities in the database is novel.

3) As detailed in Section V, the scheduling mechanism is efficient – it achieves its goals, formulated via the scheduling policy. Most common goals in heterogeneous systems of our focus can be formulated via scheduling policies.

The proposed scheduling system model is practical to achieve. We based our claim on a prototype implemented on heterogeneous database system and on preliminary promising performance evaluation.

The remaining of this paper is organized as follows. Section II gives the necessary background. The problem formulation and our proposed scheduler are described in Section III and Section IV, respectively. Section V details the implemented prototype in the Oracle database and the RAPID Data Processing Unit (DPU)-based in-memory accelerator [19][20], along with preliminary performance evaluation. The paper is concluded in Section VI.

II. PRELIMINARIES

The setup we are concerned with is one with two coupled-databases: a primary database and a secondary database that is optimized for analytical queries, such as the setup in [19][20] where a cluster of high-speed interconnected in-memory databases are used to boost analytical queries performance. The secondary database is not necessarily a fully-fledged Atomicity, Consistency, Isolation, and Durability (ACID) compliant database, and can be seen mainly as a query engine highly tuned to execute parts of SQL queries submitted through the primary. All activities are initiated through the primary database and execution on the secondary is transparent to the user. The user specifically loads some base tables into the target database at any point of time. When queries are submitted, the source database determines which queries or query-fragments, i.e., sub-queries, can be offloaded to the secondary database to boost query performance. Data changes, i.e., DMLs, are submitted and executed in the primary database. A change propagation protocol copies new or updated data to the secondary database, or informs the secondary about deletions.

The main advantage of such heterogeneous database systems is that they combine the full ACID compliant features of a traditional database (the primary) with the high efficiency and potentially highly distributed query execution of an accelerator (the secondary). The accelerator does not need to support all the features of the primary – the tradeoff between generalization and optimization via specialization allows highly optimized code for a narrower functionality. Fronting all operations from the primary also allows gradual support over releases of more complex features in the accelerator, and offloading more and more operations outside of the primary.

The source of truth, both in terms of data and query execution, in heterogeneous systems is the primary database. For space efficiency, only relations targeted to be queried in the accelerator are loaded into the secondary database. As all DML activity happens at the primary, the data has to be kept refreshed on the secondary after the initial load. As the secondary is not a fully-fledged transactional system, DML replication happens physically – by propagating the data that has changed from the primary to the secondary. However, there is no explicit requirement for synchronous data propagation. For instance, if DML activity happens on a relation not queried, then there is no need for the DML in the primary to "wait" until it is propagated to the secondary. The strict requirements are

- When a query executes on the secondary, it returns the same results as when it is executed on the primary. Therefore, when a query executes in the secondary all the DML activity on the relations references in the query has to be up-to-date (more specifically, up to the query system commit number *SCN*).

- Queries are offloaded to the secondary only when estimated to run faster than on the primary. The estimation should be such that applications run faster in the presence of the secondary and that the secondary is picked for execution whenever beneficial.

Therefore, in systems of our focus we have both a change propagation and a query submission problem, and they are interconnected: (1) when and how should changes be propagated to the secondary, and (2) how to choose between executing queries on the secondary system vs. on the primary, in order to ensure the above requirements?

Data replication has been utilized for decades either for availability reasons (i.e., backup and recovery) or for performance reasons (e.g., load balance). Therefore, propagation of data changes across data replicas is not a new problem. However, we argue that replication in analytic hybrid database systems of our focus poses new challenges. In heterogeneous database systems, the main purpose of the secondary database is to accelerate query execution and offload computation from the primary. In doing so, the hybrid system supports higher level of concurrency and faster query response than the primary system alone. The secondary database is neither a backup nor a replica of the primary database: queries are always submitted from the primary and within the primary a decision is taken to offload the query - if expected to run faster - to the secondary. If the primary goes down, the secondary is not accessible to users for query execution. Further, in most applications where replication is utilized for load balancing, data consistency can be sacrificed temporarily in order to maintain the performance at its best. For example, the eventually-consistent model [10] has been adopted by most key-value stores in this regard. However, in case of analytics queries, data consistency cannot be compromised or else wrong outdated conclusions may be deduced. Moreover, since the purpose of replication in data analytics is to boost performance, query performance cannot be compromised either. This poses a new challenge in efficiently and timely propagating data changes. Therefore, existing solutions cannot be applied per se. This paper addresses these new challenges.

The spectrum of choices of how and when to propagate changes, from a source to a target database, is quite wide. At one end, changes are propagated *eagerly* as soon as they are captured. On the other end, changes are propagated *on – demand*, i.e., only when needed at query time. Alternatives include periodic change propagation – refreshes are scheduled at certain time intervals. The pros and cons of each approach make each approach suitable for certain class of applications. For example, if changes are very frequent and queries are scarce, then one can argue that the lazy approach of pushing changes on-demand is a better choice, as it amortizes the overhead of the propagation protocol. On the other hand, if query response time is critical, a proactive approach of propagating changes as soon as they are committed would be needed to minimize query response time. This, however, comes at the expense of incurring high overhead.

Typically, most systems that employ one or the other method leave it to the user or the database administrator (DBA) to choose between the methods. For instance, the secondary system can be exposed as a cache that can be configured for one or the other types of refreshes [15]. The assumption is that the user has an expectation of the workload and pattern of data changes. Switching between different methods dynamically in response to deviations from the expected usage is not typically available.

One optimization is to combine propagating changes on-demand when a query needs them, with a *periodic* change propagation approach and an eager propagation of bulk appends [1]. The goal of such a propagation scheme is to minimize the amount, or size, of data needed to be propagated at query time to minimize the query delay. It is also meant to address run-time variations in workloads of a certain pattern – sporadic append-mainly large DMLs (such as nightly bulk data ingestion) at times of low volume of queries, with regular small online transaction processing (OLTP)-type transactions. Therefore, this approach works perfect if changes are mainly scarce and small at times of high query traffic, and it ensure strict consistency – queries are not chosen for execution on the accelerator until all dependent changes are visible to the accelerator. However, even such a hybrid scheme does not answer the following questions:

- What is a reasonable or good enough time for a query to wait for dependent changes?
- How to detect the case when changes exist while the query does not need these changes? That is, when to skip vs. when to delay a certain propagation to minimize query wait time? For example, if the changes are of a later system change number (SCN) than the query SCN, then the query does not depend on these changes and therefore does not need to wait for them to be propagated. (Note that this is similar to the query/update independence analysis of [25]-[27].)
- In the presence of multiple changes and concurrent queries, in what order should changes be propagated, and in what order should queries be submitted to the secondary?
- How to efficiently adapt to deviations in the expected pattern of DML and query activity?

There is a need to precisely formalize the change propagation model in order to answer the above questions and address the new challenges in compliance with the optimization goal.

III. PROBLEM FORMALIZATION

We formalize the change propagation problem as a real - time scheduling problem. *Tasks* to schedule are (a) the data changes to propagate, and (b) the analytic queries offloaded to the target database, that is we propose a dual query and change-propagation scheduler infrastructure. The scheduler maintains as part of its metadata the dependency information between change propagation tasks and queries. This dependency is detected and maintained to ensure valid schedules. Each task is assigned a priority based on the optimization goal. Based on the dependency between tasks and their priority, the scheduler can answer the questions that arise in case of concurrent queries and multiple data changes. For example, given the priority of each query, the scheduler can prioritize which required data change to propagate first. Also, by assigning a deadline for each query-task, as we shall explain later, the scheduler can determine when it is too long to wait for updates to be propagated, and when it is not. Finally, the scheduler can adapt different scheduling policies to suit the application and performance optimization desired. For example, one policy can optimize query throughput, another can maximize number of queries executed on the target database, say to minimize energy, and a third can minimize the query wait response time, etc.

Further, the scheduler provides infrastructure for several other functionalities. For example, one opportunity is to utilize the scheduler as a resource manager which monitors workload both on source and target databases. This allows us to add load-balance functionality. Further, the DBA or the user can monitor the system and indicate at run-time a change in the scheduling policy. In a more evolved implementation of the system, the switch between policies could happen by automatic collection of system performance and usage of simple rules for picking from available scheduling policy.

A. Change Propagation: A Scheduling Problem

Definition 1: There are two types of *tasks:*

- *query-task* (read only) - In our scheduling model a query-task actually means a query-fragment

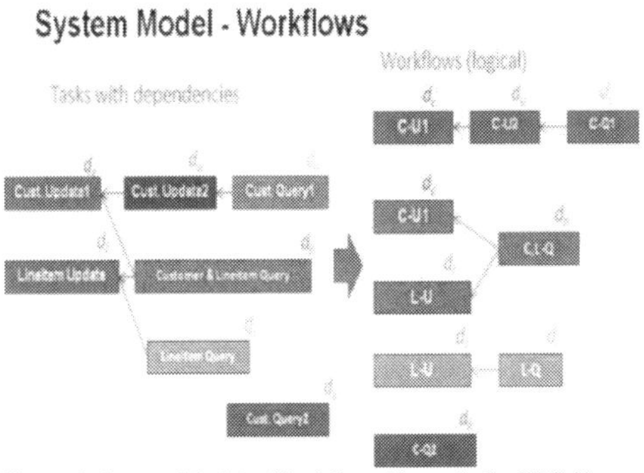

Figure 1. System Model – Workflows Example for TPC-H

that is offloaded to be executed in the secondary database to boost performance. Hence, there may be more than a one query-task per query.

- *update-task* - set of committed DMLs per object/table belonging to the same transaction.

Note that for simplicity we focus here on change propagation of committed DMLs, but the model can be naturally extended to consider uncommitted DMLs and queries submitted in a transaction after uncommitted DMLs. We note here for completeness that in the system of focus it was considered acceptable for queries running on relations in the secondary system but with uncommitted changes to be up-front executed only on the primary. Physically, update tasks can be represented in multiple formats – for instance, full post images of the changed or new rows can live in the buffer cache, on disk or in the redo log; they may also live in in-memory caches built for optimizing query execution by providing faster data access.

The dependency between tasks is defined as follows:

Definition 2: A query-task q_i and/or update-task u_j depends on update- task u_k if and only if (1) there is a common data object, and (2) u_k is executed before q_i and u_j.

We model the set of tasks as *workflows*:

Definition 3: A *workflow* is a set of tasks that has acyclic dependency relations.

A single task may then be logically present in multiple workflows. Figure 1 shows an example of seven tasks that form four workflows. The Customer update-1 task, belongs to two workflows, the first (blue) and the second (red) one. Each task (see Figure 2) has a *deadline* and a *cost*. The deadline is primarily execution driven (i.e., driven from estimated time-cost if executed in the primary database).

Definition 4: The *deadline* d_i of a query-task q_i is its estimated execution cost on the *primary* database ($c_{i,src}$). The *deadline di* of an update-task u_i is

– Infinity, if there is no query that depends on u_i

– *min{d_j , for all j, such that. query q_j depends on u_i}.*

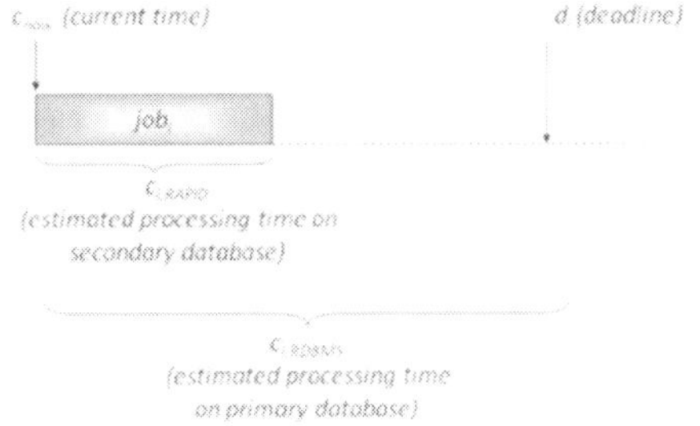

Figure 2. System Model – Individual Task

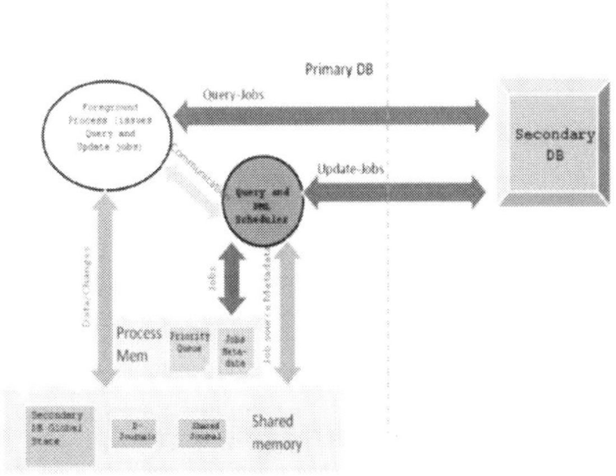

Figure 3. System Architecture

A deadline of an update-task may change, depending on arrival (addition) and departure (finish execution) of depending query-tasks. A depending query may finish before the update task it depends on, only if it is executed in the primary database, i.e., in case of fallback.

Note that the definition of cost of a query fragment is not the focus of this paper: here we rely on the fact that heterogeneous systems of our focus use a cost-based optimizer for planning a query and they are extended with cost models for execution of different query operators on the accelerator.

What is novel, however, is the usage of a query fragment cost as a deadline. In our implementation, it was a challenge to maintain, the query fragment cost as we shall discuss in Section IV. Similarly, the cost model for update tasks is not the focus of this paper. We rely on the fact that such cost models are practical, and we utilized such cost models in our prototype.

B. Change Propagation Scheduler– High Level

We assume a single propagation process with a single Propagation Priority Queue (PPQ) for the single -instance case. Figure 3 shows the System Architecture of this case. It shows that the scheduler - of queries and updates - runs in a separate process. It maintains its priority queue and tasks metadata, including dependency, in its process

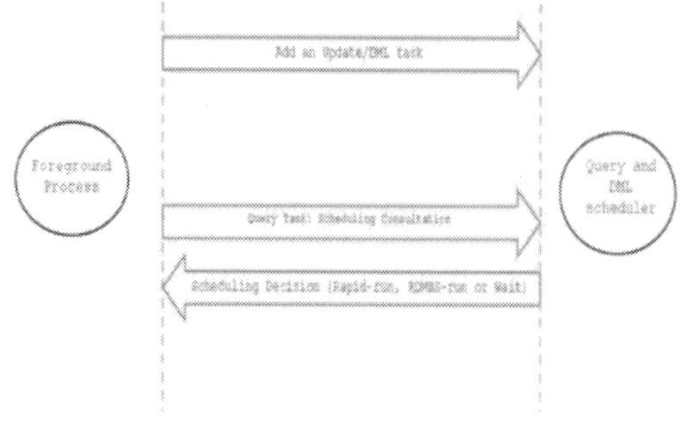

Figure 4. Communication Between Foreground And The Scheduler Process

private memory area. The query foreground processes communicate with the scheduler process to add tasks and receive scheduling decisions. This communication is depicted in Figure 4.

When a query is submitted for execution in the primary database, the query compiler determines which query fragments can be executed in the target database to boost performance. The foreground process then communicates to the scheduler each query fragment as a query-task, providing its metadata (i.e., cost, deadline, data objects, etc.).

Similarly, when a DML is submitted in the source database, updates for each data object are captured. At commit time, an update task is communicated to the scheduler process. Upon receiving a task, the scheduler updates the priority queues and tasks dependency metadata. When a DML task is due for execution, the scheduler dispatches the task shipping the updates to the secondary database. For query-tasks, on the other hand, the scheduler makes one of three decisions: (1) proceed to execute in secondary database, (2) fallback to execute on primary database, or (3) Wait. The Wait decision is basically wait for other higher priority queries, or to wait for update-task(s) this query depends on to be propagated to the secondary database first. In the following Section we provide the details of the scheduler for a single instance case.

IV. QUERIES AND DML SCHEDULER – DETAILS

In this section we detail the objectives and design for the scheduler.

A. Scheduler Objective

Our scheduler has two objectives: (1) maximize hit ratio, and (2) minimize query response time as perceived by the end-user. The *hit ratio* is the percentage of query tasks that execute within their deadlines vs. the total number of query tasks. That is the ratio of queries that meet the deadline. A task that falls back to the primary database is considered a miss. This scheduling objective also encapsulates maximizing the usage of the secondary database, which is installed to boost performance of complex analytical queries.

Existing approaches typically utilize some hybrid form of such objectives, such as MIX [2], Multiple Attribute Integration [4], and EDF & Random Hybrid [5]. All these hybrid models, however, require system parameters. An adaptive, parameter-free hybrid approach to minimize tardiness was proposed in [3]. We need a parameter-free adaptive hybrid method to maximize the hit -ratio. Shortest Remaining Processing Time (SRPT) scheduling policy is proven to provide minimal response time in case of soft-deadlines [6], i.e., when a task is allowed to run beyond its deadline. Our case however is similar to the hard-deadline one, with queries falling back to the primary.

To achieve the above two scheduling objectives, we use the invert of deadline times its secondary database cost ($p_i=1/(d_i \times c_{i,sec})$) for the task priority. Using the inverted deadline gives higher priority to more urgent tasks, to maximize hit ratio. Whereas using the inverted cost (similar to SRPT) gives higher priority to tasks that would minimize response time.

B. Scheduler Priority Queue

Each task that has no dependency, i.e., depends on no update-tasks, is inserted in the priority queue to represent a workflow. Upon task addition, (1) task dependency information is detected, and (2) if existing task priority changes (e.g., if the new task is a query then the deadline of update tasks it depends upon may get updated), then (a) the task is inserted in the list of tasks, and (b) the priority queue is updated.

The priority queue is updated when a new ready task is inserted, and when existing tasks' priority change, to reflect new priorities. At each scheduling point, the task on top of the priority queue is selected as the next task to be executed in secondary database. Note that for parallel tasks we dispatch a number of tasks that equals to the execution parallel degree.

Upon completion of a task, the workflow is updated: the ready task is deleted from list of tasks and from the priority queue. The dependency information is updated for the task(s) that depends on this completed task. If there are new ready task(s), then they are inserted into the priority queue.

Whenever the priority queue is updated, all the query-tasks in the priority queue below where the update took place are examined if they can still meet the deadline. If not, the task is scheduled to fallback, as it would take longer if it waits to get executed in the secondary database.

C. Cost Model

A precise estimation of query and DML costs is crucial for the success of our proposed scheduler, which makes cost-based decisions. Estimating a query cost is a very hard problem. However, similar to query optimizers, all that we need is a reliable cost model that enables us to compare costs of different tasks. That is, accuracy of the cost-model is relative in a sense. Therefore, we propose to use the compiler's estimated cost as the cost of a query task. In particular, the cost of a query fragment if executed in the secondary database is the query-task cost. Similarly, we use the primary database cost of this query fragment (fallback cost) to be the deadline of this query-task.

Estimating the fallback cost is not straightforward because we expose both the access path and the join order in the secondary system during query optimization in the primary. That is, there is no separate in-primary vs. in-secondary query optimization. As a result, we can retain an access path type - such as full table scan vs. index-based scan - as well as the join order that were estimated as best in the secondary system, while later on during optimization we decide to execute a larger fragment in the primary system. To provide accurate fallback cost the optimization phase had to be enhanced to remember at any point the best purely in-primary cost of each access path and join.

For update-tasks, factors that affect the cost include: (1) update granularity: cardinality of the delta relation, (2) network bandwidth/speed, (3) overhead to prepare the changes, and (4) overhead to apply the changes at the secondary database.

These cost factors are extremely hard to estimate and are workload and system-specific. Our proposed effective and accurate cost model is simply the moving-average load rate. Specifically, we maintain the load-rate as follows. While loading the table for first time to the secondary database, we observe the overall load rate *LR*, which measures how long it takes to load a single row of that table, on average. Then, we use *LR* times the number of updated rows as the cost for each DML task on that table. Once this change is uploaded, we measure the actual new load rate: *LR'*. *LR* is then updated to be the average of *LR* and *LR'* to have a new, more accurate load rate to estimate the cost of future DML tasks on this table. This way, if a table grows over time that its updates become more expensive, this will be captured by this cost model, and vice versa. In the next section we detail why it is possible for us to know the accurate number of rows for each DML task and why we do not need to rely on any typical secondary structure – like indexes – for this purpose.

V. IMPLEMENTED PROTOTYPE

We have implemented a prototype [18] of the proposed scheduler infrastructure and the above detailed scheduling policy in the Oracle general purpose database system as the primary database and the recent RAPID Data Processing Unit (DPU)-based accelerator system developed at Oracle Labs [19]
[20]. The RAPID accelerator is a main-memory system with a bandwidth-optimized architecture for big data computation. Relations in the primary are loaded into the DPUs at a given SCN, by reformatting the data in a hybrid-columnar format. In the primary database, changes post initial load are represented in memory resident transactional journals, just as typically maintained for in-memory optimized RDBMS relations [9]. As rows are logged into the journals, corresponding tasks are defined and messaged to the scheduler.

The scheduler is designed to run on both the primary and the secondary (the accelerator). The primary-side scheduler is the main scheduler that captures and maintains dependency and priority information, and decides when and what queries and DMLs to push to RAPID. It also communicates the dependency and priority information to the RAPID-side scheduler. During the initial load into the secondary system, data is scanned in parallel from the primary instance; whether the scan happens through the buffer cache, or from direct path from secondary storage, or directly from in-memory compression units using the IMCU Oracle format, we read the data at the level of the scan row source level; at this point data is vectorized, encodings can be applied, and distributed to the secondary system. In this process we know the exact number of rows we load into the Rapid nodes, and we maintain this information, together with encoding statistics, into a segment of each instance shared memory, which we call the *Rapid global state*. For each table loaded into the secondary system we enable in-memory journal tracking – by using the already developed Oracle mechanism to keep in the shared memory of each Oracle instance per relation journals of changed rows at their corresponding SCNs. Note that this journaling activity happens even if we do not require the relation to be maintained in IMCU formats – that is, for the purpose of the prototyped in-memory journaling feature has been decoupled from in-memory data encoding. As the journals are scanned and DML tasks are generated, we keep track of the exact number of rows that have been journaled at each SCN, per relation. This information is available therefore to the scheduler, and it is also used to update the number of rows loaded into the secondary and compression statistics in the Rapid global state. Once the global state statistics are updated and changes are acknowledged applied by the Rapid nodes, the in-memory journals can be truncated in case of memory pressure. For the case of direct insert/load, we make an exception and do not journal the changes; instead, entire data blocks for the appended data are scanned and changes are applied in Rapid before the transaction ends in the primary; nevertheless, in this case we also know the exact number of rows sent to Rapid and we can update the statistics in the global state. On a general note, there is no concept of pieced row in Rapid, as data is maintained in hybrid columnar format. If a pieced row is encountered during initial load or during direct path insert, the next piece is scanned recursively until the entire row is constructed, and then each column within the row is added to the respective column vector, before the vector is compressed. When scanning journaled rows, if a row is pieced we similarly traverse the links in the journal for retrieving all the pieces. The typical case when pieced rows are recurrent is when the shape of the relation is such that majority of rows are pieced (for instance, when the number of columns exceeds a certain limit); in such cases, the initial load as well as DML tasks significantly involve pieced rows. As the per-row initial cost for a relation is computed during initial load, for such typical cases this cost reflects the overhead of handling multiple pieces before forming the full row image and this overhead applies to DML tasks as well.

The RAPID-side scheduler is a distributed independent version of the scheduler that acts as an actuator: independently on each DPU, a scheduler instance makes sure that tasks are run in the right order communicated by the primary-side scheduler. By running independently, we avoid any overhead of coordination or hand-shaking protocols.

The primary-side scheduler was implemented as a background process. We used basic data structures to implement the scheduler metadata. In particular, the list of tasks and priority queue were implemented as linked lists. We relied on existing database system layer for inter-process communication. The goal of this prototype was to prove functionality and the relative benefits of the scheduler module. Our implementation was for single-instance and no parallelism, for the primary-side scheduler. In this prototype, we implemented the cost model and scheduling policy explained above. However, we implemented the hooks to enable the addition of different scheduling policies. In particular, the scheduling policy is configured as an Oracle startup parameter.

D. *Preliminary Results*

Using the 22 standard TPC-H [28] queries and the TPC-H refresh streams, we were able to demonstrate that the scheduler sometimes decides for certain query-tasks to fallback to primary database, when it is pending on many update tasks that cost more than the query deadline. Surprisingly this was the case for very small or simple queries, in addition to the intuitive case where query is pending on large updates. The reason is that for simple queries, the cost is typically very small, and hence the deadline is very close. Thus, for any reasonably large update, the query would fall back to the primary system.

We also measured the scheduler overhead on X4 machines, and with this basic implementation and experiments on small scale TPC-H (up to F=64), we found that the total query overhead ranges between 50 and 100 micro-seconds. Most of this overhead is due to inter-process communication, whereas the overhead of maintaining the scheduler metadata (i.e., the priority queue and the list of tasks) was in the order of few micro-seconds. Further, the overhead of maintaining the list of task as the priority queue grows was almost flat, i.e., grows very slowly as the priority queue grows. This shows that a scheduler module is feasible, beneficial, and has very minimal overhead that can be further optimized.

The expectation is that the scheduler overhead and load do not correlate to the workload size, since an update-task or a query-task is still a single task weather it processes gigabyte or petabytes of data.

VI. CONCLUSIONS

In this paper, we proposed a novel infrastructure for prioritizing and scheduling queries and updates between a primary and secondary database. We detailed the system model and architecture for single instance primary database case. We gave details of our implemented prototype in which we adopt a scheduling policy that maximizes hit ratio and minimizes response time. The runtime overhead incurred due to the scheduler activity was measured using TPC- H queries, with no code optimizations, and results show that the scheduler module has negligible overhead. This demonstrates that the scheduler is feasible, beneficial and effective.

ACKNOWLEDGEMENTS

We would like to acknowledge Kantikiran Pasupuleti, Seema Sundara, Adrian Schuepbach, and Benjamin Schlegel for insightful discussions and feedback.

1 Work was done while authors were member of Oracle Labs, Oracle, USA

REFERENCES

1. Oracle Patent Disclosure: A. Di Blas, B. Schlegel, S. Idicula, S. Petride and K. Pasupuleti, N. Agarwal Method for Consistent Concurrent Execution of Multiple Queries in Presence of Base Table Updates, Disclosed Jan 2015.
2. G. Buttazzo, M. Spuri, and F. Sensini. Value vs. deadline scheduling in overload conditions. In Proc. of RTSS '95, pp. 90-99, 1995.
3. S. Guirguis, M. A. Sharaf, P. K. Chrysanthis, A. Labrinidis, and K. Pruhs. Adaptive scheduling of web transactions. In ICDE, pp. 357–368, 2009.
4. W. Cao and D. Aksoy. Beat the clock: a multiple attribute approach for scheduling data broadcast. In MobiDE '05, pp. 89–96, 2005.
5. D.-Z. He, F.-Y. Wang, W. Li and X.-W. Zhang. Hybrid earliest deadline first preemption threshold scheduling for real-time systems. In *ICMLC*, pp. 433-438, 2004.
6. B. Schroeder and M. Harchol-Balter. Web servers under overload: How scheduling can help. ACM Trans. Inter. Tech., 6(1), pp. 20–52, 2006.
7. T. Lahiri, S. Chavan, M. Colgan, D. Das, M. Gleeson, S. Hase et. Al., Oracle Database In-Memory: A dual format in-memory database, ICDE 2015: 1253-1258
8. G. Marchionini, Exploratory search: from finding to understanding. Commun. ACM 49(4), pp. 41-46, 2006.
9. J. Erickson, "In-Memory Acceleration for the Real-Time Enterprise",

http://www.oracle.com/us/corporate/features/database-in-memory-option/index.html [retrieved: 04, 2018].
10. W. Vogels. "Eventually Consistent", CACM, pp. 40-44, 2009.
11. A Labrinidis and N Roussopoulos, "Balancing performance and data freshness in web database servers", VLDB, pp. 393-404, 2003.
12. Response Time references(s)
13. Oracle® Flashback Technologies, http://www.oracle.com/technetwork/database/features/availability/flashback-overview-082751.html [retrieved: 04, 2018].
14. Oracle® TimesTen In-Memory Database and TimesTen Application-Tier Database Cache, http://www.oracle.com/technetwork/database/database-technologies/timesten/overview/index.html [retrieved: 04, 2018].
15. Oracle® TimesTen Application-Tier Database Cache User's Guide: http://st-doc.us.oracle.com/12/12102/TTCAC/define.htm#TTCAC211 [retrieved: 04, 2018].
16. V. Sikka, F. Farber, W. Lehner, S. K. Cha, T. Peh and C. Bornhovd, "Efficient transaction processing in SAP HANA database: the end of a column store myth", SIGMOD, pp. 731-742, 2012.
17. H. Ma, W. Qian, F. Xia, J. Wei, C. Yu and A. Zhou, On benchmarking online social media analytical queries. In First International Workshop on Graph Data Management Experiences and Systems (GRADES), ACM, Article 10 , pp. 1-7, 2013.
18. S. Guirguis and S. Petride, Query and Change-Propagation Scheduling: A Real-Time Scheduling Model for Heterogeneous Database Systems, Patent Application, 2017.
19. V. Govindaraju, S. Idicula, S. Agrawal, V. Vardarajan, A. Raghavan, J. Wen et. al,, Big Data Processing: Scalability with Extreme Single-Node Performance, IEEE Big Data Congress, pp. 129-136, 2017.
20. S. R Agrawal, S. Idicula, A. Raghavan, E. Vlachos, V. Govindaraju, V. Varadarajan, et. al., A many-core architecture for in-memory data processing, IEEE/ACM MICRO, pp. 245-258, 2017.
21. V. Raman, G. Attaluri, R. Barber, N. Chainani, D. Kalmuk, V. KulandaiSamy, et. al., DB2 with BLU Acceleration: So Much More than Just a Column Store, VLDB Volume 6 Issue 11, pp. 1080-1091, 2014.
22. D. J. Abadi, P. A. Boncz and S. Harizopoulos. 2009. Column-oriented Database Systems. Proc. VLDB Endow. 2, 2 (Aug. 2009), pp. 1664–1665. https://doi.org/10.14778/1687553.1687625.
23. K. Lim, D. Meisner, A. G. Saidi, P. Ranganathan and T. F. Wenisch. 2013. Thin Servers with Smart Pipes: Designing SoC Accelerators for Memcached. In Proceedings of the 40th Annual International Symposium on Computer Architecture (ISCA '13). ACM, New York, NY, USA, pp. 36–47. https://doi.org/10.1145/2485922.2485926 [retrieved: 04, 2018].
24. C. Root and T. Mostak. 2016. MapD: a GPU-powered big data analytics and visualization platform. In ACM SIGGRAPH 2016 Talks (SIGGRAPH '16). ACM, New York, NY, USA, Article 73, pp. 1-2, DOI: https://doi.org/10.1145/2897839.2927468 [retrieved: 04, 2018].
25. C. Olston, A. Manjhi, C. Garrod, A. Ailamaki, B. M. Maggs and T. C. Mowry, A scalability service for dynamic web applications. CIDR, 2005.
26. Y. Huang, R. Sloan and O. Wolfson. Divergence Caching in Client Server Architectures. In Proc. 3rd International Conference on Parallel and Distributed Information Systems, 1994.
27. T. Malik, X. Wang, P. Little, A. Chaudhary and A. Thakar, A Dynamic Data Middleware Cache for Rapidly-growing Scientific Repositories, arXiv.org, arXiv:1009.3665
28. TPC-H benchmark, www.tpc.org/tpch [retrieved: 04, 2018

A Business Intelligence Solution for Supporting Making Decision in Fulfillment Process

Thi Kim Hien Le, Thuong Pham Thi, Sheng-Tun Li
Department of Industrial and Information Management
National Cheng Kung University
Tainan, Taiwan
Email: hienltk.90@gmail.com,
hocduong_2003@yahoo.com.hk
stli@mail.ncku.edu.tw

Abstract — **There are many researches about applying Business Intelligence (BI) in supporting decision in many fields but there are very few researches about how to utilize this technology to assist the decision making in business processes. To address this gap, this study aims to apply On-Line analytical processing (OLAP), which is a significant component of BI that enables users to easily and selectively extract and view data from different points of view to back the manager make better decisions in fulfillment process. This study investigates the sales management theory, as well as balanced scorecard and OLAP technology to propose the decisions and the sample reports in the process which could be supported by OLAP including: the sales volume, the main product of the company, the salary and the bonus for sales staff, the credit limit and the price policy for customers.**

Keywords-business intelligence; OLAP; fulfillment process; support decision-making; balanced scorecard .

I. Introduction

On-Line analytical processing (OLAP) involved in a decision support system provides administrators a multidimensional view, on many aspects of a problem, with large amounts of data, thereby making timely and accurate decisions, raising high competitive advantage for businesses [1].

In 2017, Bouakkaz et al. [3] have carried out a research about performing textual data, which is a key tool to demonstrate textual data analysis in OLAP for decision support systems. This investigation indicated that provided techniques and tools for both databases and data warehouses just focus mainly on numerical data. Therefore, they have provided a new classification framework to support making decision based on text mining in OLAP. Moreover, Hamoud et al. [6] applied OLAP at Iraqui Hospital to a registry data warehouse to facilitate rapid decision-making on clinical pathology. This application allowed physicians to have a multi-dimensional view of the patient's disease with large amounts of information synthesized in a short time, enabling physicians to make quick decisions about the patient condition and take timely treatment. In addition, a library management system based on data warehouses and OLAP has been developed by Xu et al. [12]. In their research, the authors proposed a data warehouse model with the management of metadata consistent with the growing amount of data in the library, the traditional way of archiving is no longer appropriate. Besides that, the paper also outlines the application of OLAP techniques to support decision-making in library management, including decisions about the selection and arrangement of books and some other critical decisions with multidimensional view supported by OLAP technology [12]. Furthermore, a study by Yin et al. [13] developed a comprehensive decision support system in the field of broadcasting and television. This support system is based on the construction of a data warehouse that aggregates data from a variety of sources, including radio and television, and application of OLAP data processing techniques and mining techniques. These techniques support the manager figure out the laws as well as provide multi-level view on multiple levels to assist media managers make decisions about the line, coverage areas and other significant decisions.

The preceding studies demonstrate the importance of applying OLAP technology to supporting decision making for managers. This paper will implement OLAP applications in decision support in the field of business, namely, the application of OLAP techniques to assisting making decision in fulfillment process.

The remainder of the paper is organized as follows. In Section 2 we discuss some fundamental theories about OLAP technology in supporting making decision as well as the benefit of OLAP in sales management and through that we propose the research model. In Section 3, we describe the OLAP report assisted for making decision in fulfillment process. Finally, Section 4 includes the findings and conclusions highlighting theoretical and practical implications, as well as points out the limitation and propose the future work.

II. Literature Review

In the literature review, we will figure out how OLAP technology could be applied to supporting decision making in sales management.

A. OLAP and supporting making decision

As presented in Figure 1, OLAP is a fundamental component of a decision support system. It provides the ability to create reports in a multidimensional, flexible, intuitive way. Furthermore, it supports to create the reports from detail to synthesis, pivot, slice, chart. Therefore, OLAP assists the decision-making process to be more efficient and effective. Besides, due to fast and timely data processing,

OLAP also supports managers to master the nature of the problem and through that makes better decisions.

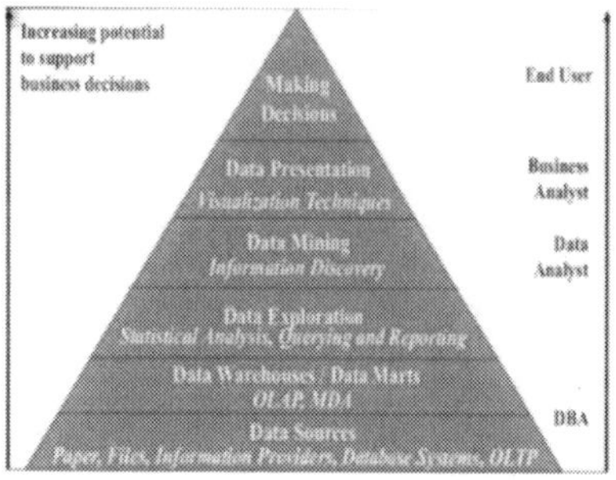

Figure 1. Supporting decision making model [5]

Business analysts must work closely with spreadsheets to capture and analyze the company's financial status. However, the creation and management of spreadsheets will be hampered by too many reports need to be created, as well as data scattered in many places. OLAP technology enables analysts to extend the spreadsheet analysis model to work with data in the data warehouse - with characteristic of greater data availability, single location focus, analysis, business elements (time, geography, and so on), capable of creating multi-dimensional reports.

B. The benefits of OLAP to sales management

OLAP provides organizations with the ability to access, display and analyze sales data in a flexible way. First, OLAP delivers data to the user through a natural intuitive data model. Users could see and understand information in a data warehouse more efficiently and thus allow organizations to more clearly appreciate the value of their data. In addition, OLAP also accelerates the transfer of information to the user, displaying multidimensional structures. The combination of easy access and fast execution allows users to view and analyze their data faster and more efficiently than using relational database systems.

Current reports have some limitations, such as "tend to shrink in their functional departments". In general, financial reports, governance, internal controls in organizations are usually prepared according to the scope of functions. For instance, business unit data is compiled from departmental and final reports will be collected as part of the overall organization picture. Another limitation of traditional reporting is that "reports do not fit into many levels of the organization." This limitation is caused by the synthesis of company-wide reporting, the aggregate staff will provide information at an increasingly high level until it becomes almost unrecognizable and becomes useless in the decision-making of most managers as well as employees [10].

With OLAP technology decision support systems, these restrictions will be eliminated. OLAP reports use data extracted from a data warehouse in which data is collected from all departments. Therefore, those reports will not be confined to functional departments. On the other hand, OLAP report with the decision-making for managers at all levels is not limited by the fact that information is too general and does not make much sense in supporting decision-making for senior leaders.

C. Fulfillment Process

The sales process goes through many different steps across many departments. At the first stage, the sales department will receive the request for quotation and order from a customer. Based on that, the credit department will examine and approve the credit limitation for this customer. Next, the warehouse department will check inventory and post goods issue and then the product will be delivered to the customer from delivery department. After the goods are received, the customer pays based on orders and delivery vouchers. Finally, the accounting department records payments from the customer [2].

Figure 2 shows the change in the sales process under the influence of internet and information systems. At each step of the sales process, we use information technology to improve performance. First, at the request for quotation step, we utilize the Customer Relationship Management (CRM) systems to manage and promote customer relationship. OLAP can be supported in CRM to assist in decision making on defining who are potential customers as well as sales volume and appropriate sales prices for each customer. Second, we use OLAP to discover the customer's financial ability to support automated credit approval at the credit review step. Finally, at the collection step, we could use OLAP to predict customer debt.

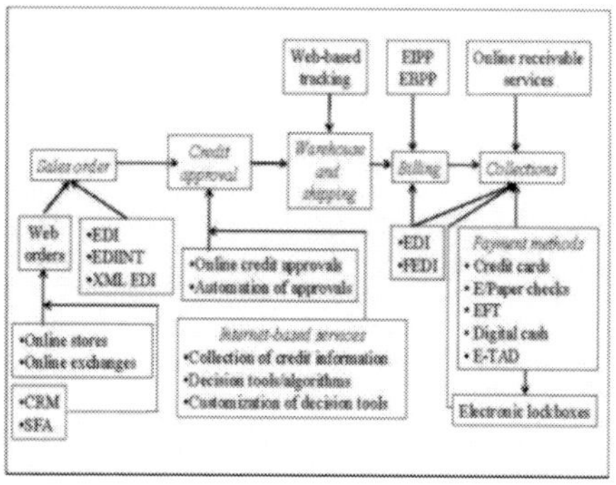

Figure 2. Fulfillment process under the influence of the Internet and information systems [2]

D. Research Methodology

We propose an appropriate research model for this study in Figure 3.

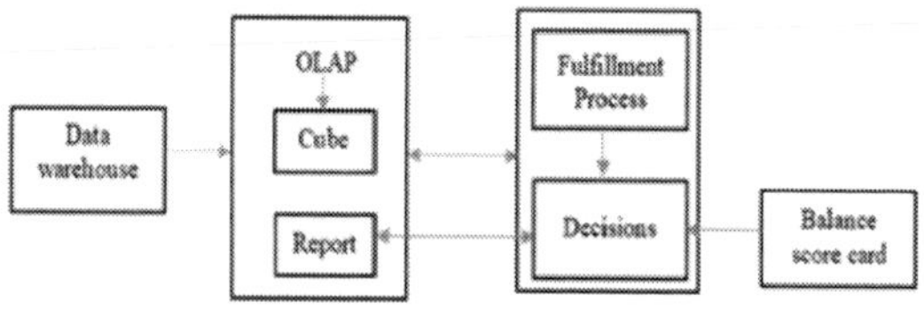

Figure 3. Research Model

First, we examine the fulfillment process and come up with a conclusion for which decisions in this process can be supported by OLAP technology. To do this, we need to investigate the steps of this process and the balanced scorecard theory. Those help to shape the decisions in fulfillment process which can be assisted by OLAP report as well as form the OLAP report context.

Second, we build the OLAP cubes based on data that was already obtained in sales data warehouse. After discovering the decisions during the fulfillment process, we build up two OLAP cubes that allows fast data analysis for two significant objectives. The first objective is the human resource objective involving all objectives that focuses on maximizing employee productivity. The second one is the financial objective covering all objectives that aim to maximize the company's profit.

Third, this study figures out the reports which are appropriate at each step in the fulfillment process. We reveal four reports that will help the manager make better decisions compared to when they do not have those reports. These are pricing policy decision, sales volume decision, company's key products decision, sale-person's salaries and compensation decision and the credit limitation decision report.

III. RESULTS

We have built up the OLAP cube with the star schema demonstrated in Figure 4. This model provides a clear view for technical aspect of an OLAP cube.

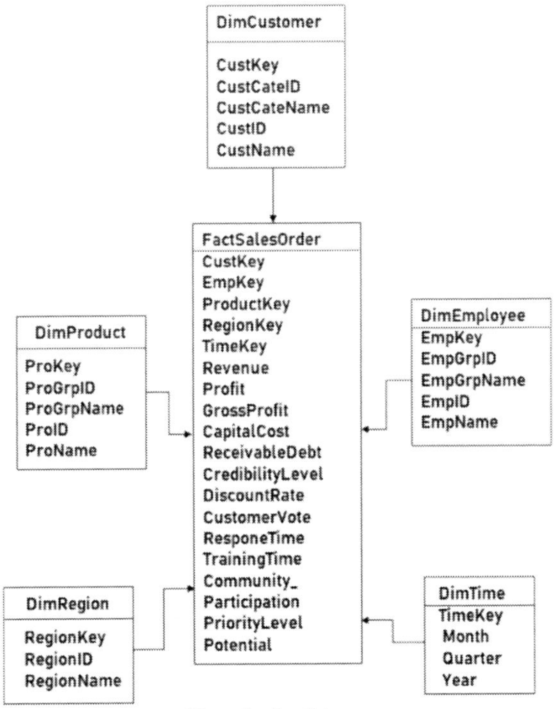

Figure 4. Star Schema

The model involves one fact table named "FactSalesOrder" linked to associated dimension tables – "DimCustomer", "DimProduct", "DimEmployee", "DimTime", "DimRegion" via primary or foreign key. Based on this cube, we propose the sample report for some sales management decisions below.

A. *Pricing policy decision*

In the sales process, at the price quotation step, enterprises need to provide information about the price and quantity of products for customers. The OLAP report will assist the sales manager in setting up appropriate pricing policies for each sales area, considering incentives for customers in the priority area of the market [8].

B. *Sales volume decision*

At the price quotation step, the company not only needs to inform the price of each product to the customer, the sales department also has to notify the quantity of each product to them. The OLAP report demonstrates sales figures and various considerable metrics for each market, thereby enabling sales managers determine the sales volume for each customer (group of customers) or each area. The report supports in allocating appropriate sales targets due to market situation and company's objectives [9].

Period	Region	Customer's Class	Customer's Name	Revenue	Profit	Gross Profit	Capital Cost	Receivable Dept	Credibility Level
2017	North	VIP							
		Loyal							
		Current							
	North Total								
	Center	VIP							
		Loyal							
		Current							
	Center Total								
	South	VIP							
		Loyal							
		Current							
	South Total								
Grand Total									

Figure 5. The OLAP report sample supports decision pricing and sales quantity

This report, which is illustrated in Figure 5, carries out an exploration of decision pricing and sales quantity based on some significant metrics, such as revenue, profit, gross profit, capital cost, receivable debt, and credibility level.

C. *Company's key products decision*

Determining the key products of the company will assist to promote the product to the right audience. Moreover, the identification of the key product will affect the production plan of the company. In the sales process, key product decisions will assist the warehouse in increasing the number of these items in stock [9]. In order to make the right decision at this step, decision makers could be supported with an OLAP report with some recommended metrics including financial and non-financial metrics, such as: revenue, profit, gross profit, market share, discount rate, customer vote.

Period	Product Category	Region	Revenue	Profit	Gross Profit	Market Share	Discount Rate	Customer Vote
2017	Group A	North						
		Center						
		South						
	Group A Total							
	Group B	North						
		Center						
		South						
	Group B Total							
	Group C	North						
		Center						
		South						
	South Total							
Grand Total								

Figure 6. OLAP report sample supports decision-making key products

Figure 6 gives a sample report with some suggestion metrics. Based on that, users could easily handle OLAP report manipulation by drill-down the dimensions to capture the detail results for any desired level.

D. *Salespersons's salaries and compensation decision*

In the fulfillment process, besides the technological infrastructure, the human factor plays a primary role, which is the decisive factor for success in implementing the process. In fact, if human resources are facilitated to promote self-efficacy and engagement with the company, then the sales force will generate a greater efficiency and stimulate the productivity for the whole process. Therefore, payroll decisions play a significant role in creating motivation for employees and also the basis for creating success for the whole process [8].

Period	Employee	Customer's Class	Revenue	Profit	Gross Profit	Respone Time	Training Time	Community Participation
2017	Group A	VIP						
		Loyal						
		Current						
	Group A Total							
	Group B	VIP						
		Loyal						
		Current						
	Group B Total							
	Group C	VIP						
		Loyal						
		Current						
	Group C Total							
Grand Total								

Figure 7. The OLAP report sample supports decision making for staff compensation

Besides the financial metrics like revenue or profit, this study proposes some other metrics, which played a critical role to evaluate the staff performance, presented in Figure 7. Some of these metrics are: respone time – the average time that a sales staff respone to a customer's order, training time – total time participated in training courses in a year, community participation – number of times this staff spent on community activities in one year.

E. *The credit limitation decision*

In the process of granting credit to customers, businesses have to deal with credit risks. As a result, the customer fails to perform or fails to fulfill his financial obligations when due. Not only that, the credit also affects the sales volume, the relationship between the customer and the company. These risks can be limited when managers are supported by flexible, historical sources of information from OLAP reports. Determining the credit limitation will assist in the credit approval step in the fulfillment process.

Period	Region	Customer's Class	Customer's Name	Revenue	Profit	Priority Level	Potential	Receivable Dept	Credibility Level
2017	North	VIP							
		Loyal							
		Current							
	North Total								
	Center	VIP							
		Loyal							
		Current							
	Center Total								
	South	VIP							
		Loyal							
		Current							
	South Total								
Grand Total									

Figure 8. The OLAP report sample supports decision making credit limitation

Each customer may have different credit limitation depending on some metrics presented in Figure 8; some of these metrics are customer's class, priority. This report provides the figure for each region and each customer's class. It is extremely useful reference channel for the sales manager to support their decision making.

IV. CONCLUSION

After carrying out the research, we came up with the conclusion about theoretical and managerial implications as well as limitation and future works.

A. *Theoretical and managerial implications*

This study adds a novel method to existing literature related to applying business intelligence to manage business process. It explores OLAP technology and the role of OLAP in decision support systems in enterprises. In addition, we also explore fulfillment process and sales management decisions which could be supported by OLAP report. This finding also highlights the contribution of non-financial measures and the importance of non-financial measures in the current economic climate.

In the managerial implication aspect, this study provides the OLAP model and sales decision support reports at the most general level - with two important decisions toward human resource goals and profitability goals (through analysis business performance) including: the sales volume, the main product of the company, the salary and the bonus for sales staff, the credit limit and the price policy for customers. According to these results, companies could build up a business intelligence system with OLAP technology to manage effectively their fulfillment process. These will support managers more convenient in building their self-report.

B. *Limitation and Futurer work*

This study discusses the application of OLAP in decision support for credits, price policy, sales volumes, key products, as well as employee compensation decisions in the fulfillment process. Besides its contributions, this study just focused on fulfillment process and analyzed the decisions in this process but there are many processes in a company. Furthermore, the database just limited on internal sources skewed on financial scales may lead to inaccuracy precision.

With the desire to contribute more to OLAP application in decision support, the author proposes to build more channels to display reports, such as website or share point. In addition, other business processes could be examined to address the question: How to apply business intelligence to support the decisions making in those processes? At the same time, the study expects to apply OLAP text-mining with the focus on text data to shape a better metric to make more accurate decisions.

REFERENCES

[1] C. Adamson, "Mastering data warehouse aggregates: solutions for star schema performance", John Wiley & Sons, 2006.

[2] A. Deshmukh, "Digital Accounting: The effects of the Internet and ERP in Accouting", 2006.

[3] M. Bouakkaz, Y. Ouinten, S. Loudcher, and Y. Strekalova , "Textual aggregation approaches in OLAP context: A survey," International Journal of Information Management, pp. 684-692, 2017.

[4] C. Adamson, "Mastering Data Warehouse Aggregates: Solution for Star Schema Performance," Wiley Publishing, 2006.

[5] TBT. Dong, "Applied OLAP technology to the deployment of information systems EIS," Workshop, A selected number of issues of information technology, pp. 248-261, 2000.

[6] A. C. Hamoud, and T. A. Obaid, "Using OLAP with Diseases Registry Warehouse for Clinical Decision Support," 2014.

[7] W. H. Inmon, "Building the data warehouse," John wiley & sons, 2005.

[8] M. W. Johnston, and Marshall, G. W., "Sales Force Management: Leadership, Innovation, Technology", Routledge, 2013.

[9] P. Kotler, and G. Armstrong, "Principles of Marketing," 15th Global Edition, Pearson, 2013.

[10] P. R Niven, "Balanced scorecard step-by-step: maximizing performance and maintaining results," John Wiley & Sons, 2002.

[11] R. Kimball and M. Ross, "The data warehouse toolkit Second edition," Willey Publishing, 2002.

[12] M. L. Xu, and X. Y. Li "Construction of the Library Management System Based on Data Warehouse and OLAP." Applied Mechanics and Materials 380, pp. 4796-4799, 2013.

[13] F. Yin, J. Chai and J. Lin., "Synthetic Decision Support of Broadcasting and Television System" In Proceedings of The Eighth International Conference on Bio-Inspired Computing: Theories and Applications (BIC-TA), Jan.2013, pp. 759-766, Springer Berlin Heidelberg.

A Distributed Collaborative Filtering Algorithm Using Multiple Data Sources

Mohamed Reda Bouadjenek[†♭], Esther Pacitti[†], Maximilien Servajean[†], Florent Masseglia[†], Amr El Abbadi[‡]
[†]INRIA & LIRMM University of Montpellier France,
[♭]The University of Toronto, Department of Mechanical and Industrial Engineering
Email: mrb@mie.utoronto.ca, {esther.pacitti, maximilien.servajean}@lirmm.fr, florent.masseglia@inria.fr
[‡]University of California, Santa Barbara, CA, USA, Email: amr@cs.ucsb.edu

***Abstract*—Collaborative Filtering (CF) is one of the most commonly used recommendation methods. CF consists in predicting whether, or how much, a user will like (or dislike) an item by leveraging the knowledge of the user's preferences as well as that of other users. In practice, users interact and express their opinion on only a small subset of items, which makes the corresponding user-item rating matrix very sparse. Such data sparsity yields two main problems for recommender systems: (1) the lack of data to effectively model users' preferences, and (2) the lack of data to effectively model item characteristics. However, there are often many other data sources that are available to a recommender system provider, which can describe user interests and item characteristics (e.g., users' social network, tags associated to items, etc.). These valuable data sources may supply useful information to enhance a recommendation system in modeling users' preferences and item characteristics more accurately and thus, hopefully, to make recommenders more precise. For various reasons, these data sources may be managed by clusters of different data centers, thus requiring the development of distributed solutions. In this paper, we propose a new distributed collaborative filtering algorithm, which exploits and combines multiple and diverse data sources to improve recommendation quality. Our experimental evaluation using real datasets shows the effectiveness of our algorithm compared to state-of-the-art recommendation algorithms.**

Keywords–Recommender Systems; Collaborative Filtering; Social Recommendation; Matrix Factorization.

I. Introduction

Nowadays, Internet floods users with useless information. Hence, recommender systems are useful to supply them with content that may be of interest. Recommender systems have become a popular research topic over the past 20 years, to make them more accurate and effective along many dimensions (social dimension [1][2][3], geographical dimension [4][5], diversification aspect [6][7][8], etc.).

Collaborative Filtering (CF) [9] is one of the most commonly used recommendation methods. CF consists in predicting whether, or how much, a user will like (or dislike) an item by leveraging the knowledge of the user preferences, as well as that of other users. In practice, users interact and express their opinions on only a small subset of items, which makes the corresponding user-item rating matrix very sparse. Consequently, in a recommender system, this data sparsity induces two main problems: (1) the lack of data to effectively model user preferences (new users suffer from the cold-start problem [10]), and (2) the lack of data to effectively model items characteristics (new items suffer from the cold-start problem since no user has yet rated them).

On the other hand, beside this sparse user-item rating matrix, there are often many other data sources that are available to a recommender system, which can provide useful information that describe user interests and item characteristics. Examples of such diverse data sources are numerous: a user social network, a user's topics of interest, tags associated to items, etc. These valuable data sources may supply useful information to enhance a recommendation system in modeling user preferences and item characteristics more accurately and thus, hopefully, to make more precise recommendations. Previous research work has demonstrated the effectiveness of using external data sources for recommender systems [1][2][3]. However, most of the proposed solutions focus on the use of only one kind of data provided by an online service (e.g., social network in [1] or geolocation information in [4][5]). Extending these solutions into a unified framework that considers multiple and diverse data sources is itself a challenging research problem.

Furthermore, these diverse data sources are typically managed by clusters at different data centers, thus requiring the development of new distributed recommendation algorithms to effectively handle this constantly growing data. In order to make better use of these different data sources, we propose a new distributed collaborative filtering algorithm, which exploits and combines multiple and diverse data sources to improve recommendation quality. To the best of our knowledge, this is the first attempt to propose such a distributed recommendation algorithm. In summary, the contributions of this paper are:

1) A new recommendation algorithm, based on matrix factorization, which leverages multiple and diverse data sources. This allows better modeling user preferences and item characteristics.
2) A distributed version of this algorithm that mainly computes factorizations of matrices by exchanging intermediate latent feature matrices in a coordinated manner.
3) A thorough comparative analysis with state-of-the-art recommendation algorithms on different datasets.

This paper is organized as follows: Section II provides two use cases; Section III presents the main concepts used in this paper; Section IV describes our multi-source recommendation model; Section V gives our distributed multi-source recommendation algorithm; Section VI describes our experimental evaluation; Section VII discusses the related work; Finally, Section VIII concludes and provides future directions.

II. USE CASES

Let us illustrate our motivation with two use cases, one with internal data sources, one with external data sources.

A. Diverse internal data sources

Consider John, a user who has rated a few movies he saw on a movie recommender system. In that same recommendation system, John also expressed his topics of interest regarding movie genres he likes. He also maintains a list of friends, which he trusts and follows to get insight on interesting movies. Finally, John has annotated several movies he saw, with tags to describe their contents.

In this example, the same recommender system holds many valuable data sources (topics of interest, friends list, and annotations), which may be used to accurately model John's preferences and movies' characteristics, and thus, hopefully to make more precise recommendations. In this first scenario, we suppose that these diverse data sources are hosted over different clusters of the same data center of the recommender system. It is obvious that a centralized recommendation algorithm induces a massive data transfer, which will cause a bottleneck problem in the data center. This clearly shows the importance of developing a distributed recommendation solution.

B. Diverse external data sources

Let us now consider that John is a regular user of a movie recommender system and of many other online services. John uses Google as a search engine, Facebook to communicate and exchange with his friends, and maybe other online services such as Epinions social network, IMDb, which is an online database of information related to films, Movilens, etc, as illustrated in Figure 1.

In this second use case, we believe that by exploiting and combining all these valuable data sources provided by different online services, we could make the recommender system more precise. The data sources are located and distributed over the clusters of different data centers, which are geographically distributed. In this second use case, we assume that the recommendation system can identify and link entities that refer to the same users and items across the different data sources. We envision that the connection of these online services may be greatly helped by initiatives like OpenID (http://openid.net/), which promotes a unified user identity across different services. In addition, we assume that the online services are willing to help the recommender system through contracts that can be established.

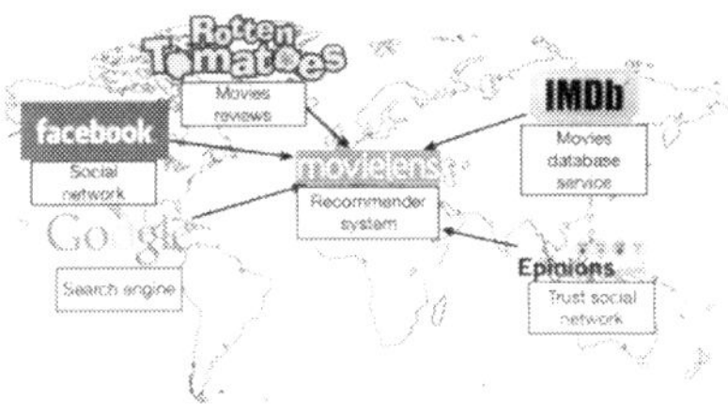

Figure 1. Use case: Movielens.

TABLE I. SAMPLE OF ATTRIBUTES.

Attribute 1	Attribute 2	Example of correlation
User	User	Similarity between the two users
User	Topic	Interest of the user in the topic
Item	Topic	Topic of the items
Item	Item	Similarity between two items

III. DEFINITIONS AND BACKGROUND

In this section, we introduce the data model we use, and a CF algorithm based on matrix factorization. Then, we describe the recommendation problem we study.

A. Data Model

We use matrices to represent all the data manipulated in our recommendation algorithm. Matrices are very useful mathematical structures to represent numbers, and several techniques from matrix theory and linear algebra can be used to analyze them in various contexts. Hence, we assume that any data source can be represented using a matrix, whose value in the i, j position is a correlation that may exist between the ith and j^{th} elements. We distinguish mainly three different kinds of data matrices:

Users' preferences history: In a recommender system, there are two classes of entities, which are referred as users and items. Users have preferences for certain items, and these preferences are extracted from the data. The data itself is represented as a matrix R, giving for each user-item pair, a value that represents the degree of preference of that user for that item.

Users' attributes: A data source may supply information on users using two classes of entities, which are referred to users and attributes. An attribute may refer to any abstract entity that has a relation with users. We also use matrices to represent such data, where for each user-attribute pair, a value represents their correlation (e.g., term frequency-inverse document frequency (tf-idf) [11]). The way this correlation is computed is out of the scope of this paper.

Items' attributes: Similarly, a data source may embed information that describes items using two classes of entities, namely items and attributes. Here, an attribute refers to any abstract entity that has a relation with items. Matrices are used to represent these data, where for each attribute-item pair, a value is associated to represent their correlation (e.g., tf-idf). The way this correlation is computed is also beyond the scope of this paper.

Table I gives examples of attributes that may describe both users and items, as well as the meaning of the correlations. It is interesting to notice that these three kinds of matrices are sparse matrices, meaning that most entries are missing. A missing value implies that we have no explicit information regarding the corresponding entry.

B. Matrix Factorization (MF) Models

Matrix factorization aims at decomposing a user-item rating matrix R of dimension $I \times J$ containing observed ratings $r_{i,j}$ into a product $R \approx U^T V$ of latent feature matrices U and V of rank K. In this initial MF setting, we designate U_i and V_j as the ith and j^{th} columns of U and V such that $U_i^T V_j$ acts as a measure of similarity between user i and item j in their respective k-dimensional latent spaces U_i and V_j.

However, there remains the question of how to learn U and V given that R may be incomplete (i.e., it contains missing entries). One answer is to define a reconstruction objective error function over the observed entries, that are to be minimized as a function of U and V, and then use gradient descent to optimize it; formally, we can optimize the following MF objective [12]: $\frac{1}{2}\sum_{i=1}^{I}\sum_{j=1}^{J} I_{ij}^R (r_{ij} - U_i^T V_j)^2$, where I_{ij} is the indicator function that is equal to 1 if user u_i rated item v_j and equal to 0 otherwise. Also, in order to avoid overfitting, two regularization terms are added to the previous equation (i.e., $\frac{1}{2}\|U\|_F^2$ and $\frac{1}{2}\|V\|_F^2$).

C. Problem Definition

The problem we address in this paper is different from that in traditional recommender systems, which consider only the user-item rating matrix R. In this paper, we incorporate information coming from multiple and diverse data matrices to improve recommendation quality. We define the problem we study in this paper as follows. Given:

- a user-item rating matrix R;
- N data matrices that describe the user preferences $\{S^{U^1}, \ldots, S^{U^n}\}$ distributed over different clusters;
- M data matrices that describe the items' characteristics $\{S^{V^1}, \ldots, S^{V^m}\}$ distributed over different clusters;

How to effectively and efficiently predict the missing values of the user-item matrix R by exploiting and combining these different data matrices?

IV. Recommendation Model

In this section, we first give an overview of our recommendation model using an example. Then, we introduce the factor analysis method for our model that uses probabilistic matrix factorization.

A. Recommendation Model Overview

Let us first consider as an example the user-item rating matrix R of a recommender system (see Figure 2). There are 5 users (from u_1 to u_5) who rated 5 movies (from v_1 to v_5) on a 5-point integer scale to express the extent to which they like each item. Also, as illustrated in Figure 2, the recommender system provider holds three data matrices that provide information that describe users and items. Note that only part of the users and items of these data matrices overlap with those of the user-item rating matrix.

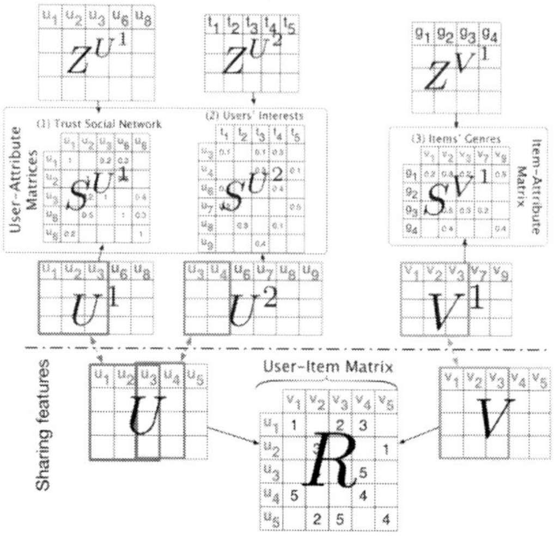

Figure 2. Overview of the recommendation model using toy data. Users and items in green are users for which we make the recommendation, whereas users and items in red are used as additional knowledge.

1) Matrix (1): provides the social network of u_1, u_2, and u_3, where each value in the matrix S^{U^1} represents the trustiness between two users.
2) Matrix (2): provides information about the interests of u_3 and u_4, where for each user-topic pair in the matrix S^{U^2}, a value is associated, which represents the interest of the user in this topic.
3) Matrix (3): provides information about the genre of the movies v_1, v_2, and v_3 in the matrix S^{V^1}.

The problem we study in this paper is how to predict the missing values of the user-item matrix R effectively and efficiently by combining all these data matrices (S^{U^1}, S^{U^2}, and S^{V^1}). Motivated by the intuition that more information will help to improve a recommender system, and inspired by the solution proposed in [1], we propose to disseminate the data matrices of the data sources in the user-item matrix, by factorizing all these matrices simultaneously and seamlessly as illustrated in Figure 2, such as: $R \approx U^T V$, $S^{U^1} \approx U^{1T} Z^{U^1}$, $S^{U^2} \approx U^{2T} Z^{U^2}$, and $S^{V^1} \approx Z^{V^1 T} V^1$, where the k-dimensional matrices U, U^1, and U^2 denote the user latent feature space, such as $U_1 = U_1^1$, $U_2 = U_2^1$, $U_3 = U_3^1 = U_1^2$, $U_4 = U_2^2$ (U_1, U_2, U_4, and U_4 refer respectively to the 1st, 2nd, 3rd, and 4th column of the matrix U), the matrices V and V^1 are the k-dimensional item latent feature space such as $V_1 = V_1^1$, $V_2 = V_2^1$, $V_3 = V_3^1$, and Z^{U^1}, Z^{U^2}, and Z^{V^1}, are factor matrices. In the example given in Figure 2, we use 3 dimensions to perform the factorizations of the matrices. Once done, we can predict the missing values in the user-items matrix R using $U^T V$. In the following sections, we present the details of our recommendation model.

B. User-Item Rating Matrix Factorization

Suppose that a Gaussian distribution gives the probability of an observed entry in the User-Item matrix as follows:

$$r_{ij} \sim \mathcal{N}(r_{ij}|U_i^T V_j, \sigma_R^2) \tag{1}$$

where $\mathcal{N}(x|\mu, \sigma^2)$ is the probability density function of the Gaussian distribution with mean μ and variance σ^2. The idea is to give the highest probability to $r_{ij} \approx U_i^T V_j$ as given by the Gaussian distribution. Hence, the probability of observing approximately the entries of R given the feature matrices U and V is:

$$p(R|U, V, \sigma_R^2) = \prod_{i=1}^{I}\prod_{j=1}^{J} \left[\mathcal{N}(r_{ij}|U_i^T V_j, \sigma_R^2)\right]^{I_{ij}^R} \tag{2}$$

where I_{ij}^R is the indicator function that is equal to 1 if a user i rated an item j and equal to 0 otherwise. Similarly, we place zero-mean spherical Gaussian priors [13][1][12] on user rating and item feature vectors:

$$p(U|\sigma_U^2) = \prod_{i=1}^{I} \left[\mathcal{N}(U_i|0, \sigma_U^2)\right], p(V|\sigma_V^2) = \prod_{j=1}^{J} \left[\mathcal{N}(V_j|0, \sigma_V^2)\right] \tag{3}$$

Hence, through a simple Bayesian inference, we have:

$$p(U, V|R, \sigma_R^2, \sigma_U^2, \sigma_V^2) \propto p(R|U, V, \sigma_R^2)p(U|\sigma_U^2)p(V|\sigma_V^2) \tag{4}$$

C. Matrix factorization for data sources that describe users

Now let's consider a User-Attribute matrix S^{U^n} of P users and K attributes, which describes users. We define the conditional distribution over the observed matrix values as:

$$p(S^{U^n}|U^n, Z^{U^n}, \sigma_{S^{U^n}}^2) = \prod_{p=1}^{P}\prod_{k=1}^{K} \left[\mathcal{N}(s_{pk}^{U^n}|U_p^{nT} Z_k^{U^n}, \sigma_{S^{U^n}}^2)\right]^{I_{pk}^{S^{U^n}}} \tag{5}$$

where $I_{pk}^{S^{U^n}}$ is the indicator function that is equal to 1 if user p has a correlation with attribute k (in the data matrix S^{U^n}) and equal to 0 otherwise. Similarly, we place zero-mean spherical Gaussian priors on feature vectors:

$$p(U^n|\sigma_U^2) = \prod_{p=1}^{P} \left[\mathcal{N}(U_p^n|0, \sigma_U^2)\right], \quad p(Z^{U^n}|\sigma_{Z^{U^n}}^2) = \prod_{k=1}^{K} \left[\mathcal{N}(Z_k^{U^n}|0, \sigma_{Z^{U^n}}^2)\right] \tag{6}$$

Hence, similar to Equation 4, through a simple Bayesian inference, we have:

$$\begin{aligned} &p(U^n, Z^{U^n}|S^{U^n}, \sigma_{S^{U^n}}^2, \sigma_U^2, \sigma_{Z^{U^n}}^2) \propto \\ &p(S^{U^n}|U^n, Z^{U^n}, \sigma_{S^{U^n}}^2)p(U^n|\sigma_U^2)p(Z^{U^n}|\sigma_{Z^{U^n}}^2) \end{aligned} \tag{7}$$

D. Matrix factorization for data sources that describe items

Now let's consider an Item-Attribute matrix S^{V^m} of H items and K attributes, which describes items. We also define the conditional distribution over the observed matrix values as:

$$\begin{aligned} &p(S^{V^m}|V^m, Z^{V^m}, \sigma_{S^{V^m}}^2) = \\ &\prod_{h=1}^{H}\prod_{k=1}^{K} \left[\mathcal{N}(s_{hk}^{V^m}|V_h^{mT} Z_k^{V^m}, \sigma_{S^{V^m}}^2)\right]^{I_{hk}^{S^{V^m}}} \end{aligned} \tag{8}$$

where $I_{hk}^{S^{V^m}}$ is the indicator function that is equal to 1 if an item h is correlated to an attribute k (in the datasource S^{V^m}) and equal to 0 otherwise. We also place zero-mean spherical Gaussian priors on feature vectors:

$$\begin{aligned} p(V^m|\sigma_V^2) &= \prod_{h=1}^{H} \left[\mathcal{N}(V_h^m|0, \sigma_V^2)\right] \\ p(Z^{V^m}|\sigma_{Z^{V^m}}^2) &= \prod_{k=1}^{K} \left[\mathcal{N}(Z_k^{V^m}|0, \sigma_{Z^{V^m}}^2)\right] \end{aligned} \tag{9}$$

Hence, through a Bayesian inference, we also have:

$$\begin{aligned} &p(V^m, Z^{V^m}|S^{V^m}, \sigma_{S^{V^m}}^2, \sigma_V^2, \sigma_{Z^{V^m}}^2) \propto \\ &p(S^{V^m}|V^m, Z^{V^m}, \sigma_{S^{V^m}}^2)p(V^m|\sigma_V^2)p(Z^{V^m}|\sigma_{Z^{V^m}}^2) \end{aligned} \tag{10}$$

E. Recommendation Model

Considering N data matrices that describe users, M data matrices that describe items, and based on the graphical model given in Figure 3, we model the conditional distribution over the observed ratings as:

$$\begin{aligned} &p(U, V|R, S^{U^1}, \ldots, S^{U^n}, S^{V^1}, \ldots, S^{V^m} \\ &\sigma_{Z^{U^1}}^2 \ldots, \sigma_{Z^{U^n}}^2, \sigma_{Z^{V^1}}^2, \ldots, \sigma_{Z^{V^m}}^2) \propto \\ &p(R|U, V, \sigma_R^2)p(U|\sigma_U^2)p(V|\sigma_V^2) \\ &\prod_{n=1}^{N} p(S^{U^n}|U^n, Z^{U^n}, \sigma_{S^{U^n}}^2)p(U^n|\sigma_U^2)p(Z^{U^n}|\sigma_{Z^{U^n}}^2) \\ &\prod_{m=1}^{M} p(S^{V^m}|V^m, Z^{V^m}, \sigma_{S^{V^m}}^2)p(V^m|\sigma_V^2)p(Z^{V^m}|\sigma_{Z^{V^m}}^2) \end{aligned} \tag{11}$$

Hence, we can infer the log of the posterior distribution for the recommendation model as follows:

$$\begin{aligned} &\mathcal{L}(U, U^1, \ldots, U^n, V, V^1, \ldots, V^m, Z^{U_1}, \ldots, Z^{U_n}, Z^{V_1}, \ldots, Z^{V_m}) = \\ &\left.\frac{1}{2}\sum_{i=1}^{I}\sum_{j=1}^{J} I_{ij}^R (r_{ij} - U_i^T V_j)^2 \right\} \text{Error over the reconstruction of } R \\ &\left.+\sum_{n=1}^{N} \frac{\lambda_{S^{U^n}}}{2} \sum_{p=1}^{P}\sum_{k=1}^{K} I_{pk}^{S^{U^n}} (s_{pk}^{U^n} - U_p^{nT} Z_k^{U^n})^2 \right\} \text{Error over the reconstruction of datasources that describe users} \\ &\left.+\sum_{m=1}^{M} \frac{\lambda_{S^{V^m}}}{2} \sum_{h=1}^{H}\sum_{k=1}^{K} I_{hk}^{S^{V^m}} (s_{hk}^{V^m} - V_h^{mT} Z_k^{V^m})^2 \right\} \text{Error over the reconstruction of datasources that describe items} \\ &\left.\begin{aligned} &+\frac{\lambda_U}{2}(\|U\|_F^2 + \sum_{n=1}^{N} \|U^n\|_F^2) \\ &+\frac{\lambda_V}{2}(\|V\|_F^2 + \sum_{m=1}^{M} \|V^m\|_F^2) \\ &+\sum_{n=1}^{N} \frac{\lambda_{Z^{U^n}}}{2} \|Z^{U^n}\|_F^2 + \sum_{m=1}^{M} \frac{\lambda_{Z^{U^m}}}{2} \|Z^{U^m}\|_F^2 \end{aligned}\right\} \text{Regularization terms} \end{aligned} \tag{12}$$

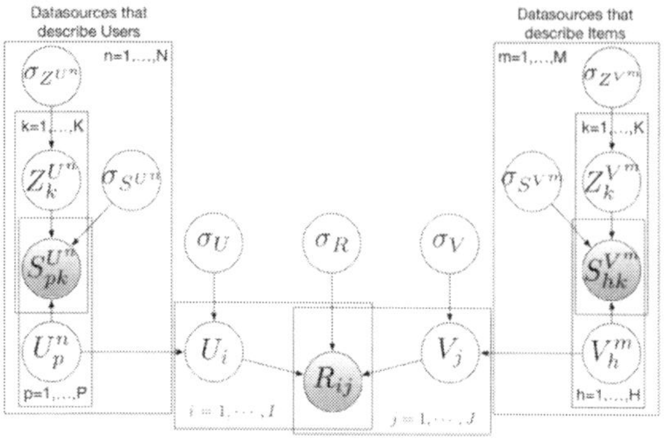

Figure 3. Graphical model for recommendation.

where $\|.\|_F^2$ denotes the Frobenius norm, and λ_* are regularization parameters. A local minimum of the objective function given by Equation 12 can be found using Gradient Descent (GD). A distributed version of this algorithm in the next section.

V. DISTRIBUTED RECOMMENDATION

In this section, we first present a distributed version of the Gradient Descent Algorithm, which minimizes Equation 12, and then we carry out a complexity analysis to show that it can scale to large datasets.

A. Distributed CF Algorithm

In this section, we show how to deploy a CF algorithm in a distributed setting over different clusters and how to generate predictions. This distribution is mainly motivated by: (i) the need to scale up our CF algorithm to very large datasets, i.e., parallelize part of the computation, (ii) reduce the communication cost over the network, and (iii) avoid to transfer the raw data matrices (for privacy concerns). Instead, we only exchange common latent features.

Based on the observation that several parts of the centralized CF algorithm can be executed in parallel and separately on different clusters, we propose to distribute it using Algorithms 1, 2, and 3. Algorithm 1 is executed by the master cluster that handle the user-item rating matrix, whereas each slave cluster that handle data matrices about users' attributes executes an instance of Algorithm 2, and each slave cluster that handles data matrices about items' attributes executes an instance of Algorithm 3.

Basically, the first step of this distributed algorithm is an initialization phase, where each cluster (master and slaves) initializes its latent feature matrices with small random values (lines 1 of Algorithms 1, 2, and 3). Next, in line 4 of Algorithm 1, the master cluster computes part of the partial derivative of the objective function given in Equation 12 with respect to U (line 4 of Algorithm 1). Then, for each user u_i, the master cluster sends its latent feature vector to the other participant slave clusters, which share attributes about that user (lines 5 and 6 in Algorithm 1). Then, the master cluster waits for responses of all these participant slave clusters (line 8 in Algorithm 1).

Algorithm 1: Distributed Collaborative Filtering Algorithm (Master Cluster 1/3)

input : The User-Item matrix R_{ij};
A learning parameter α;
Regularization parameters λ_U, λ_V;
output: Feature matrices U, V;

1 Initialize latent feature matrices to small random values.
/* Minimize $\mathcal{L}$ using gradient descent as follows: */
2 **while** $\mathcal{L} > \epsilon$ /* ϵ is a stop criterion */
3 **do**
/* Compute local intermediate results of the gradient of U as follows: */
4 $\nabla_U = \left(I^R (U^T V - R) V^T\right)^T + \lambda_U U$
5 **foreach** *user* u_i **do**
6 **Send** U_i to data sources that share information about the user u_i
7 **end**
8 **foreach** π_n *received* **do**
/* $\oplus$ is an algebraic operator given in Definition 1. */
9 $\nabla_U = \nabla_U \oplus \pi_n$
10 **end**
/* Compute local intermediate results of the gradient of V as follows: */
11 $\nabla_V = \left(I^R (U^T V - R)^T U^T\right)^T + \lambda_V V$
12 **foreach** *item* v_j **do**
13 **Send** V_j to data sources that share information about the item v_j
14 **end**
15 **foreach** π_m *received* **do**
16 $\nabla_V = \nabla_V \oplus \pi_m$
17 **end**
/* Update global U and V latent features matrices as follows: */
18 $U = U - \alpha(\nabla_U)$
19 $V = V - \alpha(\nabla_V)$
20 check U and V for convergence
21 **end**

Algorithm 2: Distributed Collaborative Filtering Algorithm (User data slave cluster 2/3)

1 Initialize latent feature matrices Z^{U^n} and U^n to small random values.
2 **Procedure** RefineUserFeatures()
input : A User-Object matrix S^{U^n};
The common user latent features matrix U;
A learning parameter α;
Regularization parameters $\lambda_{S^{U_n}}, \lambda_{Z^{U_n}}$;
3 **foreach** U_i *received* **do**
4 Replace the right latent user feature vector U_k^n with the received U_i
5 **end**
/* Compute intermediate result: */
6 $\pi_n = \lambda_{S^{U^n}} \left(I^{S^{U^n}} (U^{nT} Z^{U^n} - S^{U^n}) Z^{U^n T}\right)^T$
7 Keep in π_n vectors of users that are shared with the recommender system
8 **Send** π_n to the recommender system
/* Compute gradients of U^n and Z with respect to $\mathcal{L}$ */
9 $\nabla_{U^n} = \lambda_{S^{U^n}} \left(I^{S^{U^n}} (U^{nT} Z^{U^n} - S^{U^n}) Z^{U^n T}\right)^T + \lambda_{S^{U^n}} U^n$
10 $\nabla_Z = \left(\lambda_{S^{U^n}} \left(I^{S^{U^n}} (U^{nT} Z^{U^n} - S^{U^n})\right)^T U^{nT}\right)^T + \lambda_{Z^{U^n}} Z^{U^n}$
/* Update local latent features matrices U and Z as follows: */
11 $U^n = U^n - \alpha(\nabla_{U^n})$
12 $Z^{U^n} = Z^{U^n} - \alpha(\nabla_Z)$

Next, each slave cluster that receives users' latent features replaces the corresponding user latent feature vector U_k^n with the user latent feature vector U_i received from the master cluster (lines 3 and 4 in Algorithm 2). Then, the slave cluster computes π_n, which is part of the partial derivative of the objective function given in Equation 12 with respect to U (line 6 in Algorithm 2). Next, the slave cluster keeps in π_n, only

Algorithm 3: Distributed Collaborative Filtering Algorithm (Item data slave cluster 3/3)

Initialize latent feature matrices Z^{V^m} and V^m to small random values.
Procedure RefineUserFeatures()
  input : An Object-Item matrix S^{V_m};
    The common user latent features matrix V;
    A learning parameter α;
    Regularization parameters $\lambda_{S^{V_m}}, \lambda_{Z^{V_m}}$;
  foreach V_j *received* **do**
    Replace the right latent item feature vector V_k^m with the received V_j
  end
  /* Compute intermediate result: */
  $\pi_m = \lambda_{S^{V^m}} \left(\left(I^{S^{V^m}} (Z^{V^m T} V^m - S^{V^m}) \right)^T Z^{V^m T} \right)^T$
  Keep in π_m vectors of items that are shared with the recommender system
  Send π_m to the recommender system
  /* Compute gradients of V and Z with respect to $\mathcal{L}$: */
  $\nabla_{V^m} = \lambda_{S^{V^m}} \left(\left(I^{S^{V_m}} (Z^{V^m T} V^m - S^{V^m}) \right)^T Z^{V^m T} \right)^T + \lambda_{S^{V^m}} V^m$
  $\nabla_Z = \lambda_{S^{V^m}} \left(I^{S^{V^m}} (Z^{V^m T} V^m - S^{V^m}) V^T \right)^T + \lambda_{Z^{U^m}} Z$
  /* Update local latent features matrices V and Z as follows: */
  $V^m = V^m - \alpha(\nabla_{V^m})$
  $Z^{V^m} = Z^{V^m} - \alpha(\nabla_Z)$

vectors of users that are shared with the master cluster (line 7 in Algorithm 2). The slave cluster sends the remaining feature vectors in π_n to the master cluster (line 8 in Algorithm 2). Finally, the slave cluster updates its local user and attribute latent feature matrices Z^{U^n} and U^n (lines 9-12 in Algorithm 2).

As for the master cluster, each user latent feature matrix π_n received from a slave cluster is added to ∇_U, which is the partial derivative of the objective function with respect to U (line 9 in Algorithm 1). This addition is performed using $\oplus$, an algebraic operator defined as follows:

Definition 1.

For two matrices $A_{m,n} = (a_{ij})$ and $B_{m,p} = (b_{ij})$, $A \oplus B$ returns the matrix $C_{m,n}$ where:

$$c_{ij} = \begin{cases} a_{ij} + b_{ij} & \text{if } A_j \text{ and } B_j \text{ refer to the same user/item} \\ a_{ij} & \text{otherwise} \end{cases}$$

Once the master cluster has received all the partial derivative of the objective function with respect to U from all the user participant sites, it has computed the global derivative of the objective function given in Equation 12 with respect to U . A similar operation is performed for item slave cluster from line 11 to line 16 in Algorithm 1 to compute the global derivative of the objective function given in Equation 12 with respect to V. Finally, the master cluster updates the user and item latent feature matrices U and V, and evaluates $\mathcal{L}$ in lines 18, 19, and 20 of Algorithm 1 respectively. The convergence of the whole algorithm is checked in line 2 of Algorithm 1. Note that all the involved clusters that hold data matrices on users and items' attributes execute their respective algorithm in parallel.

B. Complexity Analysis

The main computation of the GD algorithm evaluates the objective function $\mathcal{L}$ in Equation 12 and its derivatives. Because of the extreme sparsity of the matrices, the computational complexity of evaluating the object function $\mathcal{L}$ is $O(\rho_1 + \ldots + p_n)$, where ρ_n is the number of nonzero entries in matrix n. The computational complexities for the derivatives are also proportional to the number of nonzero entries in data matrices. Hence, the total computational complexity in one iteration of this gradient descent algorithm is $O(\rho_1 + \ldots + p_n)$, which indicates that the computational time is linear with respect to the number of observations in the data matrices. This complexity analysis shows that our algorithm is quite efficient and can scale to very large datasets.

VI. Experimental Evaluation

In this section, we carry out several experiments to mainly address the following questions:

1) What is the amount of data transferred?
2) How does the number of user and item sources affect the accuracy of predictions?
3) What is the performance comparison on users with different observed ratings?
4) Can our algorithm achieve good performance even if users have no observed ratings?
5) How does our approach compare with the state-of-the-art collaborative filtering algorithms?

In the rest of this section, we introduce our datasets and experimental methodology, and address these questions (question 1 in Section VI-C, question 2 in Section VI-D, questions 3 and 4 in Section VI-E, and question 5 in Section VI-F).

A. Description of the Datasets

The first round of our experiment is based on a dataset from Delicious, described and analyzed in [14][15][16] (http://data.dai-labor.de/corpus/delicious/). Delicious is a bookmarking system, which provides to the user a means to freely annotate Web pages with tags. Basically, in this scenario we want to recommend interesting Web pages to users. This dataset contains 425,183 tags, 1,321,039 Web pages, and 318,769 users. The user-item matrix contains 2,265,207 entries (a density of $\simeq 0.0005\%$). Each entry of the user-item matrix represents the degree of which a user interacted with an item expressed on a $[0, 1]$ scale. The dataset contains a user-tag matrix with 4,598,815 entries, where each entry expresses the interest of a user in a tag on a $[0, 1]$ scale. Lastly, the dataset contains an item-tags matrix with 4,403,244 entries, where each entry expresses the coverage of a tag in a Web page on a $[0, 1]$ scale. The user-tag matrix and item-tags are used as user data matrix, and item data matrix respectively. However, to simulate having many data matrices that describe both users and items, we have manually and randomly broken the two previous matrices into 10 matrices in both columns and rows. These new matrices kept their property of sparsity. Hence, we end up with a user-item rating matrix, 10 user data matrices (with approximately 459 000 entries each), and 10 item data matrices (with approximately 440 000 entries each).

The second round of experiments is based on one of the datasets given by the HetRec 2011 workshop (http://ir.ii.uam.es/hetrec2011/datasets.html), and reflect a real use case. This dataset is an extension of the Movielens dataset, which contains personal ratings, and data coming from other data sources (mainly IMDb and Rotten Tomatoes). This dataset includes ratings that range from 1 to 5, including 0.5 steps. This dataset contains a user-items matrix of 2,113 users, 10,109 movies, and 855,597 ratings (with a density of $\simeq 4\%$). This dataset also includes a user-tag matrix of 9,078 tags describing the users with 21,324 entries on a $[0, 1]$ scale, which is used as a user data matrix. Lastly, this dataset contains four item data matrices: (1) an item-tag matrix with 51,794 entries, (2) an item-genre matrix with 20 genres and 20,809 entries, (3) an item-actor matrix with 95,321 actors, and 213,742 entries, and (4) an item-location matrix with 187 locations and 13,566 entries.

B. Methodology and metrics

We have implemented our distributed collaborative algorithm and integrated it into Peersim [17], a well-known distributed computing simulator. We use two different training data settings (80% and 60%) to test the algorithms. We randomly select part of the ratings from the user-item rating matrix as the training data (80% or 60%) to predict the remaining ratings (respectively 20% or 40%). The random selection was carried out 5 times independently, and we report the average results. To measure the prediction quality of the different recommendation methods, we use the Root Mean Square Error (RMSE), for which a smaller value means a better performance. We refer to our method Distributed Probabilistic Matrix Factorization (DPMF).

C. Data transfer

Let's consider an example where a recommender system uses a social network as a source of information to improve its precision. Let's assume that the social network contains 40 million unique users with 80 billion asymmetric connections (a density of 0.005%). It turns out that if we only consider the connections, the size of the user-user matrix representing this social network is $80 \times 10^9 \times (8B + 8B) \simeq 1.16TB$ (assuming that we need 8 bytes to encode a double to represent the strength of the relation between two users, and 8 bytes to encode a long that represents the key for the entry of the value in the user-user matrix). Hence, for the execution of the centralized collaborative filtering algorithm, $1.16TB$ of data need to be transferred through the network. However, if we assume that there are 10% of common users between the recommender system and the social network, each iteration of the DPMF algorithm requires the transfer of $4 \times 10^6 \times 10 \times 8B \times 2 \simeq 610MB$ (assuming that we use 10 dimensions for the factorization, that we need 8 bytes to encode a double value in a latent user vector, and a round trip of transfer for the latent vectors in line 6 of Algorithm 1 and line 8 of Algorithm 2). Hence, if the algorithm requires 100 iterations to converge (roughly the number of iterations needed in our experiment), the total amount of data transferred is $59GB$, which represents 5% of the data transferred in the centralized solution. Finally, the total amount of data transferred depends on the density of the source, the total

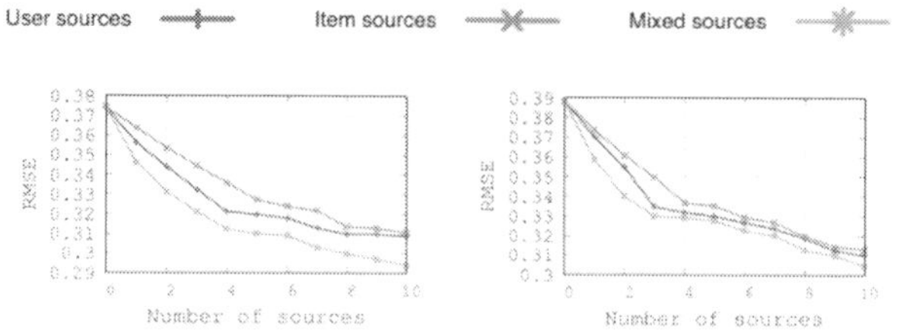

(a) Training: 80%. (b) Training: 60%.

Figure 4. Results of the impact of the number of sources on the Delicious dataset.

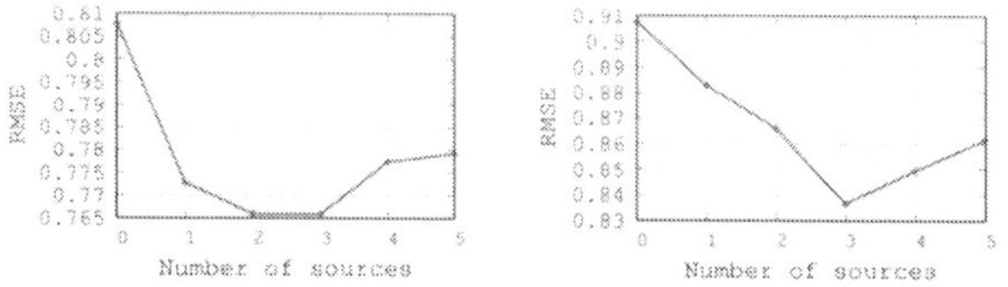

(a) Training: 80%. (b) Training: 60%.

Figure 5. Results of the impact of the number of sources on the Movielens dataset. The data matrices are added in the following order: (1) user-tag, (2) item-tag, (3) item-genre, (4) item-actor, and (5) item-location.

number of common attributes, the number of latent dimensions used for the factorization and the number of iterations needed for the algorithm to converge. These parameters can make the DPMF very competitive compared to the centralized solution in terms of data transfer.

D. Impact of the number of sources

Figures 4 and 5 show the results obtained on the two datasets, while varying the number of sources. Note that source=0 means that we factorize only the user-item matrix.

In Figure 4, the green curve represents the impact of adding item sources only, the red curve the impact of adding user sources only, and the blue curve the impact of adding both sources (e.g., 2 sources means we add 2 item and 2 user sources). First, the results show that adding more sources helps to improve the performance, confirming our initial intuition. The additional data sources have certainly contributed to refine users' preferences and items' characteristics. Second, we observe that sources that describe users are more helpful than sources that describe items (about 10% gain). However, we consider this observation to be specific to this dataset, and cannot be generalized. Third, we notice that combining both data sources provides the best performance (blue curve, about 8% with respect to the use of only user sources). Lastly, the best gain obtained with respect to the PMF method (source=0) is about 32%.

Figure 5 shows the results obtained on the Movielens dataset. The obtained results here are quite different than those obtained on the Delicious dataset. Indeed, we observe that the data matrices 1, 2 and 3 have a positive impact on the results; however, data matrices 4 and 5 decrease the performance. This is certainly due to the fact that the data embedded in these

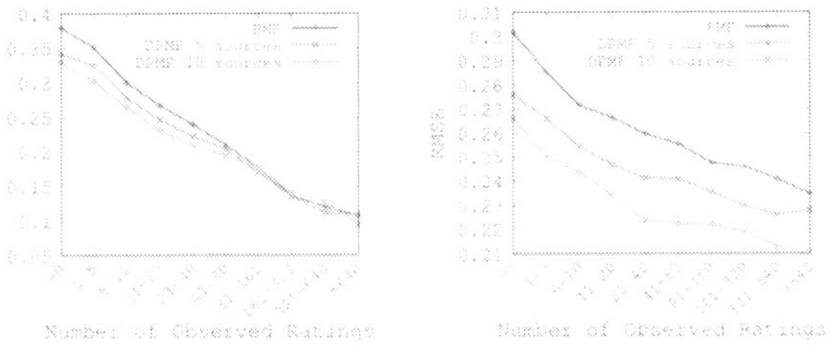

(a) Different users. (b) Different items.

Figure 6. Performance for different ratings on the Delicious dataset.

two matrices are not meaningful to extract and infer items' characteristics. In general, the best performance is obtained using the three first data matrices, with a gain of 10% with respect to PMF (source=0).

E. Performance on users and items with different ratings

We stated previously that the data sparsity in a recommender system induces mainly two problems: (1) the lack of data to effectively model user preferences, and (2) the lack of data to effectively model item characteristics. Hence, in this section we study the ability of our method to provide accurate recommendations for users that supply few ratings, and items that contain few ratings (or no ratings at all). We show the results for different user ratings in Figure 6a, and for different item ratings in Figure 6b on the Delicious dataset. We group them into 10 classes based on the number of observed ratings: "0", "1-5", "6-10", "11-20", "21-40", "41-80", "81-160", "161-320", "321-640", and ">640". We show the results for different user ratings in Figure 6a, and for different item ratings in Figure 6b on the Delicious dataset. We also show the performance of the Probabilistic Matrix Factorization (PMF) method [12], and our method using 5 and 10 data matrices. In Figure 6a, on the X axis, users are grouped and ordered with respect to the number of ratings they have assigned. For example, for users with no ratings (0 on the X-axis), we got an average of 0.37 for RMSE using the PMF method. Similarly, in Figure 6b, on the X-axis, items are grouped and ordered with respect to the number of ratings they have obtained.

The results show that our method is more efficient in providing accurate recommendations compared to the PMF method for both users and items with few ratings (from 0 to about 100 on the-X axis). Also, the experiments show that the more we add data matrices, the more the recommendations are accurate. However, for clarity, we just plot the results obtained for our method while using 5 and 10 data matrices. Finally, we also noticed that the performance is better for predicting ratings to items that contain few ratings, than to users who rated few items. This is certainly due to the fact that users' preferences change over time, and thus, the error margin is increased.

F. Performance comparison

To demonstrate the performance behavior of our algorithm, we compared it with eight other state-of-the-art algorithms: **User Mean:** uses the mean value of every user; **Item Mean:** utilizes the mean value of every item; **NMF** [18]; **PMF** [12], **SoRec** [1]; **PTBR** [19]; **MatchBox** [20]; **HeteroMF** [21]. The results of the comparison are shown in Table II. The optimal parameters of each method are selected, and we report the final performance on the test set. The percentages in Table II are the improvement rates of our method over the corresponding approaches.

First, from the results, we see that our method consistently outperforms almost all the other approaches in all the settings of both datasets. Our method can almost always generate better predictions than the state-of-the-art recommendation algorithms. Second, only Matchbox and HeteroMF slightly outperform our method on the Movielens dataset. Third, the RMSE values generated by all the methods on the Delicious dataset are lower than those on Movielens dataset. This is due to the fact that the rating scale is different between the two datasets. Fourth, our method outperforms the other methods better on the Delicious dataset, than on the Movielens dataset (10% to 33% on Delicious and -0.05% to 11% on Movielens). This is certainly due to the fact that: (1) the Movilens dataset contains less data (fewer users and fewer items), (2) there are less data matrices in the Movielens dataset to add, and (3) the data matrices of the Delicious dataset are of higher quality. Lastly, even if we use several data matrices in our method, using 80% of training data still provides more accurate predictions than 60% of training data. We explain this by the fact that the data of the user-item matrix are the main resources to train an effective recommendation model. Clearly, an external source of data cannot replace the user-item rating matrix, but can be used to enhance it.

VII. Related Work

Enhanced recommendation: Many researchers have started exploring social relations to improve recommender systems (including implicit social information, which can be employed to improve traditional recommendation methods [22]), essentially to tackle the cold-start problem [23][1][10]. However, as pointed in [24], only a small subset of user interactions and activities are actually useful for social recommendation.

In collaborative filtering based approaches, Liu and Lee [25] proposed very simple heuristics to increase recommendation effectiveness by combining social networks information. Guy et al. [26] proposed a ranking function of items based on social relationships. This ranking function has been further improved in [19] to include social content such as related terms to the user. More recently, Wang et al. [27] proposed a novel method for interactive social recommendation, which not only simultaneously explores user preferences and exploits the effectiveness of personalization in an interactive way, but also adaptively learns different weights for different friends. Also, Xiao et al. [28] proposed a novel user preference model for recommender systems that considers the visibility of both items and social relationships.

In the context of matrix factorization, following the intuition that a person's social network will affect her behaviors on the Web, Ma et al. [1] propose to factorize both the users' social network and the rating records matrices. The main idea is to fuse the user-item matrix with the users' social trust networks by sharing a common latent low-dimensional user

TABLE II. PERFORMANCE COMPARISON USING RMSE. OPTIMAL VALUES OF THE PARAMETERS ARES USED FOR EACH METHOD (K= 10).

Dataset	Training	U. Mean	I. Mean	NMF	PMF	SoRec	PTBR	Matchbox	HeteroMF	DPMF
Delicious	80%	0.4389 33,03%	0.4280 31,33%	0.3814 22,94%	0.3811 22,88%	0.3566 17.58%	0.3499 16.00%	0.3297 10.85%	0.3301 10.96%	0.2939 Improvement
	60%	0.3965 23,15%	0.4087 25,44%	0.3779 19,37%	0.3911 22,09%	0.3681 17.22%	0.3599 15.33%	0.3387 10.03%	0.3434 11.26%	0.3047 Improvement
Movielens	80%	0.8399 8,82%	0.8467 9,55%	0.7989 4,14%	0.8106 5,52%	0.774 1.05%	0.7801 1.83%	**0.7605** **-0.69%**	0.7788 1.66%	0.7658 Improvement
	60%	0.9478 11,74%	0.9667 13,46%	0.9011 7,16%	0.9096 8,03%	0.882 5.15%	0.8912 6.13%	0.8399 0.40%	**0.8360** **-0.05%**	0.8365 Improvement

feature matrix. This approach has been improved in [29] by taking into account only trusted friends for recommendation while sharing the user latent dimensional matrix. Almost a similar approach has been proposed in [30] and [31] who include in the factorization process, trust propagation and trust propagation with inferred circles of friends in social networks respectively. In this same context, other approaches have been proposed to consider *social regularization terms* while factorizing the rating matrix. The idea is to handle friends with dissimilar tastes differently in order to represent the taste diversity of each user's friends [2][3]. A number of these methods are reviewed, analyzed and compared in [32].

Also, few works consider cross-domain recommendation, where a user's acquired knowledge in a particular domain could be transferred and exploited in several other domains, or offering joint, personalized recommendations of items in multiple domains, e.g., suggesting not only a particular movie, but also music CDs, books or video games somehow related with that movie. Based on the type of relations between the domains, Fernández-Tobías et al. [33] propose to categorize cross-domain recommendation as: (i) content based-relations (common items between domains) [34], and (ii) collaborative filtering-based relations (common users between domain) [35][36]. However, almost all these algorithms are not distributed.

Distributed recommendation: Serveral decentralized recommendation solutions have been proposed mainly from a peer to peer perspective, basically for collaborative filtering [37], search and recommendation [38]. The goal of these solutions is to decentralize the recommendation process.

Other works have investigated distributed recommendation algorithms to tackle the problem of scalability. Hence, Liu et al. [25] provide a multiplicative-update method. This approach is also applied to squared loss and to nonnegative matrix factorization with an "exponential" loss function. Each of these algorithms in essence takes an embarrassingly parallel matrix factorization algorithm developed previously and directly distributes it across a MapReduce cluster. Gemulla et al. [39] provide a novel algorithm to approximately factor large matrices with millions of rows, millions of columns, and billions of nonzero elements. The approach depends on a variant of the Stochastic Gradient Descent (SGD), an iterative stochastic optimization algorithm. Gupta et al. [40] describe scalable parallel algorithms for sparse matrix factorization, analyze their performance and scalability. Finally, Yu et al. [41] uses coordinate descent, a classical optimization approach, for a parallel scalable implementation of matrix factorization for recommender system. More recently, Shin et al. [42] proposed two distributed tensor factorization methods, CDTF and SALS. Both methods are scalable with all aspects of data and show a trade-off between convergence speed and memory requirements.

However, note that almost all the works described above focus mainly on decentralizing and parallelizing the matrix factorization computation. To the best of our knowledge, none of the existing distributed solutions proposes a distributed recommendation approach using diverse data sources.

VIII. CONCLUSION

In this paper, we proposed a new distributed collaborative filtering algorithm, which uses and combines multiple and diverse data matrices provided by online services to improve recommendation quality. Our algorithm is based on the factorization of matrices, and the sharing of common latent features with the recommender system. This algorithm has been designed for a distributed setting, where the objective was to avoid sending the raw data, and parallelize the matrix computation. All the algorithms presented have been evaluated using two different datasets of Delicious and Movielens. The results show the effectiveness of our approach. Our method consistently outperforms almost all the state-of-the-art approaches in all the settings of both datasets. Only Matchbox and HeteroMF slightly outperform our method on the Movielens dataset.

REFERENCES

[1] Hao Ma, Haixuan Yang, Michael R. Lyu, and Irwin King. Sorec: Social recommendation using probabilistic matrix factorization. In *Proceedings of the 17th ACM Conference on Information and Knowledge Management*, CIKM '08, pages 931–940, New York, NY, USA, 2008. ACM.

[2] Hao Ma, Dengyong Zhou, Chao Liu, Michael R. Lyu, and Irwin King. Recommender systems with social regularization. In *Proceedings of the Fourth ACM International Conference on Web Search and Data Mining*, WSDM '11, pages 287–296, New York, NY, USA, 2011. ACM.

[3] Joseph Noel, Scott Sanner, Khoi-Nguyen Tran, Peter Christen, Lexing Xie, Edwin V. Bonilla, Ehsan Abbasnejad, and Nicolas Della Penna. New objective functions for social collaborative filtering. In *Proceedings of the 21st International Conference on World Wide Web*, WWW '12, pages 859–868, New York, NY, USA, 2012. ACM.

[4] J. J. Levandoski, M. Sarwat, A. Eldawy, and M. F. Mokbel. Lars: A location-aware recommender system. In *2012 IEEE 28th International Conference on Data Engineering*, pages 450–461, April 2012.

[5] Hao Wang, Manolis Terrovitis, and Nikos Mamoulis. Location recommendation in location-based social networks using user check-in data. In *Proceedings of the 21st ACM SIGSPATIAL International Conference on Advances in Geographic Information Systems*, SIGSPATIAL'13, pages 374–383, New York, NY, USA, 2013. ACM.

[6] Sofiane Abbar, Sihem Amer-Yahia, Piotr Indyk, and Sepideh Mahabadi. Real-time recommendation of diverse related articles. In *Proceedings of the 22Nd International Conference on World Wide Web*, WWW '13, pages 1–12, New York, NY, USA, 2013. ACM.

[7] Cai-Nicolas Ziegler, Sean M. McNee, Joseph A. Konstan, and Georg Lausen. Improving recommendation lists through topic diversification. In *Proceedings of the 14th International Conference on World Wide Web*, WWW '05, pages 22–32, New York, NY, USA, 2005. ACM.

[8] Mi Zhang and Neil Hurley. Avoiding monotony: Improving the diversity of recommendation lists. In *Proceedings of the 2008 ACM Conference on Recommender Systems*, RecSys '08, pages 123–130, New York, NY, USA, 2008. ACM.

[9] Paul Resnick and Hal R Varian. Recommender Systems. *Commun. ACM*, 40(3):56–58, 1997.

[10] Suvash Sedhain, Scott Sanner, Darius Braziunas, Lexing Xie, and Jordan Christensen. Social collaborative filtering for cold-start recommendations. In *Proceedings of the 8th ACM Conference on Recommender Systems*, RecSys '14, pages 345–348, New York, NY, USA, 2014. ACM.

[11] Ricardo A Baeza-Yates and Berthier Ribeiro-Neto. *Modern Information Retrieval*. Addison-Wesley Longman Publishing Co., Inc., 2 edition, 2010.

[12] Ruslan Salakhutdinov and Andriy Mnih. Probabilistic matrix factorization. In *Proceedings of the 20th International Conference on Neural Information Processing Systems*, NIPS'07, pages 1257–1264, USA, 2007. Curran Associates Inc.

[13] Delbert Dueck and Brendan J Frey. Probabilistic sparse matrix factorization. Technical report, 2004.

[14] Robert Wetzker, Carsten Zimmermann, and Christian Bauckhage. Analyzing Social Bookmarking Systems: A del.icio.us Cookbook. In *ECAI*, 2008.

[15] Mohamed Reda Bouadjenek, Hakim Hacid, and Mokrane Bouzeghoub. SoPRa: A New Social Personalized Ranking Function for Improving Web Search. In *Proceedings of the 36th International ACM SIGIR Conference on Research and Development in Information Retrieval*, SIGIR '13, pages 861–864, New York, NY, USA, 2013. ACM.

[16] Mohamed Reda Bouadjenek, Hakim Hacid, Mokrane Bouzeghoub, and Athena Vakali. Persador: Personalized social document representation for improving web search. *Information Sciences*, 369:614 – 633, 2016.

[17] A. Montresor and M. Jelasity. Peersim: A scalable p2p simulator. In *Peer-to-Peer Computing, 2009. P2P '09. IEEE Ninth International Conference on*, pages 99–100, Sept 2009.

[18] Daniel D Lee and H Sebastian Seung. Learning the parts of objects by non-negative matrix factorization. *Nature*, 401(6755):788–791, 1999.

[19] Ido Guy, Naama Zwerdling, Inbal Ronen, David Carmel, and Erel Uziel. Social media recommendation based on people and tags. In *Proceedings of the 33rd International ACM SIGIR Conference on Research and Development in Information Retrieval*, SIGIR '10, pages 194–201, New York, NY, USA, 2010. ACM.

[20] David H. Stern, Ralf Herbrich, and Thore Graepel. Matchbox: Large scale online bayesian recommendations. In *Proceedings of the 18th International Conference on World Wide Web*, WWW '09, pages 111–120, New York, NY, USA, 2009. ACM.

[21] Mohsen Jamali and Laks Lakshmanan. Heteromf: Recommendation in heterogeneous information networks using context dependent factor models. In *Proceedings of the 22Nd International Conference on World Wide Web*, WWW '13, pages 643–654, New York, NY, USA, 2013. ACM.

[22] Hao Ma. An Experimental Study on Implicit Social Recommendation. In *SIGIR*, 2013.

[23] Jovian Lin, Kazunari Sugiyama, Min-Yen Kan, and Tat-Seng Chua. Addressing cold-start in app recommendation: Latent user models constructed from twitter followers. In *Proceedings of the 36th International ACM SIGIR Conference on Research and Development in Information Retrieval*, SIGIR '13, pages 283–292, New York, NY, USA, 2013. ACM.

[24] Suvash Sedhain, Scott Sanner, Lexing Xie, Riley Kidd, Khoi-Nguyen Tran, and Peter Christen. Social affinity filtering: Recommendation through fine-grained analysis of user interactions and activities. In *Proceedings of the First ACM Conference on Online Social Networks*, COSN '13, pages 51–62, New York, NY, USA, 2013. ACM.

[25] Fengkun Liu and Hong Joo Lee. Use of social network information to enhance collaborative filtering performance. *Expert Syst. Appl.*, 37(7):4772–4778, 2010.

[26] Ido Guy, Naama Zwerdling, David Carmel, Inbal Ronen, Erel Uziel, Sivan Yogev, and Shila Ofek-Koifman. Personalized recommendation of social software items based on social relations. In *Proceedings of the Third ACM Conference on Recommender Systems*, RecSys '09, pages 53–60, New York, NY, USA, 2009. ACM.

[27] Xin Wang, Steven C.H. Hoi, Chenghao Liu, and Martin Ester. Interactive social recommendation. In *Proceedings of the 2017 ACM on Conference on Information and Knowledge Management*, CIKM '17, pages 357–366, New York, NY, USA, 2017. ACM.

[28] Lin Xiao, Zhang Min, Zhang Yongfeng, Liu Yiqun, and Ma Shaoping. Learning and transferring social and item visibilities for personalized recommendation. In *Proceedings of the 2017 ACM on Conference on Information and Knowledge Management*, CIKM '17, pages 337–346, New York, NY, USA, 2017. ACM.

[29] Hao Ma, Irwin King, and Michael R. Lyu. Learning to recommend with social trust ensemble. In *Proceedings of the 32Nd International ACM SIGIR Conference on Research and Development in Information Retrieval*, SIGIR '09, pages 203–210, New York, NY, USA, 2009. ACM.

[30] Mohsen Jamali and Martin Ester. A matrix factorization technique with trust propagation for recommendation in social networks. In *Proceedings of the Fourth ACM Conference on Recommender Systems*, RecSys '10, pages 135–142, New York, NY, USA, 2010. ACM.

[31] Xiwang Yang, Harald Steck, and Yong Liu. Circle-based recommendation in online social networks. In *Proceedings of the 18th ACM SIGKDD International Conference on Knowledge Discovery and Data Mining*, KDD '12, pages 1267–1275, New York, NY, USA, 2012. ACM.

[32] Xiwang Yang, Yang Guo, Yong Liu, and Harald Steck. A survey of collaborative filtering based social recommender systems. *Computer Communications*, 41(0):1–10, 2014.

[33] Ignacio Fernández-Tobías, Iván Cantador, Marius Kaminskas, and Francesco Ricci. Cross-domain recommender systems: A survey of the state of the art. *Proceedings of the 2nd Spanish Conference on Information Retrieval. CERI*, 2012.

[34] Fabian Abel, Eelco Herder, Geert-Jan Houben, Nicola Henze, and Daniel Krause. Cross-system user modeling and personalization on the social web. *User Modeling and User-Adapted Interaction*, 23(2):169–209, Apr 2013.

[35] Pinata Winoto and Tiffany Tang. If You Like the Devil Wears Prada the Book, Will You also Enjoy the Devil Wears Prada the Movie? A Study of Cross-Domain Recommendations. *New Generation Computing*, 26(3):209–225, June 2008.

[36] Shlomo Berkovsky, Tsvi Kuflik, and Francesco Ricci. Mediation of user models for enhanced personalization in recommender systems. *User Modeling and User-Adapted Interaction*, 18(3):245–286, August 2008.

[37] Anne-Marie Kermarrec and Francois Taiani. Diverging towards the common good: Heterogeneous self-organisation in decentralised recommenders. In *Proceedings of the Fifth Workshop on Social Network Systems*, SNS '12, pages 1:1–1:6, New York, NY, USA, 2012. ACM.

[38] Fady Draidi, Esther Pacitti, and Bettina Kemme. P2prec: A P2P recommendation system for large-scale data sharing. *T. Large-Scale Data- and Knowledge-Centered Systems*, 3:87–116, 2011.

[39] Rainer Gemulla, Erik Nijkamp, Peter J. Haas, and Yannis Sismanis. Large-scale matrix factorization with distributed stochastic gradient descent. In *Proceedings of the 17th ACM SIGKDD International Conference on Knowledge Discovery and Data Mining*, KDD '11, pages 69–77, New York, NY, USA, 2011. ACM.

[40] Anshul Gupta, George Karypis, and Vipin Kumar. Highly scalable parallel algorithms for sparse matrix factorization. *IEEE Trans. Parallel Distrib. Syst.*, 8(5):502–520, May 1997.

[41] Hsiang-Fu Yu, Cho-Jui Hsieh, Si Si, and Inderjit Dhillon. Scalable coordinate descent approaches to parallel matrix factorization for recommender systems. In *Proceedings of the 2012 IEEE 12th International Conference on Data Mining*, ICDM '12, pages 765–774, Washington, DC, USA, 2012. IEEE Computer Society.

[42] Kijung Shin, Lee Sael, and U Kang. Fully scalable methods for distributed tensor factorization. *IEEE Trans. on Knowl. and Data Eng.*, 29(1):100–113, January 2017.

Interactive Graph Query Language for Multidimensional Data in Collaboration Spotting Visual Analytics Framework

Adam Agocs*, Dimitrios Dardanis*, Jean-Marie Le Goff*, Dimitrios Proios*
*CERN, CH-1211 Geneva 23, Switzerland
E-mail: {Adam.Agocs, Dimitrios.Dardanis, Jean-Marie.Le.Goff, Dimitrios.Proios}@cern.ch

Abstract—**Human reasoning in visual analytics of data networks relies mainly on the quality of visual perception and the capability of interactively exploring the data from different perspectives. Visual quality strongly depends on networks' size and dimensional complexity while network exploration capability relies upon the intuitiveness and expressiveness of user frontends. The approach taken in this paper aims at addressing the above by decomposing data networks into multiple networks of smaller dimensions and building an interactive graph query language that supports full navigation across the sub-networks. Within sub-networks of reduced dimensionality, structural abstraction and semantic techniques can then be used to enhance visual perception further.**

Keywords–Visual analytics; labelled graph; graph query language; visualisation; patents and publications

I. Introduction

According to an English idiom, "A picture is worth a thousand words". Visual analytics aims to combine the power of visual perception with high performance computing in order to support human analytical reasoning. Since Wong et al. [1] in 2004, visual analytics has been widely used in various fields, such as biology or national security but also in other fields, such as climate monitoring [2][3] or social networks analysis, the field originally addressed by the Collaboration Spotting project (CS). Multidimensional networks built out of interconnected elements contained in datasets and represented as directed and labelled graphs are a natural means of representing data for visual analytics. These graphs - often referred to as knowledge graphs - comprise labelled nodes and relationships and their data schemas are graphs of labels that correspond to the networks' dimensions.

Graphs as database models and graph query languages defined over these models have been investigated for some 30 years [4]. These models and languages have been used in many applications using a wide spectrum of data (e.g., biology, social network and criminal investigation data), clearly indicating that the combination of visual analytics with graph query languages has become quite popular.

According to Wong et al. [5], one of the biggest challenges in visual analytics is *User-Driven Data Reduction* which calls for "*a flexible mechanism that users can easily control according to their data collection practices and analytical needs*" to reduce the amount of data [6]. This essentially entails an improvement of the visualization clarity and an escalation of data processing performances irrespective of the increasing complexity of the data over the years. To meet this challenge, semantic and structural abstraction techniques, such as clustering, collapsing, extraction and demonstration of relationships among graph entities can be used [7] at the expanse of a loss of information on the network content [8].

Dimension reduction is central to the visualization of data networks since it enables users to increase their insight into the data. The approach taken in the Collaboration Spotting project is to reduce the dimensional complexity of data networks while maintaining the information about their content. It consists in decomposing directed and labelled graphs into multiple directed and weighted graphs of lesser dimensions - named views - and in building an interactive graph query language that supports user-specified views and full navigation across the data networks using these views as a support to the operations of the language. Within a view, structural abstraction techniques can then be used to enhance the visual perception further. The novelty of the approach taken is to combine *Visual graph representation* and *User interactions* [9] at the graph query language level with a view to supporting interactive dimension reduction based on the concept of blueprint where the architectural plan is distributed across different navigable views. In this context, users can select and combine labels according to their semantic understanding of the network models and visualize the corresponding network structures.

Section II gives a short overview on visualisation techniques for visual analytics (focusing on social networks) and on graph query languages fit to data networks. Section III gives a short description of the mathematical background supporting the approach. Section IV, introduces how views are constructed and Section V shows how the basic operations of the query language enable users to conduct their analysis. In Section VI, the use-case that inspired the Collaboration Spotting project and the graphical query language are presented. This paper ends with conclusions and future work in Section VII.

II. Related Work

The related work is twofold since it combines multiple visual analytics techniques with the power of graph query languages. In the last 15 years, a lot of visual analytics articles were published with the aim of showing processes of transformation of multidimensional data into node-link diagrams [9][10].

A lot of articles have been published, especially on the *coordinated multiple views* topic, which introduces a visual analytics paradigm supported by an interactive query language or by a set of operations. These articles can be divided into four different groups:

- OLAP [11] inspired paradigms that are using operations like *slice*, *roll-up*, *dice*, etc. The most relevant papers are PivotGraph [12], ScatterDice [13], GraphDice [14], MatrixCube [15] and Orion [16].

- Relational algebra-related solutions such as Cross-filter views [17] which uses *grouping*, *filtering*, *projection* and *selection* operations. Polaris [18] that introduces and maps its algebra to SQL and Ploceus [19], which works with first-order logic language.
- Other solutions such as Cross-filter views with hyper-graph query language [20], JUNG [21] and Gephi [22] that allow users to use other programming languages (JAVA in these cases).
- Literature on graph query languages is huge [23]–[30]. It covers the use of different graph models reflecting the variety of requirements for applications and languages.

The visual analytics model introduced in this paper promotes a different approach to graph query language. The language operates on a directed, labelled graph that is managed via user interactions treated as query inputs and follows the semantic web query language concepts, SPARQL [31] and Cypher [32][33]. This approach allows users to generate graph patterns and evaluate them directly on the graph. Reducing the complexity of network is not a novel idea [34]. The main differences between existing solutions and the one proposed in this paper are i) the introduction of a proper mathematical model based on labelled graphs; ii) a label-based complexity reduction (views); iii) basic operations to support navigation across views and iv) an intuitive user interface to drive these operations.

III. Basic Graph and Views

Let graph G be a directed, labelled graph defined as a four-element tuple $G = (V, E, L, \alpha)$ where V represents a set of nodes and $E \subseteq V \times V$, a set of edges defined as a subset of the Cartesian products of these nodes. L is a set of node labels and $\alpha : V \to L$ is a mapping function from nodes to the corresponding labels. Figure 1 shows an example of such a graph. We define the reachability graph over graph G as

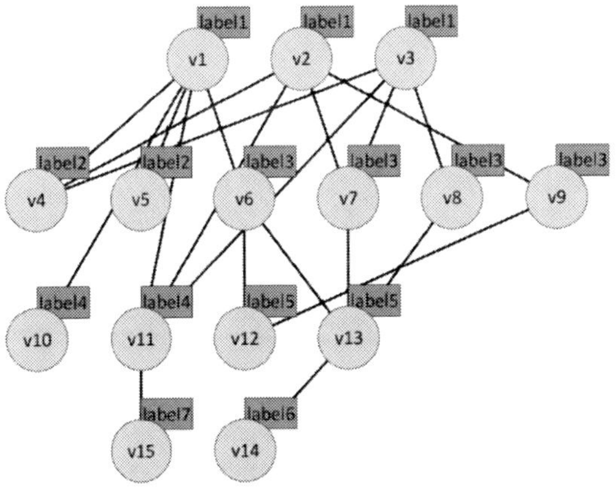

Figure 1. Example of graph G where $V = \{v1, \dots v15\}$ and $L = \{label1, \dots label7\}$

$G_{reachability} = (L, E_{reachability})$ where nodes are labels of graph G, $E_{reachability} \subseteq L \times L$ is defined as the Cartesian product of the labels where any two nodes of $G_{reachability}$ are connected if and only if there exists two connected nodes in graph G and their respective labels correspond to the two nodes of graph $G_{reachability}$. Graph $G_{reachability}$ is a description of graph G, it is also called the graph schema of graph G. Graph schema helps users view graph G via different sub-graphs of lesser dimensionality using labels of G as dimensions and facilitates the generation of approximately optimal user-defined graph queries. Let graph $G_{pattern} = (V_{pattern}, E_{pattern})$ be a graph pattern where $V_{pattern} \subseteq L$ and $E_{pattern} \subseteq E_{reachability} \cap V_{pattern} \times V_{pattern}$. To process the answer to a graph query, one needs to find all possible isomorphic subgraphs of G that are homomorphic to a graph pattern $G_{pattern}$ corresponding to the query. This is a graph pattern matching problem, a well-known part of Mathematics [35]. In this case, one defines Graph $G' = (V', E', L, \alpha)$, a subgraph of graph G as a sample matching the graph pattern $G_{pattern}$ if and only if:

- $\forall v' \in V' : \exists v \in V_{pattern}, \alpha(v') = v$,
- $\forall (u', v') \in E' : (\alpha(u'), \alpha(v')) \in E_{pattern}$.

The answer to a graph query is a view containing the set of subgraphs of G matching $G_{pattern}$. To build such a view, one needs first to introduce the graph pairing function $pair$ and the set $Pattern$. Let $G_{pattern_1}$ and $G_{pattern_2}$ be two graph patterns. These graph patterns are paired iff

- $V_{pattern_1} = V_{pattern_2}$ and
- $\exists! a, b \in V_{pattern_1}$:
  path(a,b) $\in E_{pattern_1}$ and path(a,b) $\notin E_{pattern_2}$,
  path(b,a) $\notin E_{pattern_1}$ and path(b,a) $\in E_{pattern_2}$,
  $E_{pattern_1} \setminus$ path(a,b) $= E_{pattern_2} \setminus$ path(b,a).

Where a path is an alternate non-empty sequence of nodes and edges, starting and ending with nodes and requiring that all edges and nodes be distinct from one another. path(a,b) $\in E_{pattern_1}$ indicates that all edges of this path are in set $E_{pattern_1}$. The $pair$ function is defined as

$$pair(G_{pattern}) := \begin{cases} G^{pair}_{pattern} & \text{if } G^{pair}_{pattern} \text{ pair of } G_{pattern} \\ (\emptyset, \emptyset) & \text{else.} \end{cases}$$

And $Pattern$, the set of these pairs is defined as $Pattern := \{(g, g') | g, g' \text{are patterns}, g' = pair(g)\}$.

A view of graph G is defined as a six-element tuple $G_q = (C_q, B_q, E_q, L_q, \epsilon_q, v_q,)$ where

- $C_q \subset V, L_C := \{\alpha(v) | v \in C_q\}$,
- $B_q \subset V, L_B := \{\alpha(b) | b \in B_q\}$,
- $L_q \subseteq L$ and $L_q = L_C \cup L_B$,
- $E_q := \{(u, v) |$
  $u, v \in C_q, \exists G', G'' \subseteq G,$
  $\exists (G_{pattern}, pair(G_{pattern})),$
  $(G'_{pattern}, pair(G'_{pattern})) \in$ *Patterns* :
  G' *matches to* $G_{pattern}$,
  G'' *matches to* $pair(G'_{pattern})$,
  $\exists b \in B_q$: path$(u, b) \in G'$, path$(b, v) \in G''\}$,
- $\epsilon_q : E_q \to \mathcal{P}(B_q), \epsilon_q((u, v)) = \{b |$
  $b \in B_q, \exists G', G'' \subseteq G,$
  $\exists (G_{pattern}, pair(G_{pattern})),$
  $(G'_{pattern}, pair(G'_{pattern})) \in$ *Patterns* :
  G' *matches to* $G_{pattern}$,
  G'' *matches to* $pair(G'_{pattern})$,
  path$(u, b) \in G'$, path$(b, v) \in G''\}$,

- $v_q : C_q \rightarrow \mathcal{P}(B_q), v_q(u) = \{b | b \in B_q, \exists G' \subseteq G, \exists (G_{pattern}, pair(G_{pattern})) \in Patterns : G' \text{ matches to } G_{pattern}, \text{path}(u, b) \in G'\}$.

The use of multiple graph patterns for the construction of graph G_q is required since the cardinality of set L_B and set L_C are not necessary equal to 1 (see details in Section IV-A). To ease the reading, graph G_q is noted $G_{L_B}^{L_C}$ to refer directly to the set of labels used in the construction of the view. Also, in practice, we use an aggregation function on edges, respectively on nodes in graph G_q for determining their respective weights instead of the elements in set B_q (for instance, the number of elements). Figure 2 shows an example of a view when the two graph patterns are $G_{pattern} = (\{label1, label3\}, \{(label1, label3)\})$ and pair$(G'_{pattern}) = (\{label1, label3\}, \{(label3, label1)\})$.

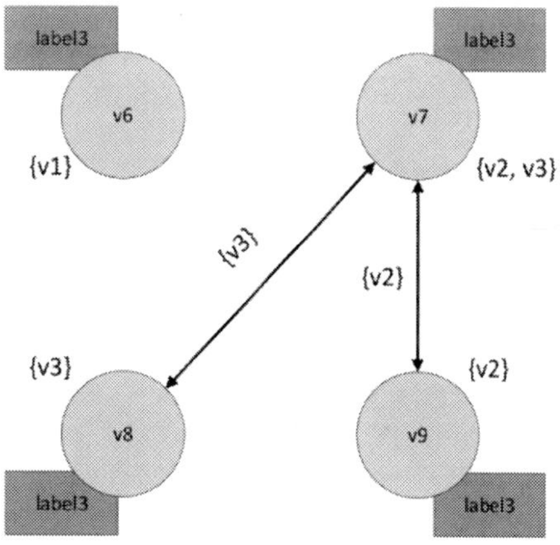

Figure 2. Example of a view where $C_q = \{v6, \ldots, v9\}$, $B_q = \{v1, \ldots, v3\}$, $L_C = \{label3\}$, $L_B = \{label1\}$.

IV. Graph Creation from User Interactions

In this section, we introduce how graph patterns and views can be created as a result of the following user interactions:

- Selection of different nodes in the current view,
- Removal of all nodes with the same label selected in one of the previous views,
- Navigation from one view to another.

Users can modify set L_C and set L_B when performing any of the above interactions. Let $F \subseteq V$ be the set of nodes corresponding to a user selection, we define from F:

1) $L_F := \{l \in L | \exists f \in F : \alpha(f) = l\}$ which contains the labels of nodes in set F and,
2) $F_{|L^*} := \{f \in F | \alpha(f) \in L^*\}$ with $L^* \subseteq L$, a subset of set F, restricted to nodes having their respective labels in set L^*.

In order for set F to operate as a filter, the matched sample definition of Section III has to be restricted by requiring that $\forall v' \in V', \alpha(v') \in L_F \Rightarrow v' \in F$. Example 1 below shows the content of L_F for user selection $F = \{v_4, v_6, v_7, v_{13}\}$ from the graph G depicted in Figure 1.

Example 1.

$$F = \{v_4, v_6, v_7, v_{13}\} \quad (1)$$

$$L_F = \{label_2, label_3, label_5\} \quad (2)$$

A. Graph pattern construction

This section shows how to construct a graph pattern with set L_F containing all the labels of nodes in set F. We exploit the fact that graph patterns are actually only needed when constructing edges in $G_{L_B}^{L_C}$ and their respective weights. A pair of graph patterns are required for each combination of labels in set L_C and set L_B since paths connecting nodes from set L_C and set L_B can have different directions, due to the construction of edges between nodes of C_q and nodes of B_q. Each pattern has to satisfy the following criteria:

- It must be a connected and directed graph,
- It must be minimal,
- Labels from set $L \setminus L_F$ can be used as intermediate nodes in the pattern.

These requirements exactly fit a Steiner Minimal Tree problem [36], known to be NP-complete[37] and for which we use a minimal spanning tree solver as an approximation algorithm. Algorithm 3 describes the full process of pair generation. Figure 4 shows the graph schema of graph G depicted in Figure 1 and the generated patterns pair for $\{v_4, v_6, v_7, V_{13}\}$ as set F, with $L_C = \{label4\}$ and $L_B = \{label1\}$.

Algorithm 3 Pattern generator algorithm

function PatternGenerator(F_L, L_B, L_C)
  $Patterns \leftarrow \emptyset$
  $B \leftarrow L_B$
  while $B \neq \emptyset$ **do**
    $from, B \leftarrow from \in B, B \setminus \{from\}$
    $E \leftarrow L_C$
    while $E \neq \emptyset$ **do**
      $to, E \leftarrow to \in E, E \setminus \{to\}$
      $Left \leftarrow SpanningTree(F_L \cup \{from, to\}, from, to)$
      $Right \leftarrow SpanningTree(F_L \cup \{from, to\}, to, from)$
      $Patterns \leftarrow Patterns \cup \{(Left, Right)\}$
    end while
  end while
  return $Patterns$
end function

B. Connecting user interactions and views

Now that graph patterns ($Patterns$) have been created using set F, set L_C and set L_B, one can introduce the gen function $gen : \mathcal{P}(V) \times \mathcal{P}(L) \times \mathcal{P}(L) \rightarrow G_{L_B}^{L_C}$ that generates views from user interactions, ($F \subseteq \mathcal{P}(V)$ and $L_C, L_B \subset \mathcal{P}(L)$) as $gen(F, L_C, L_B) := {}^F G_{L_B}^{L_C} = ({}^F C_q, {}^F B_q, E_q, L_q, v_q, \epsilon_q)$ where

$${}^F C_q := \begin{cases} V \cap F_{|L_C} & \text{if } V \cap F_{|L_C} \neq \emptyset \\ V_{|L_C} & \text{else} \end{cases}$$

are the nodes of graph ${}^F G_{L_B}^{L_C}$ and

$${}^F B_q := \left\{ b \in V'_{|L_B} \;\middle|\; \begin{array}{l} \exists G' = (V', E', L, \alpha) \subseteq G, : \\ G' \text{ matches to } G_{pattern}, \forall v' \in V' : \\ (v' \in F \text{ or } \alpha(v') \notin L_F) \end{array} \right.$$

are the "interconnection" nodes: The other members of the six-tuple G_q are unchanged since

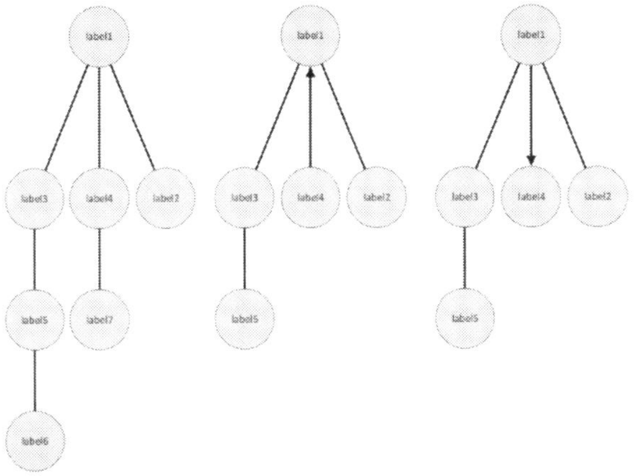

Figure 4. On the left hand-side, the graph schema of graph G; On the middle and on the right hand-side, an example of a graph pattern pair.

- labels (set L_q) are not modified and since
- edge definition (set E_q) and weighting functions (v_q and ϵ_q) only depend on set ${}^F C_q$ and set ${}^F B_q$.

V. Operations on Graphs

User interactions will result in the following graph operations:

- *Selection*: The user selects nodes in a view,
- *Expansion*: The user expands a view by removing in his previous selection, nodes having the same labels,
- *Navigation*: The user navigates from a view to another.

To define these operations one needs first to introduce the concepts of visual equivalence and minimal views since there can be views with nodes of null weight that are hidden to the user and hence non-selectable. Let F_1 and F_2 be two different filters on the same view complying with $F_1 \setminus F_{1|L_C} = F_2 \setminus F_{2|L_C}$. In essence, this means that there is no difference in the sets of nodes with labels contained in $L \setminus L_C$ which technically should be empty. View ${}^{F_1}G^{L_C}_{L_B}$ and view ${}^{F_2}G^{L_C}_{L_B}$ generated using F1 and F2 are said to be visual equivalent if and only if

Definition 1. *(Vis-equivalent)*

$${}^{F_1}G^{L_C}_{L_B} \sim {}^{F_2}G^{L_C}_{L_B} \Leftrightarrow \begin{array}{l} \forall v \in V_1 \setminus V_2 : v_q(v) = \emptyset, \\ \forall v' \in V_2 \setminus V_1 : v_q(v') = \emptyset, \end{array}$$

where V_1 (V_2) represents the nodes of view ${}^{F_1}G^{L_C}_{L_B}$ (${}^{F_2}G^{L_C}_{L_B}$). Intuitively visual equivalence guaranties that nodes that are not common to two views have empty weights. It provides equivalence classification on views. It is easy to prove that for each class of views there is only one which does not have nodes with empty weights. This view is called the minimal view.

A. Selection on graphs

Let F_{select} be the set of user selected nodes within a view. $F_{select} \subseteq V$ and $F_{select} \subseteq V'$ where V' is a set of nodes from the minimal view which is visual-equivalent to graph ${}^F G^{L_C}_{L_B}$. The selection operator $\sigma : G_q \times \mathcal{P}(V) \to G_q$ is defined as

Definition 2. *(Selection)*

$$\sigma({}^F G^{L_C}_{L_B}, F_{select}) := gen((F \setminus F_{|L_C}) \cup F_{select}, L_C, L_B).$$

where $F_{|L_C} = \{f | f \in F, \alpha(f) \in L_C\}$. It is to be noted that at view creation the selection operator uses a more general definition of the gen function. Figure 6a and 6b show how the selection operator works. As a result of applying this operator, set L_C and L_B will only contain those nodes that are "related" to this user selection.

B. Expansion on graphs

The expansion operator ξ is in some sense the "inverse" of the selection operator. It is defined as

Definition 3. *(Expansion)*

$$\xi({}^F G^{L_C}_{L_B}, L_{C'}) := gen(F \setminus F_{|L_{C'}}, L_{C'}, L_B).$$

The expansion operator changes view when $L_{C'} \neq L_C$ and removes all nodes in set F that are labelled with labels in L_C. Figure 6d and 6e show how the expansion operator works.

C. Navigation through graphs

By selecting a subset of labels from L_C one can build views of graph G with reduced dimensional complexity. Navigation across views is required to enable users to apprehend the full graph G. Therefore the navigation function η goes from view ${}^F G^{L_C}_{L_B}$ to a view labelled as $L_{C'}$ and $L_{B'}$ and is defined as:

Definition 4. *(Navigation)*

$$\eta({}^F G^{L_C}_{L_B}, L_{C'}, L_{B'}) := gen(F, L_{C'}, L_{B'})$$

Figure 6b and 6c show how the navigation between views works.

D. Navigation history

The navigation history can be represented as a navigation graph G_{nav} where nodes represent navigation states and edges navigation steps between states. $G_{nav} = (N_{nav}, E_{nav})$ complies to

- $N_{nav} \subset \mathcal{P}(V) \times \mathcal{P}(L) \times \mathcal{P}(L)$,
- $E_{nav} \subseteq N_{nav} \times N_{nav} \times \{\sigma, \xi, \eta\}$,

where there is a navigation step between node $n_1 = (F_1, L_{C_1}, L_{B_1})$ to node $n_2 = (F_2, L_{C_2}, L_{B_2})$ if and only if one of the following statements is true:

1) $\sigma(gen(F_1, L_{C_1}, L_{B_1}), F_2 \setminus F_1) = gen(F_2, L_{C_2}, L_{B_2})$, and $L_{C_1} = L_{C_2}, L_{B_1} = L_{B_2}$;
2) $\xi(gen(F_1, L_{C_1}, L_{B_1}), L_{C_2}) = gen(F_2, L_{C_2}, L_{B_2})$, and $F_2 = F_1 \setminus F_{1|L_{C_2}}, L_{B_1} = L_{B_2}$;
3) $\eta(gen(F_1, L_{C_1}, L_{B_1}), L_{C_2}, L_{B_2}) = gen(F_2, L_{C_2}, L_{B_2})$ and $F_1 = F_2$.

In E_{nav}, the third component of an edge is always one of the operations σ, ξ or η. It indicates how the step was processed. The proper size of N_{nav} is $2^n * (3^m - 2^{m+1} + 1)$ where $n = |V|$ and $m = |L|$. A particular navigation history corresponds to a walk in G_{nav}. An example of such a walk is given below.

Example 2 (Walk on graph).

$(F_0, L_{C_0}, L_{B_0}), \eta, (F_1, L_{C_1}, L_{B_1}), \sigma, \ldots, \xi, (F_f, L_{C_v}, L_{B_b})$

In practice, a particular set of labels L_{C_0} is used to create an entry view from which all the above mentioned operations can then be performed.

VI. USE-CASE

In the framework of AIDA [38], an FP7 project on Advanced European Infrastructures for Detectors at Accelerators, researchers needed to identify key players from academia and industry for technologies considered as strategic for the particle physics programme. To this end, the Collaboration Spotting project was launched in 2012 with a view to enabling users to search for terms describing particular technologies in titles and abstracts of publications and patents and viewing the organisation, subject category, keywords, city and country landscapes for each of these searches individually. Individual technology searches are represented as nodes in a view named Technogram, used as the user entry view in which edges represent publications and/or patents common to searches.

A. Data

Two different sources are used for searching. The metadata records of publications from Web of Science^{TM} Core Collection [39] developed by Clarivate Analytics (in the past, Thomson Reuters) and the metadata records of patents from PATSTAT developed by the European Patent Office [40]. Although the two sources have a number of labels in common, such as *Organisation*, *City* and *Country* there are others like *Subject Category* and *Keyword* that only belong to publications. The subset of data from the two sources corresponding to the labels of interest for users was used to construct graph G and its schema $G_{reachability}$.

B. Storing data in a graph database (Neo4j)

Graph G is stored in a Neo4j graph database [41], in which individual metadata records are stored as subgraphs of labelled nodes using *Published item, Organisation, Subject Category, Author Keyword, City, Region* and *Country* as labels. Figure 5 represents the reachability graph (graph schema) of this network (Light color nodes represent nodes uploaded by the data administrator and the dark nodes are created by the system itself by using search and authentication modules). Besides these labels, additional labels have been introduced to support user authentication and authorisation (*User*) and technology searches (*Graph* and *Technology*). Searches use full text indices of the Apache Lucene project [42] that have been integrated into the Neo4j database as legacy indices [41].

Statistic of the graph data: Searches on publications and patents metadata records from the 2000 - 2014 period can be performed. The resulting data network contains 45 million nodes and 150 million edges. Its breakdown is given in Table I. and Table II.

As can be noticed, the number of region edges is smaller than the number of country edges due to the use of the 2nd level of Nomenclature of Territorial Units For Statistic [43] created by the European Commission, which covers Europe only.

C. Navigation

The entry point for this use case is individual users. Using the terminology introduced above, the initial values for set F are user IDs.

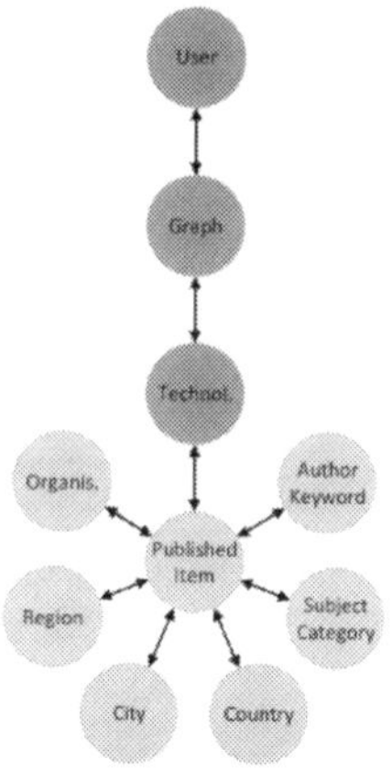

Figure 5. The database schema (reachability graph)

TABLE I. NUMBER OF NODES BY NODE LABELS

TYPE OF NODES	NUMBER OF NODES
Patents	15.000.442
Publications	20.087.904
Organisations	2.918.060
Author Keywords	8.193.604
Subject Categories	230
Cities	7.741
Regions	946
Countries	128
Total	46.209.055

TABLE II. NUMBER OF EDGES BY NODE LABELS. A PATENT DOES NOT HAVE AUTHOR KEYWORDS OR SUBJECT CATEGORIES PROPERTY

	PATENTS	PUBLICATIONS	TOTAL
Organ.	12.440.903	36.672.677	49.113.580
Author Key.	-	48.941.098	48.941.098
Subject Cat.	-	32.566.806	32.566.806
Cities	3.193.709	8.826.222	12.019.931
Regions	265.421	2.504.441	2.769.862
Count.	3.156.449	8.020.648	11.177.097
Total	19.056.482	137.531.892	156.588.374

Limitations: In the current implementation there is a restriction on the size of L_C and L_B fixed to a single label *Published Item* and the visualization system only supports undirected edges. This calls for the generation of only one graph pattern instead of two making the system faster.

In Figure 6, a series of pictures illustrate how navigation operations work. A user enters the system in a technology view (nodes are labelled with the *Technology* label). In the example, this view contains four "technologies" (obtained as results of searches using Lucene-indices), namely *Database, Language, Graph Language* and *Visual Analytics*. Links between nodes indicate publications and patents common to technology searches. As indicated in the reachability graph of Figure 5, users can access other views via nodes labelled with the *Published Item* label. The user selects two *technology* nodes from Figure 6a, giving F_{select} ={*Visual Analytics, Language*}. Figure 6b shows the result of this selection: *Language* and

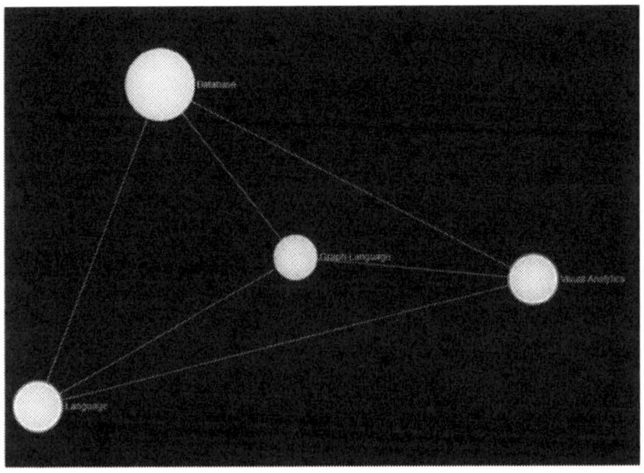

(a) Technology view: ($L_C = \{Technology\}$, $L_B = \{Published\ Item\}$); Selecting two technologies ($F_{select} = \{Visual\ Analytics, Language\}$)

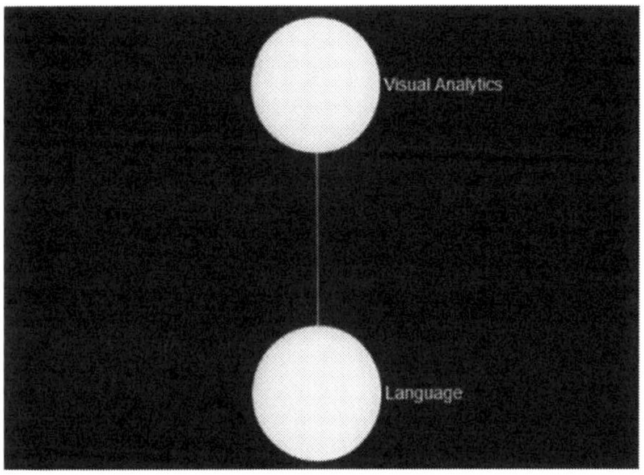

(b) Result of the selection

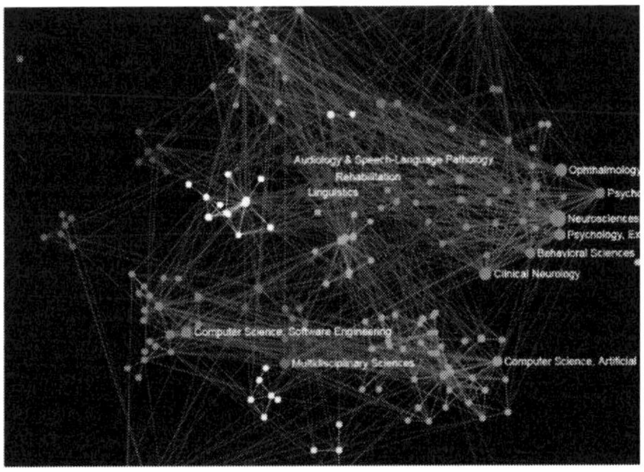

(c) Navigation to the "Subject Category view"

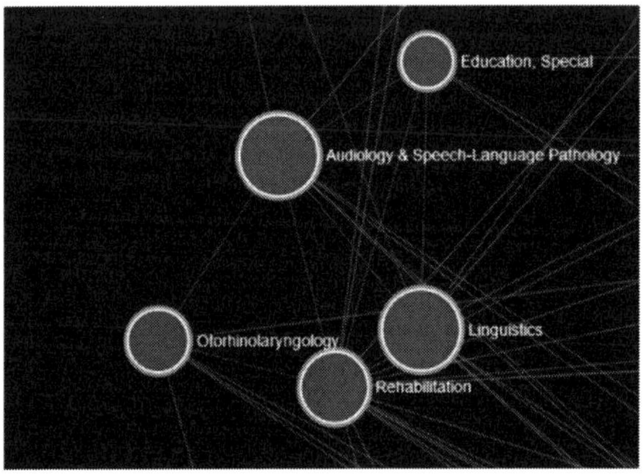

(d) Selecting a cluster in the Subject Category view; expanding the view and going back to the Technology view

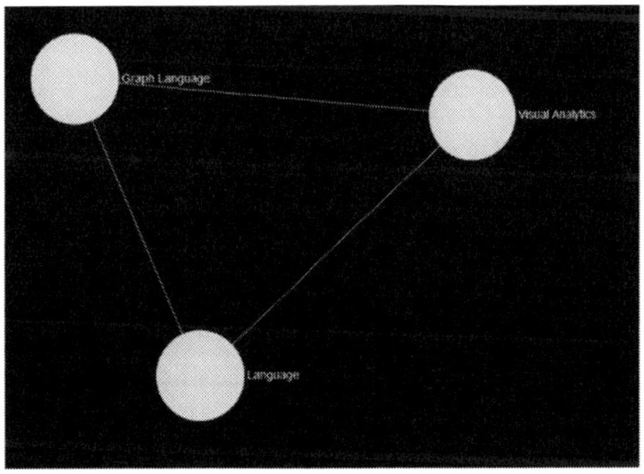

(e) Technology view with $F = \{Language, Linguistics \ldots Rehabilitation\}$ filter

Figure 6. Example of operations; navigation, selection and expansion on views

Visual Analytics. Changing set L_C from value $\{Technology\}$ to value $\{Subject\ Category\}$ enables the navigation operation to reach the *Subject Category* view corresponding to the two previously selected *technology* nodes. Figure 6c shows the view resulting from this operation. It is optained using the (L_C = {*Subject Category*}, L_B = {*Published Item*}, F = {*Language, Visual Analytics*}) triplet. In Figure 6d, the user selects a few nodes from the view of Figure 6c (i.e., the F filter was extended with *Linguistic, ...,* values). After selection of the value {*Technology*} for L_C, the expansion and navigation operations bring the user back to the *technology* view of Figure 6e. This view shows the *technology* nodes having publications with nodes labelled with the *Subject Category* label corresponding to the last user selection.

VII. Conclusion and Future Work

The current version of Collaboration Spotting running at CERN [44] addresses the implementation of the concepts using patents and publications metadata records. It is a new experimental service that aims to provide the High Energy Physics community (such as HEPTech [45]) with information on Academia & Industry main players active around key technologies, with a view to fostering more inter-disciplinary and inter-sectoral R&D collaborations, and giving the procurement service the opportunity of reaching a wider selection of high-tech companies for bidding purposes. Collaboration Spotting is generic in its concepts and implementation. It can support visual analytics of any kind of data and its backend is implemented using a Neo4j graph database [41]. Conference papers, technical & business news, trademarks & designs and financial data are amongst the data targeted to enrich the information on technologies that one can obtain from publications and patents. The choice of data sources will depend on users' priorities. The tool can be of use to other communities, in particular in dentistry [46] but also to policy makers and investors if data in the knowledge graph is enriched with technical & business news and financial data. Collaboration Spotting also addresses other types of data, such as compatibility and dependency relationships in software and meta-data [47][48] of the LHCb experiment at CERN.

As an interactive graph query language, Collaboration Spotting is intended to provide a fully customisable visual analytics environment. In the current version, data processing supports searches and contextual queries. In the future, labelled & directed relationships and attributes on nodes will be included in the labelled property graph representation of the data network and the processing will be extended to more complex operations directly on the graph resulting from searches and queries with a view to enhancing the visual perception of users.

Acknowledgment

We are very thankful to Richard Forster, Sotiris Fragkiskos, Tim Hertweck, Nikos Kasfikis, Xavier Ouvrard and Eirik Skogstad from CERN for their hard work in implementing the first prototypes of Collaboration Spotting. We are also thankful to Bernard Denis from CERN and Emanuele Leonardi from INFN who provided very valuable feedback when testing the early version of the tool; Thierry Lagrange from CERN for ensuing sufficient funding to support the development.

References

[1] P. C. Wong and J. Thomas, "Visual analytics," IEEE Comput. Graph. Appl., vol. 24, no. 5, pp. 20–21, Sep. 2004, ISSN 0272-1716, doi: 10.1109/MCG.2004.39.

[2] J. B. Kollat, P. M. Reed, and R. M. Maxwell, "Many-objective groundwater monitoring network design using bias-aware ensemble Kalman filtering, evolutionary optimization, and visual analytics," Water Resour. Res., vol. 47, no. 2, pp. 1:1–1:18, 2011, ISSN 1944-7973, doi: 10.1029/2010WR009194,, w02529.

[3] A. Scharl, A. Hubmann-Haidvogel, A. Weichselbraun, H. P. Lang, and M. Sabou, "Media watch on climate change – visual analytics for aggregating and managing environmental knowledge from online sources," in 2013 46th Hawaii Int. Conf. System Sciences, Jan 2013, pp. 955–964, ISSN 1530-1605, doi: 10.1109/HICSS.2013.398.

[4] P. T. Wood, "Query languages for graph databases," SIGMOD Rec., vol. 41, no. 1, pp. 50–60, Apr. 2012, ISSN 0163-5808, doi: 10.1145/2206869.2206879.

[5] P. C. Wong, H. W. Shen, C. R. Johnson, C. Chen, and R. B. Ross, "The top 10 challenges in extreme-scale visual analytics," IEEE Comput. Graph. Appl., vol. 32, no. 4, pp. 63–67, July 2012, ISSN 0272-1716, doi: 10.1109/MCG.2012.87.

[6] E. Namey, G. Guest, L. Thairu, and L. Johnson, "Data reduction techniques for large qualitative data sets," in Handbook for team-based qualitative research, vol. 2, pp. 137–161, ISBN 978-0-7591-1373-2.

[7] T. A. Davis and Y. Hu, "The university of Florida sparse matrix collection," ACM Trans. Math. Softw., vol. 38, no. 1, pp. 1:1–1:25, Dec. 2011, ISSN 0098-3500, doi: 10.1145/2049662.2049663.

[8] Z. Shen, K.-L. Ma, and T. Eliassi-Rad, "Visual analysis of large heterogeneous social networks by semantic and structural abstraction," IEEE Trans. Vis. Comput. Graphics, vol. 12, no. 6, pp. 1427–1439, Nov 2006, ISSN 1077-2626, doi: 10.1109/TVCG.2006.107.

[9] T. von Landesberger et al., "Visual analysis of large graphs: state-of-the-art and future research challenges," Comput. Graph. Forum, vol. 30, no. 6, pp. 1719–1749, 2011, ISSN 1467-8659, doi: 10.1111/j.1467-8659.2011.01898.x.

[10] J. Kehrer and H. Hauser, "Visualization and visual analysis of multi-faceted scientific data: A survey," IEEE Trans. Vis. Comput. Graphics, vol. 19, no. 3, pp. 495–513, March 2013, ISSN 1077-2626, doi: 10.1109/TVCG.2012.110.

[11] J. Gray et al., "Data Cube: A relational aggregation operator generalizing group-by, cross-tab, and sub-totals," Data Min. Knowl. Discov., vol. 1, no. 1, pp. 29–53, Mar 1997, ISSN 1573-756X, doi: 10.1023/A:1009726021843.

[12] M. Wattenberg, "Visual exploration of multivariate graphs," in Proc. SIGCHI Conf. Human Factors in Computing Systems, ser. CHI '06. New York, NY, USA: ACM, 2006, pp. 811–819, ISBN 1-59593-372-7, doi: 10.1145/1124772.1124891.

[13] N. Elmqvist, P. Dragicevic, and J. D. Fekete, "Rolling the dice: Multidimensional visual exploration using scatterplot matrix navigation," IEEE Trans. Vis. Comput. Graphics, vol. 14, no. 6, pp. 1539–1148, Nov 2008, ISSN 1077-2626, doi: 10.1109/TVCG.2008.153.

[14] A. Bezerianos, F. Chevalier, P. Dragicevic, N. Elmqvist, and J. D. Fekete, "Graphdice: A system for exploring multivariate social networks," in Proc. 12th Eurographics / IEEE - VGTC Conf. Vis., ser. EuroVis'10. Chichester, UK: The Eurographs Association and John Wiley & Sons, Ltd., 2010, pp. 863–872, doi: 10.1111/j.1467-8659.2009.01687.x.

[15] B. Bach, E. Pietriga, and J.-D. Fekete, "Visualizing dynamic networks with matrix cubes," in Proc. SIGCHI Conf. Human Factors in Computing Systems, ser. CHI '14. New York, NY, USA: ACM, 2014, pp. 877–886, ISBN 978-1-4503-2473-1, doi: 10.1145/2556288.2557010.

[16] J. Heer and A. Perer, "Orion: A system for modeling, transformation and visualization of multidimensional heterogeneous networks," Inf. Vis., vol. 13, no. 2, pp. 111–133, 2014, doi: 10.1177/1473871612462152.

[17] C. Weaver, "Cross-filtered views for multidimensional visual analysis," IEEE Trans. Vis. Comput. Graphics, vol. 16, no. 2, pp. 192–204, March 2010, ISSN 1077-2626, doi: 10.1109/TVCG.2009.94.

[18] C. Stolte, D. Tang, and P. Hanrahan, "Polaris: a system for query, analysis, and visualization of multidimensional relational databases," IEEE Trans. Vis. Comput. Graphics, vol. 8, no. 1, pp. 52–65, Jan 2002, ISSN 1077-2626, doi: 10.1109/2945.981851.

[19] Z. Liu, S. B. Navathe, and J. T. Stasko, "Network-based visual analysis of tabular data," in 2011 IEEE Conf. Visual Ana-

lytics Science and Technology (VAST), Oct 2011, pp. 41–50, doi: 10.1109/VAST.2011.6102440.

[20] R. Shadoan and C. Weaver, "Visual analysis of higher-order conjunctive relationships in multidimensional data using a hypergraph query system," IEEE Trans. Vis. Comput. Graphics, vol. 19, no. 12, pp. 2070–2079, Dec 2013, ISSN 1077-2626, doi: 10.1109/TVCG.2013.220.

[21] J. O'Madadhain, D. Fisher, S. White, and Y. Boey, "The JUNG (Java universal network/graph) framework," University of California, Irvine, California, 2003. [Online]. Available: http://jung.sourceforge.net/index.html 2018.04.03

[22] M. Bastian, S. Heymann, and M. Jacomy, "Gephi: an open source software for exploring and manipulating networks," 3rd Int. AAAI Conf. Weblogs and Social Media (ICWSM), vol. 8, pp. 361–362, 2009.

[23] J. Hidders and J. Paredaens, "Goal, a graph-based object and association language," in Adv. Database Systems: Implementations and Applications, J. Paredaens and L. Tenenbaum, Eds. Vienna: Springer Vienna, 1994, pp. 247–265, ISBN 978-3-7091-2704-9, doi: 10.1007/978-3-7091-2704-9_13.

[24] J. Paredaens, D. V. Gucht, J. V. den Bussche, and M. Gyssens, "A graph-oriented object database model," IEEE Trans. Knowl. Data Eng., vol. 6, pp. 572–586, 08 1994, ISSN 1041-4347, doi: 10.1109/69.298174.

[25] J. Hidders, "Typing graph-manipulation operations," in Database Theory — ICDT 2003, D. Calvanese, M. Lenzerini, and R. Motwani, Eds. Berlin, Heidelberg: Springer Berlin Heidelberg, 2003, pp. 394–409, ISBN 978-3-540-36285-2, doi: 10.1007/3-540-36285-1_26.

[26] R. H. Güting, "GraphDB: modeling and querying graphs in databases," in Proc. 20th Int. Conf. Very Large Data Bases, ser. VLDB '94. San Francisco, CA, USA: Morgan Kaufmann Publishers Inc., 1994, pp. 297–308, ISBN 1-55860-153-8.

[27] H. S. Kunii, "DBMS with graph data model for knowledge handling," in Proc. 1987 Fall Joint Computer Conf. Exploring Technology: Today and Tomorrow, ser. ACM '87. Los Alamitos, CA, USA: IEEE Computer Society Press, 1987, pp. 138–142, ISBN 0-8186-0811-0.

[28] P. Barceló Baeza, "Querying graph databases," in Proc. 32nd Symp. Principles of Database Systems, ser. PODS '13. New York, NY, USA: ACM, 2013, pp. 175–188, ISBN 978-1-4503-2066-5, doi: 10.1145/2463664.2465216.

[29] J. Paredaens, P. Peelman, and L. Tanca, "G-Log: a graph-based query language," IEEE Trans. Knowl. Data Eng., vol. 7, no. 3, pp. 436–453, Jun 1995, ISSN 1041-4347, doi: 10.1109/69.390249.

[30] J. Yang, S. Zhang, and W. Jin, "DELTA: indexing and querying multi-labeled graphs," in Proc. 20th ACM Int. Conf. Information and Knowledge Management, ser. CIKM '11. New York, NY, USA: ACM, 2011, pp. 1765–1774, ISBN 978-1-4503-0717-8, doi: 10.1145/2063576.2063832.

[31] S. Harris, A. Seaborne, and E. Prudhommeaux. (2013) Sparql 1.1 query language. [Online]. Available: https://www.w3.org/TR/sparql11-query/ 2018.04.03

[32] J. Webber, "A programmatic introduction to Neo4J," in Proc. of the 3rd Annual Conference on Systems, Programming, and Applications: Software for Humanity, ser. SPLASH '12. New York, NY, USA: ACM, 2012, pp. 217–218, ISBN 978-1-4503-1563-0, doi: 10.1145/2384716.2384777.

[33] Neo Technology. openCypher project. [Online]. Available: http://www.opencypher.org 2018.04.03

[34] R. M. Martins et al., "Multidimensional projections for visual analysis of social networks," Journal of Computer Science and Technology, vol. 27, no. 4, pp. 791–810, Jul 2012, ISSN 1860-4749, doi: 10.1007/s11390-012-1265-5.

[35] B. Gallagher, "Matching structure and semantics: A survey on graph-based pattern matching," AAAI Fall Symp. Capturing and Using Patterns for Evidence Detection, vol. 6, pp. 45–53, 2006.

[36] F. K. Hwang, D. S. Richards, and P. Winter, "Introduction," in The Steiner Tree Problem, ser. Annals of Discrete Mathematics. Elsevier, 1992, vol. 53, pp. 3–19, ISSN 0167-5060, doi: 10.1016/S0167-5060(08)70192-4.

[37] M. R. Garey, R. L. Graham, and D. S. Johnson, "The complexity of computing Steiner minimal trees," SIAM J. Appl. Math., vol. 32, no. 4, pp. 835–859, 1977, ISSN 0036-1399, doi: 10.1137/0132072.

[38] AIDA Collaboration. AIDA - website. [Online]. Available: http://aida2020.web.cern.ch/content/aida 2018.04.03

[39] Clarivate Analytics. Web of Science^{TM}. [Online]. Available: http://webofknowledge.com 2018.04.03

[40] European Patent Office. PATSTAT - worldwide patent statistical database. [Online]. Available: http://www.epo.org/searching-for-patents/business/patstat.html 2018.04.03

[41] Neo4j, The Neo4j manual, November 2015, Release 2.3.2. [Online]. Available: http://neo4j.com/docs/stable/index.html 2018.04.03

[42] Lucene^{TM}/Solr^{TM} Committers. Apache Lucene^{TM} Documentation. [Online]. Available: https://lucene.apache.org/core/documentation.html 2018.04.03

[43] European Commision. NUTS - Nomenclature of territorial units for statistics. [Online]. Available: http://ec.europa.eu/eurostat/web/nuts/overview 2018.04.03

[44] Collspotting Developerment Team. Collspotting. [Online]. Available: http://collspotting.web.cern.ch 2018.04.03

[45] HEPTech Collaboration. HEPTech - website. [Online]. Available: http://heptech.web.cern.ch 2018.04.03

[46] E. Leonardi, A. Agocs, S. Fragkiskos, N. Kasfikis, J. Le Goff, M. Cristalli, V. Luzzi, and A. Polimeni, "Collaboration spotting for dental science," Minerva Stomatologica, vol. 63, no. 9, pp. 295–306, Sep 2014.

[47] M. Cattaneo, M. Clemencic, and I. Shapoval, "LHCb software and conditions database cross-compatibility tracking system: A graph-theory approach," in 2012 IEEE Nuclear Science Symp. and Medical Imaging Conf. Record (NSS/MIC), Oct 2012, pp. 990–996, ISSN 1082-3654, doi: 10.1109/NSSMIC.2012.6551255.

[48] I. Shapoval, M. Clemencic, and M. Cattaneo, "ARIADNE: a tracking system for relationships in LHCb metadata," J. Phys. Conf. Ser., vol. 513, no. 4, pp. 1:1–1:7, 2014, 042039.

Interactive Search and Exploration of Entity-entity Relationships in a Huge Document Corpus

Andreas Schmidt[*†] and Steffen Scholz[*]
[*] Department of Computer Science and Business Information Systems,
Karlsruhe University of Applied Sciences
Karlsruhe, Germany
Email: andreas.schmidt@hs-karlsruhe.de
[†] Institute for Automation and Applied Informatics
Karlsruhe Institute of Technology
Karlsruhe, Germany
Email: andreas.schmidt@kit.edu, steffen.scholz@kit.edu

Abstract—**This paper presents an interactive tool developed for the search and exploration of named entities and their relationships. The tool sits on top of an entity-based search engine, which previously has extracted and indexed all entities from a potentially huge document corpus. Relatedness between different entities is calculated based on entity n-tuples in the document corpus. The relatedness measure between entities is calculated during indexing time, which makes the algorithm very fast and usable for interactive application. Furthermore, the user can search for entities and their relationships to other entities using an interactive auto-completion and suggestion service. Related entities can then be filtered further by a multi-prefix search as well as based on type restrictions from an existing classification taxonomy. Another powerful feature is the merging of multiple entities into a group which allows the extraction of entities related to this group. A graphical interface is proposed with an entity or entity group as a central point, surrounded by the most n-related entities, based on some restrictions formulated by the user.**

Keywords*–*Interactive graph; entity-based search engine; relationship exploration; graphical representation.

I. Introduction

A. Motivation

The advent of information-driven technologies has recently initiated massive document collections, the so-called Big Data, to exist and has enabled an exponentially growing demand for collecting as much relevant data as possible. Although these data collections can give access to rich knowledge, such a large scale of gathered information could technically preclude timely and effective data processing and hence be one of the main barriers to further growth and development of Big Data technology. This issue is not only restricted to general information, which can be obtained from the Web, but also applies to specific data in different fields [1] e.g., aviation, bank and security exchanges, medicine, engineering, and technology, and many others. This has motivated researchers to address such a challenging issue with the objective of advancing relevant computing technologies.

B. Problem

Processing a large collection of documents initially requires understanding the content of the documents. This is a process allowing the relevant entities or concepts (persons, cities, organizations, materials, diseases, etc.), and the way in which they are related to each other. Subsequently, and based on this step, further cognitive processes take place, which are mostly influenced by prior background knowledge of the human reader. Due to the huge amount of data, these steps cannot be done by a human for all documents available.

C. Solution

Having an automatic tool, which extracts the entities and their relationships, can give a first insight into a given document collection. With the emergence of Named Entity Recognition (NER) [2], Named Entity Disambiguation (NED) [3], and entity-based search engines [4] now exists reliable tools to help identify and extract entities from document collections. Also, complex concepts, consisting of multiple different entities can be extracted [5].

STICS [4], for example, is a search engine, which works on entities instead of on words. In particular, rather than building an inverted index from words, STICS identifies named entities in the text and uses these entities for building the index. Additionally, STICS performs the so-called disambiguation step [3], which identifies the correct meaning of the entity. As an example, consider the word "Paris", which could be the french capital, a greek deity, the biological name of a plan, or a blonde hotel heiress. The correct meaning can be extracted from the context, by looking for other entities in the surrounding. As a result of this entity recognition and disambiguation step, we have a clear picture of which entities occur at which places in the indexed documents.

The system presented in this paper, uses the previously mentioned technologies for identification and disambiguation of entities inside a document corpus and presents the entities and their relationships in an interactive graph, which ultimately allows the search and exploration of entities and their quantitative relationships to other entities of interest. It is worth emphasizing that in contrast to the large body of the relevant reported approaches in this field, this research study is not only focused on bilateral relationships, but it is extended to allow the acummulation of entities into groups and look for further related entities. For example, we can accumulate the entities "*Emmanuel Macron*" and "*Germany*" to form a group and find out which other entities are related to this group. Figure 1 illustrates a visual representation of the user interface, which

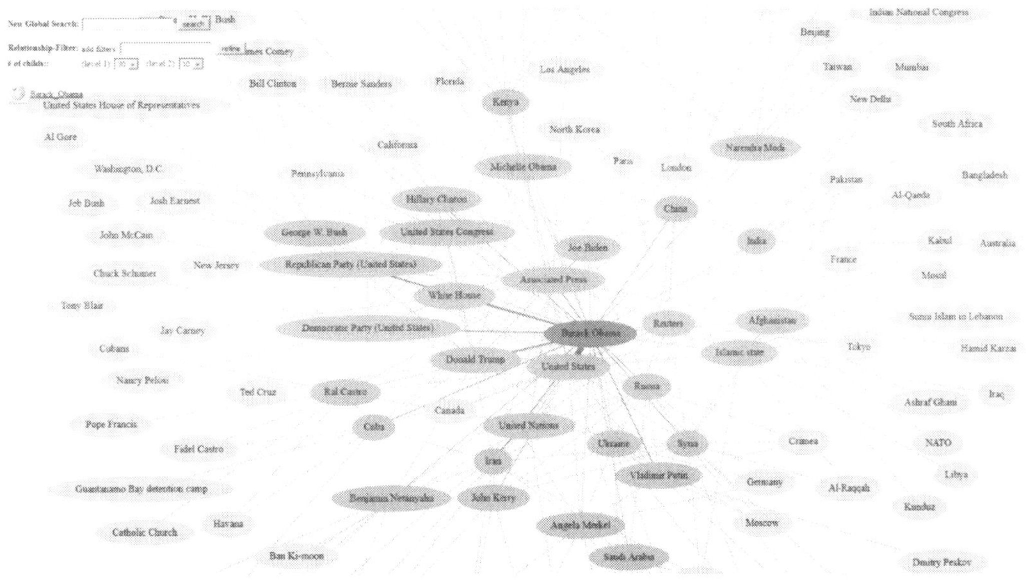

Figure 1. Screenshot of the graph-based interface.

allow navigation along entities and their relationships by just clicking on the nodes and edges.

The main contribution of this papers are the following: (1) Visual representation of the relationships of fully automatically extracted entities from a large document corpus. (2) Introduction of the concept of entity groups to formulate more complex concepts consisting of several entities and integrating them into the relationship graph.

The structure of the paper is as follows: In Section II we discuss what "relatedness" between entities mean. Then, in Section III we introduce the concept of our graph-based GUI. Section IV gives a short overview over related work and the last section finishs the paper with a conclusion and an outlook for further research avenues.

II. Relatedness Measure

The relatedness between two or more entities is based on the occurrence of the entities inside a sliding window of a predefined size. By shifting the window over the text of the documents, tuples, triples, and quadruples, along with other sequences of different entities can be extracted. The distance between different entities, as well as the number of times when a combination of entities appears inside the document corpus is used to calculate a co-occurrence measure. Please note that details about the exact calculation can be found in [6].

A. *Realtime Aspects*

Since the tool should allow of an interactive exploration, we need an adequate data structure to support our queries. Besides an inverted index for fast retrieval of entities, based on prefixes, the information about the co-occurrence measure must be provided. This is done by precalculating the co-occurrences of all possible combinations. Figure 2 shows the result of this process. Although, this sounds very expensive with respect to space requirements and computational effort, the number of combinations is much smaller than the theoretical maximum value, based on all possible combinations, which was already approved in [6]. Accordingly, one can argue that the chosen data structure can also be used for incremental updates.

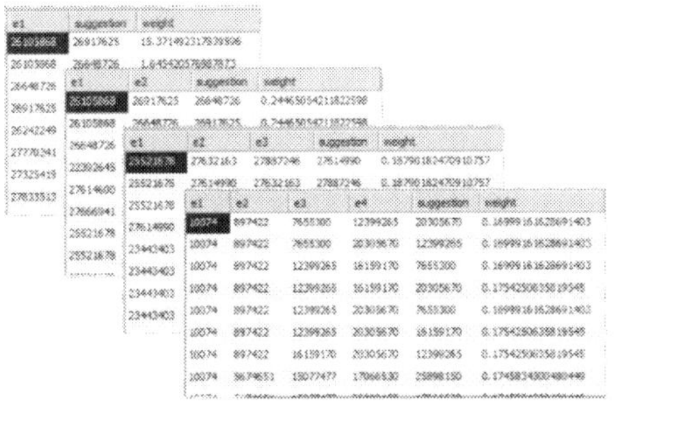

Figure 2. Precalculated materialized views for tuples, triples, quadruples and quintuples.

III. Interactive Exploration

A. *Search for Entities*

The starting point for an interactive exploration is the selection of an initial entity. To rapidly identify an entity or category, a multi-prefix search is implemented. The search is combined with an auto-suggestion mode, as shown in Figure 3. The disambiguation tool used to identify the entities in the text is AIDA [7], which itself utilizes YAGO [8] as a knowledge base. This means that about 4.3 million entities can be identified. Additionally, about 660 thousand categories are available, which can be selected also.

1) Entity Groups: An entity group is a combination of two and more entities. Semantically, when we search for related entities of an entity group, the combination of all entities in the entity group and a further related entity appear at least

Figure 3. Auto-Suggestion, based on multiple prefixes.

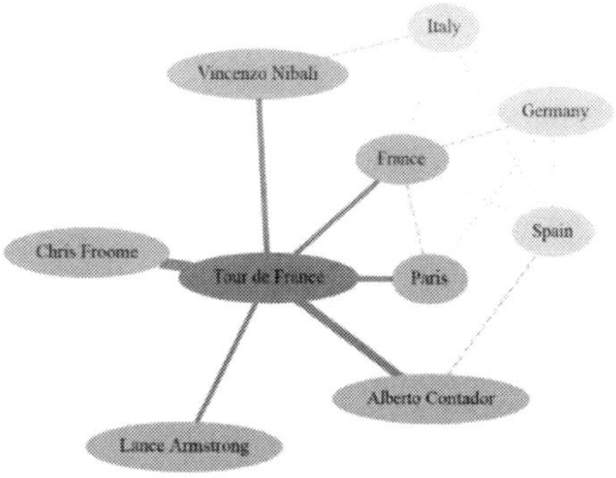

Figure 4. Tour de France with most related entities.

somewhere in the document corpus within k-words. (k represents the window size from Section II). The maximum number of entities in a group is only limited by the precalculation step, where we collect n-tuples of entities. For a given n, groups up to $n-1$ entities can be build. A meaningful value of n depends on the window size. The smaller the window size, the smaller n is, since only a limited number of entities appear within a certain window size. In our current setting the maximum number of entities in a group is 4.

2) Category Taxonomy: Every entity belongs to one or more categories. In our system we use a modified version of the Wikipedia categories. In contrast to the original category system, our approach encompasses a proper tree, where the categories are used to filter related entities.

B. Navigation

After having been chosen, the entity is displayed as a central node in a graph (shown in red). Figure 4 shows this situation around the central entity *Tour de France*. Grouped entities around (shown in dark blue), are the most related n-entities, where n is a choosable parameter between 5 and 50. The widths of the red edges represent the strengths of the relationships. Optionally, a percentile value along the edge, can quantify the relative strength of the relationship compared to the other related entities. In addition, for each of the related entities, another m-entities (light blue) can be displayed (m choosable between 0 and 5). This offers additional information about the context of the central entity.

Hence, you can select every entity in the graph as a next central entity, by simply clicking on it. Alternatively, you can click onto one of the edges, which merges the two related entities into a group and makes them the next central node in the graph. Figure 5 shows the result, after clicking on the edge

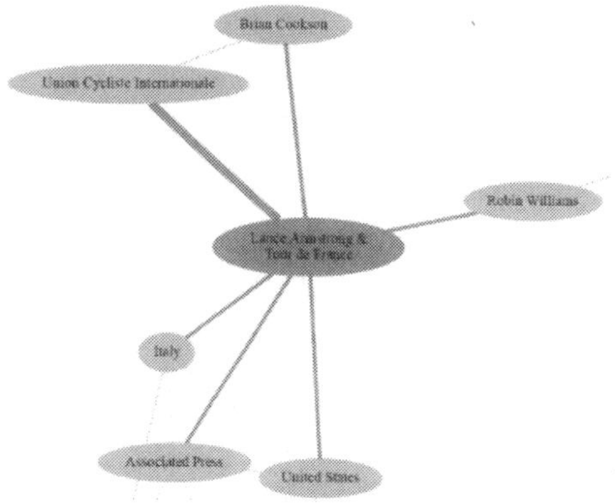

Figure 5. *Tour de France* & *Lance Armstrong* as entity group.

between the entities "*Tour de France*" and "*Lance Armstrong*", merging them into a single node and showing entities around, which are most related to the combination of these two entities.

C. Entity & Type Suggestions

A graph can also be refined, by applying filters to the related entities. Hence, for example, if we want to know which are the most famous passes along the route through France, we start entering the prefix "col" (French word for "pass") in the relationship filter field. While typing, all entities and categories, matching the prefix (or prefixes) are diplayed, making it easy to select the right one or further restrict the actual selection. It must be noted that only entities and categories, which actually are related to the central entity (here: *Tour de France*) are displayed and, thus, no suggestion would lead to a non-existing relationship. Additionally, the order of the entities and categories is context-sensitive to the specified central entity starting with the most relevant entity and category. Figure 6 shows the situation after the three characters "col" have been typed. In this situation, possible related entities, as well as categories are displayed.

At this point, there are three possibilities:

1) If we find a prefix or combination of prefixes covering all relevant entities (i.e., a family name) we can simply press the `refine` button and only the displayed entities will be considered in the graph.
2) Alternatively, we can select a category on the right, so that only entities, which fall into this category (also transitively) are selected. This feature can be applied multiple times.
3) The third option we have is selecting an entity from the left side of the selection box. In this case, the selected entity is added to the actual central entity or entity group and forms an entity group with it. This is the same as clicking on the edge between two entities or an entity and an entity group.

If the user is not interested in entities and categories matching a given prefix but wants to see all possible entities and categories, he simply has to type the asterisk symbol '*' into the search field. Figure 7 shows an extraction of the suggested entities and categories sorted by their relevance. In this way, one can find all related entities, and not only fifty most, as shown in the graph.

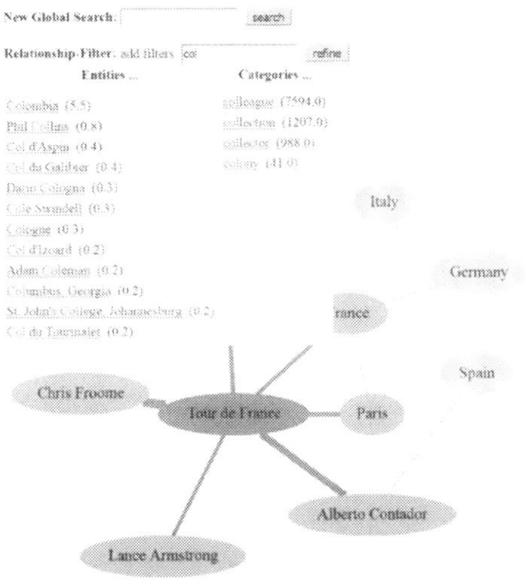

Figure 6. Entity *Tour de France* with related entities and categories, satisfying the given prefixes `col`.

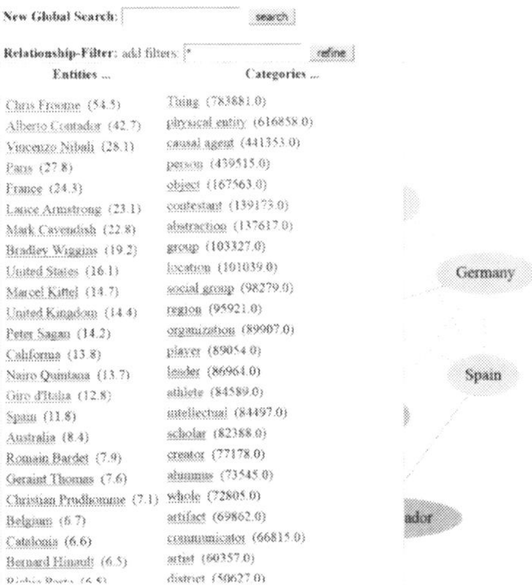

Figure 7. All possible (related) entities and categories for entity *Tour de France*, sorted by their relevance.

IV. Related Work

Our work is comparable with previous works in the field of entity recommendation, particularly which what is reported by Bi et al. [9]. Unlike what was described for our method, the related entities came from a knowledge graph and the click behavior of a user. In our approach, the knowledge is extracted from a document corpus. Schmidt et al. [10] have published a related work where related entities matching a prefix are suggested in the search interface to speed up query formulation (context-sensitive suggestions). This work, on the contrary, explicitly shows relations between entities in a graphical and navigational manner. Indeed, the data structures used are partly the same.

V. Conclusion and Further Work

The paper reported on a system for identifying and analyzing entities and their relationships. The system enables navigation along entity relationships as well as filtering relationships based on prefixes and/or categories. However, calculating the relationships at indexing time makes our system usable for interactive exploration of hidden relationships in a given document corpus. The relationships are automatically extracted from a given text corpus. The system not only considers bidirectional relationships, but also relationships between more entities (the so-called entity groups).

For further work, we intend to extend our interface, so that the documents most relevant to an entity or entity group can be inspected along with the parts of the documents, providing the most needed boost for that entity or entity type. The same can be implemented considering the edges of the graph, which represent the relationships between entities (entity groups).

Our approach of representing the most relevant entities and relationships can be applied to single documents rather than to multiple documents, by simply building a relationship graph for a single document (containing the m most relevant entities and relationships). This graph can potentially be used as a filter for searching for similar documents. In the case presented, the similarity of graphs [11] has to be computed.

References

[1] S. Seufert, K. Berberich, S. J. Bedathur, S. K. Kondreddi, P. Ernst, and G. Weikum, "Espresso: Explaining relationships between entity sets," in Proceedings of the 25th ACM International Conference on Information and Knowledge Management (CIKM'16), 2016, pp. 1311–1320.

[2] J. R. Finkel, T. Grenager, and C. Manning, "Incorporating non-local information into information extraction systems by gibbs sampling," in Proceedings of the 43rd Annual Meeting on Association for Computational Linguistics, ser. ACL '05. Stroudsburg, PA, USA: Association for Computational Linguistics, 2005, pp. 363–370.

[3] J. Hoffart, "Discovering and disambiguating named entities in text," Ph.D. dissertation, Universität des Saarlandes, Saarbrücken, 2015.

[4] J. Hoffart, D. Milchevski, and G. Weikum, "STICS: searching with strings, things, and cats," in SIGIR 2014, 2014, pp. 1247–1248.

[5] A. Schmidt, D. Kimmig, and M. Dickerhof, "Search and graphical visualization of concepts in document collections using taxonomies," in HICSS 2013, 2013, pp. 1429–1434.

[6] A. Schmidt and S. Scholz, "Quantitative considerations about the semantic relationship of entities in a document corpus," in HICSS 2018, 2018, pp. 933–942.

[7] M. A. Yosef, J. Hoffart, I. Bordino, M. Spaniol, and G. Weikum, "AIDA: an online tool for accurate disambiguation of named entities in text and tables," PVLDB, vol. 4, no. 12, 2011, pp. 1450–1453.

[8] F. M. Suchanek, G. Kasneci, and G. Weikum, "Yago: A core of semantic knowledge," in WWW 2007, 2007, pp. 697–706.

[9] B. Bi, H. Ma, B. P. Hsu, W. Chu, K. Wang, and J. Cho, "Learning to recommend related entities to search users," in WSDM 2015, 2015, pp. 139–148.

[10] A. Schmidt, J. Hoffart, D. Milchevski, and G. Weikum, "Context-sensitive auto-completion for searching with entities and categories," in Proceedings of the 39th International ACM SIGIR conference on Research and Development in Information Retrieval, SIGIR 2016, Pisa, Italy, July 17-21, 2016, 2016, pp. 1097–1100.

[11] M. Dehmer, F. Emmert-Streib, and J. Kilian, "A similarity measure for graphs with low computational complexity," Appl. Math. Comput., vol. 182, no. 1, Nov. 2006, pp. 447–459.

Towards using a Graph Database and Literature-based Discovery for Interpretation of Next Generation Sequencing Results

Dimitar Hristovski
Medical faculty
Ljubljana, Slovenia
dimitar.hristovski@mf.uni-lj.si

Gaber Bergant
KIMG, UMC Ljubljana
Ljubljana, Slovenia
gaber.bergant@kclj.si

Andrej Kastrin
Medical faculty
Ljubljana, Slovenia
andrej.kastrin@guest.arnes.si

Borut Peterlin
KIMG, UMC Ljubljana
Ljubljana, Slovenia
borut.peterlin@kclj.si

Abstract—**The arrival of high-throughput sequencing technologies in routine diagnostic medicine has enabled the large scale use of these technologies; however, the challenges of interpreting the results for diagnostic purposes has recently become evident. For this reason, we aim to develop a bioinformatics tool for clinical genetics diagnostics support. We gathered the data for this project from several different sources, including semantic relations extracted with SemRep from the MEDLINE bibliographic database, clinical phenotype observations from clinical geneticists and finally genotype data produced by Next-Generation Sequencing (NGS) annotated with population data and several theoretical pathogenicity prediction algorithms. We stored this data in a Neo4j graph database and employed it using a closed discovery approach to Literature-Based Discovery (LBD) as a complementary method in diagnostic NGS data analysis. All algorithms were implemented using the Cypher query language. The goal of the study was first to determine the usability of graph databases to represent heterogeneous clinical genomic data and secondly to determine the potential benefits of using LBD as a complementary approach in a diagnostic setting using NGS.**

Keywords- Literature-based discovery; Next-generation sequencing; Genomic data analysis; Semantic MEDLINE; Graph database; Neo4j.

I. INTRODUCTION

Next Generation Sequencing (NGS), also known as high-throughput sequencing, is a term collectively describing several different technologies that integrate a massively parallel sequencing approach, thus enabling the sequencing of whole human genomes within reasonable timescales. The development of NGS technologies successfully spread the utility of (clinical) Deoxyribonucleic Acid (DNA) sequencing by reaching unprecedented speed at reduced cost, enabling wide spread clinical and research use and thus fueling the rapid growth of genomic sciences. This presents a challenge in that pursuing and incorporating the newly discovered data in analytical pipelines becomes more and more difficult. Targeting this issue, we present our preliminary research in using the Literature-Based Discovery (LBD) paradigm to improve the interpretation of NGS results.

II. METHODS

The goal of LBD is to generate novel hypotheses by analyzing the literature and optionally other knowledge sources [1]. For a recent review of LBD tools and approaches see [2]. We can approach LBD with one of two paradigms, either open or closed discovery. For this project we selected closed discovery. We also chose Neo4j [3] as a graph database for storing the collected data. Briefly, we deal with the data from a single patient at a time. The input is two sets of data for each patient, the genotype of discovered genomic variants and the phenotype as observed by the clinical geneticist. The genotype set X contains the genes with mutations as found by diagnostic NGS. The phenotype set Z contains the clinical observations provided by the clinical geneticist described using the human phenotype ontology (HPO) terms.

After gathering the relevant datasets, we constructed a graph database in Neo4j. The graph database consists of two major types of nodes, patients and concepts of several types including phenotypes, genes, proteins, cell functions, genetic disorders and many other biomedical types. Connecting these nodes, we have several different relationship types. For example, the relationship PHENO connects patients with their corresponding phenotype nodes and the relationship GENO connects patients with their respective mutated genes. This relationship also holds the information of the variant location, the specific mutated nucleotide, the severity of the mutation type (mainly differentiating missense and loss of function variants), predictions of theoretical algorithms for pathogenicity prediction and population data from the repository of the Genome Aggregation Database (gnomAD) [4]. We used this additional information for filtration and prioritization of candidate genes, thus reducing the workload required for manual result review by a clinical expert. Additionally, we have included the 30 different types of semantic relations as extracted by SemRep [5] from all of MEDLINE (titles and abstracts) serving as a backbone for patient and phenotype node connection. SemRep is a rule-based, symbolic natural language processing system that extracts semantic relationships in clinical medicine, substance interactions, genetic etiology of disease, and pharmacogenomics (e.g., TREATS, INHIBITS, STIMULATES, CAUSES, PREDISPOSES, AUGMENTS). These relationships are publicly available as SemMedDB [6] (a MySQL database). This work is a continuation and extension of our previous work [7] in which we explained how to construct a Neo4j graph database from SemMedDB and how to implement generic LBD with Cypher.

We assumed that the feasibility of our approach in routine clinical practice depended heavily on the development of intuitive algorithms for final result filtration and prioritization. We also expected this to prove especially useful in the clinical setting where expert time is limited. Therefore, we implemented a practical prioritization algorithm, which outputs an ordered list of genes awaiting expert review. For this purpose, we used the integrated relevant statistical data, such as population frequencies extracted from several population databases encompassing worldwide healthy control populations as well as theoretical pathogenicity predictions from several available prediction algorithms. Finally, we programmatically employed the prioritization algorithm in the Cypher query language on a per patient basis, extracting a prioritized list of genes, hopefully leading to further diagnostic and research steps, possibly also improving the diagnostic yield of NGS.

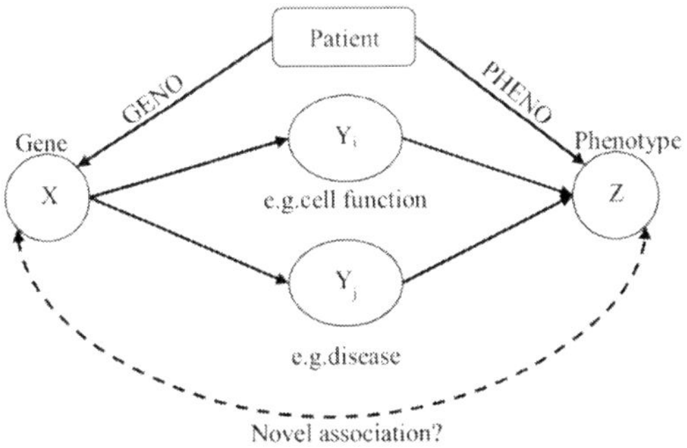

Figure 1. Illustration of novel clinical association prediction. Based on clinical genetic data and current biomedical knowledge (solid lines) we predict novel clinical associations (dashed arcs).

Figure 1 illustrates our approach. The output of the algorithm is a set of relevant intermediate concepts Y (such as genetic functions and/or diseases) that link the genotype X to the phenotype Z. These Y concepts should provide a hypothesis that explains the mechanisms for the novel associations that link the genotype to the phenotype. Our algorithm is meant as a discovery support step in a clinical NGS data processing pipeline. We generate hypotheses (explanations and novel associations); however, a knowledgeable human expert is needed for the critical evaluation of these hypotheses.

III. RESULTS

The network we constructed consists of 1205 patient nodes. There are 262132 GENO relationships linking the patients to 15294 gene nodes. Multiple GENO relations are possible between a particular patient and a particular gene because sometimes there are multiple mutations (genetic variants) in the same gene for a particular patient. There are 4751 PHENO relations between the patients and the corresponding phenotypes represented with 1450 HPO terms (represented as nodes). The 1450 HPO terms were mapped to 982 UMLS concepts, which are used as arguments in the SemRep semantic relations. With SemRep we extracted 91567597 semantic relation instances from 55551193 sentences from 27263265 MEDLINE bibliographic records. The semantic relations instances were aggregated into 20818782 semantic relations between 277160 biomedical concept nodes, and were stored in our Neo4j database. The SemRep semantic relations represent general biomedical knowledge. The clinical patient data (the genotype and phenotype) are linked to the general biomedical knowledge through common concepts (represented as nodes).

Essential for the clinical implementation of the graph database was the storage of genotype data within multiple relationships between the patient and the specific gene, where the mutations occurred, as that allowed for the possibility of storing sequencing information regardless of the number of variants occurring in this gene.

IV. DISCUSSION AND FURTHER WORK

In this preliminary work, we constructed the necessary bioinformatics infrastructure in such a way that it allows efficient import of clinical data and simple extraction of relevant results, which are necessary for its inclusion in the diagnostic pipeline. However, several challenges remain to be solved. From the clinical genomics perspective, we noticed that within the SemMed database, the relationships between some genes and their correlated biomedical concepts are underrepresented while other genes are highly connected with non-informative concepts. Another issue is that some concepts are too general and highly connected to other concepts rendering them non-informative. We plan to find ways for filtering out non-informative concepts by using network analysis centrality measures and community detection algorithms. Furthermore, within the ranking algorithm, we face Cypher language efficiency issues, which we plan to address by query optimization. We also plan to develop an interactive visualization tool, enabling a quick and easy visual analytics. And finally, we plan to evaluate the usefulness of our approach from the clinical genetics point of view.

V. CONCLUSION

Although the LBD paradigm has been used in a research context for some time, it has been underappreciated in the clinical genetic diagnostic setting. With this preliminary study we show the potential of using LBD as a complementary method in clinical diagnostics of genetic disorders, with the emphasis on novel gene-phenotype associations. Furthermore, we determined that using a graph database such as Neo4j is suitable for storing heterogeneous genomic data needed for clinical genetics diagnostic support.

ACKNOWLEDGMENT

We thank Thomas C. Rindflesch for his comments and suggestions regarding this manuscript.

REFERENCES

[1] D. R. Swanson, "Fish oil, Raynaud's syndrome, and undiscovered public knowledge," Perspectives in Biology and Medicine, vol. 30, no. 1, pp. 7-18, 1986.

[2] D. Hristovski, T. Rindflesch, and B. Peterlin, "Using literaturebased discovery to identify novel therapeutic

approaches," Cardiovascular & Hematological Agents in Medicinal Chemistry, vol. 11, no. 1, pp. 14-24, 2013.

[3] Neo4j website. Available at: http://neo4j.com. Last accessed March 10th 2018.

[4] M. Lek, K. J. Karczewski, E. V. Minikel et al. Exome Aggregation Consortium. Analysis of protein-coding genetic variation in 60,706 humans. Nature. 2016 Aug 18;536(7616):285-91.

[5] T. C. Rindflesch and M. Fiszman, "The interaction of domain knowledge and linguistic structure in natural language processing: Interpreting hypernymic propositions in biomedical text," Journal of Biomedical Informatics, vol. 36, no. 6, pp. 462-477, 2003.

[6] H. Kilicoglu, D. Shin, M. Fiszman, G. Rosemblat, and T. C. Rindflesch, "SemMedDB: A PubMed-scale repository of biomedical semantic predications," Bioinformatics, vol. 28, no. 23, pp. 3158-3160, 2012.

[7] D. Hristovski, A. Kastrin, D. Dinevski, and T. C. Rindflesch, "Towards implementing semantic literature-based discovery with a graph database," Proceedings of the GraphSM 2015, The Second International Workshop on Large-scale Graph Storage and Management, pp. 180-184, 2015.